N £1·60s

SO-ATU-217

THE MISSIONARY FACTOR IN EAST AFRICA

'The only purely spiritual phenomena are good intentions, and we all know what portion of the universe is paved with them.'

WILLIAM TEMPLE,
International Missionary Conference,
Jerusalem 1928.

THE MISSIONARY FACTOR
IN EAST AFRICA

by

ROLAND OLIVER, M.A., Ph.D.

Sometime Scholar and Reginald John Smith Student
King's College, Cambridge

Professor of African History
in the University of London

LONGMAN

LONGMAN GROUP LIMITED

London

*Associated companies, branches and representatives
throughout the world*

First published	.	. .	1952
Second edition	.	. .	1965
New impression	.	. .	1970

ISBN 0 582 60847 3

PRINTED IN GREAT BRITAIN BY
LOWE AND BRYDONE (PRINTERS) LTD, LONDON

CONTENTS

LIST OF MAPS

INTRODUCTION

AFTER some considerable hesitation I have decided that the continued demand for this book must be met by reprinting it in its original form. The reason is not that I hold the high artistic view of history as the vision of a subject set down once and for all and never to be recaptured. I do believe that all worthwhile historical writing is primarily an artistic exercise, consisting in an attempt to master a large body of facts and to present a small selection of them in the proportion and form that seems most meaningful at a particular moment in time. And, obviously, the closer that point to the events discussed, the more it will affect what is written. All the same, an historian's view, deliberately set down, should be sufficiently detached to stand for twenty years, and therefore at any time within that period it should be capable of being brought up to date. My difficulty is simply that this book was five years in the making, and that properly to master the events of the past fifteen years and to reduce them into a new final chapter would take another year or eighteen months, which I do not have at my disposal. It would require, above all, another extensive journey through East Africa such as I was fortunate enough to be able to make in 1949 and 1950, when I was able to see a representative cross-section of the work of all the Christian forces on the ground, and to supplement four years of study by discussions with the living practitioners of the Christian propaganda.

It needs to be said, therefore, that this book was written between 1947 and 1951, during what was for East Africa still the tranquil twilight of the colonial period. 1947 was the year of Kwame Nkrumah's return to West Africa as Secretary of the United Gold Coast Convention. 1951 was the year of his release from prison as Leader of Government Business in a Cabinet still presided over by Sir Charles Arden-Clarke. The idea of independence for the African colonies was in the air, but only just. Certainly in relation to East Africa it was felt to be a still very distant target. Young Englishmen who came out to East Africa during those years as cadets in the Colonial Service never imagined that their own careers would be foreshortened by it. In Kenya the influence of the European settlers upon the government of the country was still extremely strong. It is no wonder, therefore, that in a study of the missionary contribution to East African history undertaken at this time the relationship of missions with colonial governments should have occupied such a dominating role. What is surprising in 1etrospect is that the danger to the Churches inherent in such a relationship should have been evident enough to call for comment in the closing pages of the book.

It was between the writing of the book and its publication that there burst upon Kenya the sudden and violent tempest of the Mau Mau rebellion, when Christianity was denounced as the religion of the imperialist, and when it was temporarily alleged that more than ninety per cent of Kikuyu Christians had abandoned all connection with the Churches. Then indeed it seemed that, not in Kenya only, but perhaps in most of Africa, Christianity and colonialism would stand on trial together, with Christian leaders forced by the nature of the revolution into an explicit defence of colonial law and order. It was then that one wondered most whether the long-term results of the missionary movement would bear any comparison at all with those of its colonial heyday.

And yet, save for the southern Sudan and parts of the Congo, the events of the past twelve years have not so far justified those particular fears. The Kenya situation was stabilised by military action, and subsequent claims for independence in the African countries were peacefully stated, often by political leaders who were practising Christians, and nearly always by methods which the Churches could approve. The colonial powers, reacting to world pressures, abdicated while negotiation was still possible, and phased and orderly transfers of power were the rule rather than the exception. The Churches blessed the new states at their inauguration, and within the Churches the transfer of offices from expatriate to indigenous personnel went steadily forward, without traumatic haste. In general, foreign missionaries have continued to be as welcome as other bearers of aid without strings.

Superficially at least, it would seem that there has been a remarkable contrast between the institutional stability of the Churches in East Africa and the rapidity of political change within the African states. In the political field the scene has changed since independence almost beyond recognition. It is not merely that colonial governments have been replaced by African ones. It is that the political model presented by the colonial power has been deliberately cast aside. Democracy on the Westminster pattern has been abandoned even as a goal. The current political philosophy is that of the single revolutionary party, dominating the central legislature, permeating the civil service and the armed forces, and exercising through party officials a detailed control over the provincial and district administration. The Churches, however, have undergone no such drastic changes. Africans have progressively taken the places of Europeans, but have continued to do the same jobs and to teach the same doctrines. To a very large extent East African Christianity has retained its world-wide denominational structures, while experiencing from within them the mutual attractions arising from the ecumenical movement, which has been such a marked feature of our time. If there is a historical explanation for this contrast, it must surely be that the planters of East African Christianity were wiser in their generation than their secular colonialist counterparts in their early willingness to share the positions of leadership with their African successors.

And yet there is a vital question about the Churches' leadership, which I posed in the final chapter of this book, and to which, so far as I am aware, no reassuring answer can yet be given. It concerns the utter failure of the Churches, ever since the 1920's, to attract into the Christian ministry even a handful of the best educated East Africans. During the first three decades of the colonial period this had not been so. Of the first literate generation of East Africans the élite had become either chiefs or churchmen. But with the development of secondary education, and with the widening of secular opportunities, the Churches began to be outpaced in the competition for the best educated men. With the

beginnings of higher education the situation grew still
more serious. In the early 'fifties, when the University
College of East Africa began to put forth its first graduates,
there was still not a single ordained minister in any of the
Churches who had received even the beginnings of a
secondary education in any of the lay schools. If the Roman
Catholic seminaries provided a partial exception to this rule,
it was only by pursuing a policy of isolating possible candidates for the ministry from a very early age. During the
last decade, while hundreds of East Africans have been
studying in the universities of Europe, Asia and North
America, a tiny trickle of Roman Catholic clergy has been
flowing to the Gregorian University, but other Christian
denominations still lack a single African graduate in the
ordained ministry. The élite which won political independence and now exercises political control is thus an entirely
secular élite, with which the clergy can scarcely communicate effectively. Thus the Church's work is most evident
still in the villages, but the life of the towns, and especially of
the capitals, has largely passed it by. As I wrote in 1951, the
danger is that under the stress of political and social change
organised Christianity may start to disintegrate at the centre
while it is still expanding at the circumference. Though I do
not know the present situation in anything like the same
detail as it knew it in 1951, my impression is that this
danger is today even more insistent than it was then.

My great regret is that I cannot in a new final chapter
look afresh at this question with the detailed attention that
it deserves. With what is actually written I am relatively
content. The book was a first foray into the field of mission-

ary history in East Africa. As such, it is a little rough in places, but for the present it can stand. Some more specialised studies have appeared since it was published, and more are on the way. First and foremost, there is F. B. Welbourn's *East African Rebels*, comprising a series of essays on the independent church movements in East Africa, an important subject, to which I barely alluded when writing this book. Next, there is John Taylor's *The Growth of the Church in Buganda*, a deeply original study of the faith and practice of Christianity as it has emerged through the missionary and ecclesiastical pipelines into the daily life of a group of country hamlets in north-eastern Buganda. Some interesting new conclusions on the Christian revolution in Buganda during the earliest part of the colonial period were published by D. A. Low in his essay on the Uganda Agreement in *Buganda and British Overrule*. These will perhaps be carried further when he publishes his major work on *The British and Uganda*, based amongst other things on a more complete examination of the Church Missionary Society's archives than I was able to undertake. Some fresh monographs are also to hand on the work of particular missionary societies in East Africa. There is already H. P. Gale's *Uganda and the Mill Hill Fathers*. There will soon be J. A. Kieran's study of the Holy Ghost Fathers in East Africa, and Marcia Wright's comprehensive work on the Evangelical Lutheran missionary societies. The archives of the Universities Mission to Central Africa are at last open to students, and are being examined from some particular points of view by E. A. Alpers. Above all, it is to be hoped that a major work will soon be set in train on the East

African missions of the White Fathers, to whose archives, recently transferred from Algiers to Rome, I was offered access only some years after this book had been published.

What is of even more importance, however, than the further examination of European missionary archives is that a deliberate effort should be made to assemble and preserve the Christian records still existing in East Africa, and to use them to write the history of the Churches as opposed to that of the missions. After all, the early Christians of East Africa were usually known as 'readers'. Literacy was one of the qualities that distinguished them from the pagan world in which they lived. To be sure, they must have created records in considerable quantity, and a portion of these records must still survive at diocesan headquarters and mission stations, in presbyteries, schools and private houses throughout the length and breadth of East Africa. Where writing is still a marvel and the arrival of letters an event, papers are apt to be treasured, and it is certain that many a simple clay-built house with an earthen floor and a roof of thatch nevertheless contains a tin trunk full of family papers preserved since the early days of mission and colonial contact. Research students and archivists working hand in hand have recently proved this to be the case in Nigeria, and there is no reason to doubt that in East Africa it will be the same. It is no less certain that a high proportion of these early records will have a Christian interest. They will show parents writing to school authorities, village evangelists writing to their supervising clergy, and parish clergy to their ecclesiastical superiors. There will be a mass of illuminating financial details about school fees, church dues and building projects. There will be registers of baptisms and confirmations and marriages and burials. There will be accounts of disciplinary issues affecting both clergy and laity, from which more than from any other source the developing impact of Christian morality upon pre-existing beliefs and customs will be able to be traced. It is from sources such as these rather than from missionary records that the history of the East African Churches will have to be built up. And it will be work on these lines which will more and more supersede in relevance the history of the missionary founders of the Church. Meanwhile it seems that this little book may still have a useful purpose to perform.

R.O.

LONDON,
JULY 1964.

ACKNOWLEDGEMENT

Acknowledgement is due to Mrs. George Bambridge, Messrs. Methuen & Co. Ltd., Messrs. Doubleday & Co. Inc., and The Macmillan Company of Canada Ltd., for permission to include a verse from 'The White Man's Burden' from *The Five Nations* by Rudyard Kipling. Copyright 1899 by Rudyard Kipling.

NOTE ON NAMES OF TRIBES AND PLACES

For those who have no personal knowledge of East Africa it may be helpful to know that the vowels in African words and place-names are pronounced as in Italian; also that the meanings of Bantu word-roots are amplified by prefixes, of which those relevant to this book are: U- and Bu-, signifying place; A-, Wa- and Ba-, signifying people; Ki-, Lu- and Chi-, signifying language. Thus, if we take the word 'Nyamwezi', which is the name of the tribal group living round Tabora in Central Tanganyika, the people are Wanyamwezi, the country is Unyamwezi, and the language is Kinyamwezi. If these rules are borne in mind, the only names that need cause confusion are Uganda and Buganda. Ganda is the name of a tribal group inhabiting the northern shores of Lake Victoria. The people are Baganda; their country is Buganda. But the Arab traders and early European travellers used the Kiswahili form of the locative and called it Uganda, and this word was later used to designate the whole area of the British Protectorate, which includes many other tribal areas than Buganda proper. In this book Buganda has been used for the tribal area, Uganda only for the wider region, of which Buganda is a part. It is also important to remember that from 1895 till 1919 'British East Africa' meant the area now known as Kenya. The new name was adopted to eliminate confusion when the greater part of the former German East Africa became the British mandated territory of Tanganyika.

ABBREVIATIONS

A.	*Africa:* Journal of the International African Institute.		preserved at the Public Record office.
AFER.	*Africanae Fraternae Ephemerides Romanae.*	*IRM.*	*International Review of Missions.*
A.I.M.	Africa Inland Mission.	(KP)	Sir John Kirk's copies of
AMZ.	*Allgemeine Missionszeitschrift.*		Foreign Office prints deposited at Rhodes House, Oxford.
CA.	*Central Africa.*	L.M.S.	London Missionary Society.
CMI.	*Church Missionary Intelligencer.*	*MC.*	*Missions Catholiques.*
		U.M.C.A.	Universities Mission to Central Africa.
CMR.	*Church Missionary Review.*		
C.M.S.	Church Missionary Society.	U.M.M.	United Methodist Mission.
C.S.M.	Church of Scotland Mission.	*ZMW.*	*Zeitschrift fur Missionswissenschaft.*
F.O.	Foreign office correspondence		

Chapter One

THE MISSIONARY OCCUPATION OF EAST AFRICA

I

IN 1856 LIVINGSTONE returned to England after crossing Central Africa from the Angolan port of St. Paul de Loanda to the Zambezi delta at Quilimane. At this time European interests in East Africa were concentrated, with one exception, on the island of Zanzibar. During a reign of fifty years just ended, the great Sultan Seyyid Said of Muscat had consolidated his dominion over the Arab-settled towns of the East African coast and had moved his capital to Zanzibar, which had become under his influence the nodal point of trade between East Africa and the outside world. It was through his custom-houses that the traditional exports of the mainland, slaves and ivory and gum-copal, passed into the hands of the Arab and Indian merchants and sea captains who conveyed them to their Asiatic destinations; and by encouraging the cultivation of cloves on the island itself, he had further stimulated a direct trade with the nations of Europe and North America in the small arms and hardware and cloth which were his most-needed imports. By 1856 three American firms, dealing in cheap calico, had agents at Zanzibar and a trade valued at about £250,000 a year. Four German firms, all from Hamburg, brought hardware and did a three-cornered trade by carrying cowrie-shells to West

Africa for use as currency. Two French firms came mostly with brandy and bought sesamum. Direct trade with Britain was negligible, but some hundreds of Indians, British subjects, carried on a trade even greater than that of the Americans.[1]

For all their growing importance, however, there was nothing in these European commercial activities which was likely to promote their own direct extension to the mainland. East Africa was no Eldorado. It was only through the genius of Said that the meagre products of the interior had been channelled to Zanzibar in sufficient quantities to justify the visits of European traders, who had little incentive to call at the smaller ports and still less to attempt to penetrate the interior. Consuls had been appointed to Zanzibar, by the United States in 1837, by Great Britain in 1841 and by France in 1844; but this did not mean that there was any reason strong enough to interest a European power in East African conquests at this time. Had there been total indifference on the part of other nations, France, with her base at Réunion and her growing interest in Madagascar and the Comoros, might have been tempted to intervene; but her first tentative intrusions into the politics of the area in the forties and early fifties provoked sharp protests from the British Foreign Office;[2] and after a final endeavour to undermine the British diplomatic ascendancy at Zanzibar after Said's death in 1856, she was to sign in March 1862 a joint

---

[1] For the earlier history of the East African coast the reader is referred to the standard work by Sir Reginald Coupland, *East Africa and its Invaders*, Oxford, 1938, and, for the general historical background to the first half of this book, to the same author's *The Exploitation of East Africa, 1856-90*, London, 1939.

[2] Coupland, *Invaders*, p. 439 *sqq.*

declaration with Britain pledging herself to respect the independence of the new Sultan, Seyyid Majid. French ambitions apart, the principal British political interest in East Africa was the control of the slave-trade; and here again the solution was imagined at this period to lie rather in the building up of the Sultan's authority over the coastlands and in the exercise of diplomatic influence through him, than in any direct British interference in his dominions. As early as 1822 Seyyid Said had been prevailed upon to limit the trade to the north-western quarter of the Indian Ocean;[1] and in 1845 this area had been further reduced so as to exclude all trade beyond the Sultan's African dominions.[2] But it cannot be too strongly emphasised that the East African slave-trade was at this period only engaging the attention of certain officials and experts with a limited mandate and with still more limited funds at their disposal. Philanthropic energy was still focused on the trans-Atlantic trade. The seven or so cruisers available for the Indian Ocean, attempting to police a 4,000-mile coast line, could catch only a few hundred out of perhaps 10,000 slaves annually exported from the treaty area;[3] and it can hardly be doubted that the British Government's highest expectation of success was to prevent the importation of slaves into its own possessions in India and Aden and the Persian Gulf. It was only between twenty and thirty years later, when Livingstone, Stanley, Cameron and many other

[1] The so-called Moresby Treaty. This very inadequate limitation enabled the Sultan to carry on the trade with the other half of his dominion at Muscat.

[2] The legal status of slavery was abolished in India in 1843.

[3] Coupland, *Exploitation*, p. 164, gives 2,645 liberated as against 37,000 safely smuggled during the three years, 1867–9.

eye-witnesses had painted the inland horrors of the trade and demonstrated that a comparatively trivial export figure implied a depopulation of Africa by perhaps half a million human beings a year,[1] that any large section of European opinion became aware that counteraction was necessary by land, and far inland at that.

From the point of view of European commerce and politics, therefore, East Africa was in 1856 a backwater, contact with which was best limited strictly to the coast, with its floating aristocracy of Arabs who still kept some touch with their homelands around the Persian Gulf, and its settled 'Swahili' population, of mixed race and nominally Muhammedan religion. Of the vast territory which stretched inland from the palm-fringed coast line through arid foothills to the highland plateaux and the fertile and densely populated regions of the great lakes Europeans knew nothing. Of its peoples they knew only the degraded and inarticulate slave labour employed in the clove plantations of Zanzibar and the maltreated human cargoes of the slave-dhows. The solitary exception, the only European interest already operating on the East African mainland and determined to push its influence beyond the coastal belt, was the C.M.S. mission at Rabai on the hill-side behind Mombasa.

The Church Missionary Society had travelled far since Charles Simeon in his Cambridge rooms used fondly to describe India as his diocese.[2] Its 170 missionaries were now

---

[1] This estimate was Cameron's, that accepted by most of the leading propagandists of the next generation including Lavigerie and Horace Waller.

[2] Stock, *History of the Church Missionary Society*, 3 vols., 1899, I, p. 59.

spread abroad in India, China, West Africa, Canada and New Zealand, and were supported at home by a comprehensive propaganda network, designed to draw the guineas of the rich, but even more the pennies of the poor and the farthings of children, by magazines and missionary boxes, by sermons and special meetings.[1] Like all other missionary societies, its home constituency was more genuinely popular than that of any other factor in the nineteenth-century expansion of Europe; unlike many other societies, its policy and the expenditure of its £125,000 income[2] was largely controlled by lay-opinion and not by an ecclesiastical hierarchy. Every subscriber of a guinea was entitled to speak and vote at the monthly meetings of the General Committee; and among those who had the leisure and the interest to do so were many influential men in business, in politics and in the government services, men like Sir James Stephen, Sir T. F. Buxton and Sir John Kennaway.

For all the growing prosperity of the C.M.S., it was more by accident than design that the Church of England was thus early represented in the East African field; and it is a significant fact that until 1874 the only men it could find to face the rigours of the climate were Lutherans trained at Basel.[3] Johann Krapf had been a missionary in Abyssinia.

---

[1] In 1882 it was receiving support from 5,375 parishes out of a total of 15,700. About £100,000 of the income was accounted for as follows: Annual subscriptions, £35,000; Collections at Special Sermons, £34,000; Special meetings, £10,000; Missionary boxes, £18,000; *CMI.*, £2,193. *CMI.* 82. 191–6.

[2] *Proceedings of the Church Missionary Society, 1856–7*, p. 15.

[3] Krapf, like many of the German and Danish Lutherans employed by the C.M.S. and the S.P.C.K. in South India, never received Anglican orders. Rebmann and Erhardt both took a short divinity course at the C.M.S. training college at Islington and were received into Anglican orders.

Frustrated in his attempt to work among the Gallas in the Kingdom of Shoa, in 1844 he sought and obtained permission from the Home Committee to attempt to reach the same tribe from a south-eastern base at Mombasa. Rebmann was sent to join him in 1846, Erhardt in 1849. These three sad and other-worldly men achieved no great evangelistic success among the scattered and socially incoherent Wanyika tribesmen who were their neighbours at Rabai. Colonel Playfair, the British Consul at Zanzibar, who visited their station in 1864, found six baptised converts with another six under tuition and 'several well-built and commodious houses, but all in a state of semi-completion'.[1] But Krapf and Rebmann, if they were somewhat impractical, had vision, tenacity and boundless courage. They were filled with the assurance that others of their calling would follow them, and they regarded themselves from the first as the pioneers of a continental system. Reporting in 1848 that one youth gave 'strong evidence of the grace of God operating upon his mind', Krapf continued: 'The coast mission must have a broad basis towards the west, and be the first link of a mission-chain between East and West Africa.'[2]

Between 1847 and 1849 Krapf and Rebmann set out by turns across the parched and thorny Nyika desert, Rebmann to Kilimanjaro and the Chagga people living on its southern slopes, Krapf southwards to the well-organised little kingdom of Usambara with its centre in the hills behind the

[1] Playfair to Havelock, Officiating Secretary of the Bombay Government, Zanzibar, 9.iv.64. Secretariat Archives, Zanzibar, kindly communicated by Sir J. M. Gray.
[2] *CMI*. 49. 55

port of Tanga, and north-westwards to the haunts of the pastoral Akamba on the eastern fringes of the Kenya Highlands.[1] In 1850 Krapf with Erhardt coasted southwards by dhow from Mombasa to the mouth of the Rovuma, gleaning on the way important intelligence about the geography of the interior.[2] Erhardt supplemented this information during a subsequent stay at Tanga and published it in 1856 in a famous map which was to be the main inspiration of Burton and Speke in their expedition of 1858.[3]

Yet the fact remains that it was Livingstone the individual, and not the C.M.S. missionaries with their twelve years' start and their powerful society behind them, who set in motion the missionary invasion of East Africa. Their linguistic work laid a solid foundation for all who came after. Their explorations forged a vital link in the discovery of the Great Lakes and the Nile sources. In the Chagga and the Shambaa they made contact with two tribes which proved eminently responsive to Christian teaching at a later date. Usambara in particular, with its absolute and friendly disposed monarch Kimweri, seemed to offer in miniature all the circumstances which were to prove so advantageous in Buganda. Under Kimweri missionaries would have been safe from violence and theft. Youths from the most influential families would have been detailed to attend the mission for instruction, and they would have come with a

[1] Coupland, *Invaders*, pp. 391–9.
[2] J. L. Krapf, *Travels, Researches and Missionary Labours in East Africa*, London, 1860, p. 411 *sqq.*
[3] See the mean references in R. F. Burton, *The Lake Regions of Central Africa*, London, 1860, I, p. 3 and II, p. 170; *infra*, p. 27.

sense of discipline and purpose unknown in the more loosely organised societies. An able missionary would certainly have become, if only for his knowledge of the wider world, a trusted adviser at Kimweri's court; and had prolonged contact led to the King's conversion, the sequel would have been the same as in Anglo-Saxon England. But these openings were not followed up. Krapf returned to Europe broken in health in 1853,[1] Erhardt in 1855, and Rebmann was left to work on at Rabai for twenty more years alone. Several causes contributed to this interesting failure. The Home Committee had decided in 1850 that the extensive schemes of the Rabai missionaries were 'the sober calculation of wise men' and not the 'dreams of enthusiasts'; and six more Germans had been detailed to accompany Krapf on his return to Mombasa in 1851.[2] In the event, through withdrawals and ill-health, none of these men lived to do effective missionary work. But the C.M.S. had sustained worse disasters on the west coast of Africa, and it can hardly be doubted that, placed in the forefront of their propaganda, the claims of East Africa would have met with some response. For a decade from 1852, however, India was the burning question: first the gigantic battle for government subsidies in education, then the problems of rebuilding and extension raised by the Mutiny.[3] But India alone does not explain the

---

[1] Krapf returned to Mombasa in 1861 in order to help Charles New of the United Methodist Free Church to establish a small mission station at Ribé. This isolated and frequently deserted station makes only a brief appearance in this story in connection with the freed slave troubles at Mombasa in the 1880's.

[2] Stock, *op. cit.*, II, p. 131.

[3] *ibid.*, II, p. 235 *sqq.* Expenditure rose by £30,000 between 1853 and 1863, of which £23,000 on India. *CMI*. 65. 1.

absolute dearth of candidates for East Africa.[1] Krapf, it must be remembered, though surrounded by domestic slavery, scarcely penetrated as far south as the great slave-trading routes. Nor, in his day, had European fire-arms appreciably multiplied the horrors of inter-tribal slave-raiding. And the Rabai missionaries were all Lutherans, Pietists of the old school. For some or all of these reasons they saw the negro primarily as 'fallen man'.[2] Livingstone saw him primarily as 'suffering'. As a result, where Krapf's views commanded the respect of a well-informed committee, Livingstone's were received with emotion by a whole country.

If it was Livingstone's last journey and his later attacks on the Arab slave-trade which chiefly caught the popular imagination, it was during his early years, while he was in the service of the London Missionary Society,[3] that he addressed himself to the peculiar missionary problems of tropical Africa, of work among primitive peoples in countries still unsettled by Europeans. His conclusions were revolutionary. They attracted an England obsessed with the idea of progress; and they did much to promote the wider than ecclesiastical policies which missions came to pursue. His first contact with a Bechuanaland tribe untouched by any Christian influence made him realise how great had been the

[1] *CMI*. 52. 211 stresses dearth of candidates. 'Can we be surprised that when we send out missionaries to other fields, they are removed before they have been enabled to put their hand to the work, if that Mission which most needs help and has been longest importuning it, is left unaided.' *ibid*, 56. 15.

[2] *e.g.* 'The deep fall of man from his Creator shows itself in these countries especially in the circumstance that nature exercises its full dominion over him, while he has been appointed to subject it to himself.' Rebmann, *ibid.*, 49. 15.

[3] He left the service of the L.M.S. in 1856, and thereafter worked as a free-lance.

indirect effects of mission-work farther south, and led him to stress 'those other than saving influences of Christianity, which so materially modify the social system at home.'[2] Eleven years later the same idea was foremost in his mind:

If we call the actual amount of conversions the direct result of Missions, and the wide diffusion of better principles the indirect, I have no hesitation in asserting that the latter are of infinitely more importance than the former. I do not undervalue the importance of the conversion of the most abject creature that breathes: it is of overwhelming worth to him personally, but viewing our work of wide sowing of the good seed relatively to the harvest which will be reaped when all our heads are low, there can, I think, be no comparison. . . . Time is more important than concentration.[3]

That a pioneer missionary should make it a part of his duty to introduce the arts and sciences of civilisation was itself a proposition not universally accepted in Protestant circles: that he should consciously aim at the indirect results, and press on into unexplored regions, leaving half- or even unevangelised peoples behind him, was quite startling. But Livingstone went further. As he travelled down the Zambezi, observing not one Bantu people but a score, he became convinced that the chief hindrance to the Gospel lay not so much in the refractory wills of individuals as in the great social evils of African society, in the poverty which bound it to material ambitions, in the ignorance which surrounded it

---

[1] D. Livingstone, *Missionary Travels and Experiences in South Africa*, 1857, p. 226.

[2] D. Chamberlin, *Some Letters from Livingstone*, London, 1940, p. 70. From Mabotsa, 1844.

[3] *ibid.*, p. 252. Livingstone to Tidman from Linyanti, 1855.

with fear, in the mutual repulsion of its tribal groupings[1] which laid it ever open to violence. When, finally, drawing towards the east, he saw the slavers at their work and realised that this was a country invaded by Coastmen whose exploitation of it carried few mitigating features, he concluded that the task would only be accomplished by the impact of civilised and Christian society as a whole.

Naturally, in 1856, Livingstone was thinking in terms of commerce rather than imperialism. He was convinced that the Zambezi region was suitable for cotton, and he visualised the growth of a steady trade with Europe which would relieve the poverty, integrate the several tribes and kill the illegitimate trade by the legitimate.[2] Though still first and foremost a Christian missionary, he chose for his own part in this movement the search for a navigable river, by which steamships could enter the interior. This was the 'open path for commerce and Christianity' to which he referred in his celebrated appeal in the Senate House at Cambridge in December 1857. At the end of his *Missionary Travels*, which appeared early in the following year, he said that he regarded 'the end of the geographical feat as the beginning of the

[1] In view of the modern tendency to idolise the 'tribal system' and to deplore its passing, it is interesting to note how little it attracted the early travellers, who, if their examination was superficial, at least saw it before it was controlled by European administration: *e.g.* Sir Bartle Frere in *East Africa as a Field for Missionary Labours*, London, 1874, p. 70, writes: 'At present there is nothing to counteract the action of the cold materialism which, teaching selfishness as the highest wisdom, isolates every man from his neighbour. This, perhaps, is one of the natural religions of mankind; but by counteracting the formation of any social ties higher than those which keep together a herd of bison, it is an effectual obstacle to anything like permanent civilisation.'

[2] *i.e.* (i) by teaching the people to pay for their imports with raw cotton instead of human beings, (ii) by substituting mechanical transport for porterage, which was in itself a stimulus to the slave-trade, in that the slaves carried the ivory to the coast.

missionary enterprise', including in that expression 'every effort made for the amelioration of our race, the promotion of all these means by which God in His Providence is working, and bringing all His dealings with man to a glorious consummation.'[1]

Livingstone's appeal resulted in the foundation by a group of English High Churchmen of the Universities Mission to Central Africa. As an organisation it grew from the first along radically different lines from the C.M.S., in a way which powerfully affected its methods and its influence. Partly as a result of Anglo-Catholic views on episcopacy,[2] and partly because the mission worked in a single geographical area,[3] the bishop on the spot came to occupy the key position, while the Home Committee merely raised the funds and found the candidates. Naturally such humble functions did not attract the services of the influential laymen, who, while ruling the C.M.S. bishops with a rod of iron, provided important connections between Salisbury Square and Westminster.[4] In other ways, too, the U.M.C.A. missionaries bought their independence dear. Funds were difficult to

---

[1] D. Livingstone, *Missionary Travels*, p. 673.

[2] It is significant that whereas the U.M.C.A. sent out a bishop in charge of its very first expedition, the C.M.S. did not appoint a bishop for East Africa till 1883.

[3] *i.e.* because the Home Committee could not grasp excessive powers on the grounds that it had to allocate funds between different fields of work.

[4] 'Ours is an actual mission living and working in the country. . . . It has been the custom to think of missionaries as an inferior set of men, sent out, paid and governed by a superior set of men formed into a committee in London. Of course then you must have examiners and secretaries and an office to see that the inferior men are not too inferior; and you must have a set of cheap colleges in which the inferior men may get an inferior education and you must provide an inferior sort of ordination which will not enable them to compete in England with the superior men.' Bishop Steere in the *Guardian*, 8.vi.81. Quoted in R. M. Heanley, *A Memoir of Bishop Steere*, London, 1888, p. 298.

raise in competition with the two larger societies.[1] Support came mostly from the very pious, who were neither very numerous nor very rich; and, for economic more than doctrinal reasons, a system grew up whereby missionaries received only their keep and were usually retired on marriage. Stations were often poorly equipped and supplied, the incidence of disease was high, and comparatively few men stayed for longer than a single tour of service.

Livingstone's influence was clearly marked in the new society's plan of action, which was to establish 'centres of Christianity and civilisation for the promotion of true religion, agriculture and lawful commerce'. Moreover, the clergy were to be accompanied by a doctor, a Lay Superintendent 'and a number of artificers, English and native, capable of conducting the various works of building, husbandry, and especially of the cultivation of the cotton plant'.[2] The outcome was a disaster so serious that it temporarily discredited Livingstone as a missionary theorist. Bishop Mackenzie and his party arrived at the mouth of the Zambezi in 1861 to find that Livingstone's second expedition had disproved the existence of an open path, at least for commerce. No navigable entry had been found to the Zambezi and rapids had been located on the main stream above Tete. The ascent of its northern tributary, the Shiré, though leading to the discovery of Lake Nyasa, had been

---

[1] *i.e.* the C.M.S. and the Society for the Propagation of the Gospel.

[2] H. Goodwin, *A Memoir of Bishop Mackenzie*, Cambridge, 1864, p. 188. Krapf also used to recommend this type of work: 'The Hamitic race is sunk so low that spiritual and temporal means must be applied at one and the same time. Christian families of various secular professions should invariably be connected with every missionary, to represent Christianity intuitively to a people who have left off reasoning.' *CMI.* 49. 87.

impeded by the Murchison cataracts, necessitating a sixty miles' porterage. Worse, the whole Shiré Valley with its weak and disorganised Mang'anja population had recently become the scene of devastating raids by a branch of the fierce Yao tribe, which, with its centre to the south-east of Lake Nyasa, had long been acting the part of middleman to the Arab slave-traders of Kilwa and the half-caste Portuguese of Ibo.[1] It was inevitable that any European settlement in the valley would become a place of refuge for the helpless Mang'anja and would therefore find itself at war with the Yao invaders. Yet it was to the centre of this very district that Livingstone, after proving that the Rovuma, too, was unnavigable, led the members of the Universities Mission; and he was a conscious party to their initial and determining blunder in liberating some ninety Mang'anja slaves from their Yao captors. Regarding these freedmen as a God-sent nucleus for his Christian village, Mackenzie was in fact left facing the toughest of all missionary problems, the responsibility for detribalised Africans in the midst of a tribal society. Religion apart, he had to feed, govern and defend ninety uprooted strangers, not at the coast with access to food and consular protection, but with few fire-arms and limited barter-goods in the most unhealthy part of the interior, surrounded by hostile tribes and possessing only the most tenuous communications with the outside world. A few months and he was defending them by force against the antagonised Yao of the district; a few months more and he was dead, from fever.[2] Three of his companions died the

[1] S. S. Murray, *A Handbook of Nyasaland*, London, 1932, p. 80.
[2] For the full story see R. Coupland, *Kirk on the Zambezi*, Oxford, 1928, pp. 185-240.

next year: others had to be invalided home. His successor, Bishop Tozer, stayed only long enough to try out a healthier site on Mount Morambala before deciding with great prescience,[1] and in the face of Livingstone's scathing reproaches,[2] to transfer the mission to a new base at Zanzibar.

*   *   *   *

2

Tozer had suffered a violent reaction against Livingstone's methods; and agriculture as well as commerce might have gone by the board had events at Zanzibar not forced the Missions to take on wider commitments than purely religious considerations would have suggested. In spite of preventive measures the sixties witnessed an expansion of the slave-trade in the interior. It would seem that between 50,000 and 70,000 slaves were reaching the coast every year.[3] The British warships were catching about 900 of those illicitly exported and their disposal was becoming a serious problem.[4] Hitherto the majority had been landed at Mauritius or the Seychelles and distributed as free labourers

[1] See Tozer to Woodcock of 16.xi.63 *apud* G. Ward, *Bishop Tozer's Letters*, London, 1902.

[2] What would Gregory the Great have said if St. Augustine had landed in the Channel Islands? D. Livingstone, *Narrative of an Expedition to the Zambezi and its Tributaries*, London, 1865, p. 571.

[3] The custom-house records at Kilwa alone showed a a steady rise from 18,500 in 1862 to 22,000 in 1866, and these were for export only, and did not include the large numbers which were smuggled. *CMI.* 72. 91., cf. F. M. Zahn in *AMZ.* 81. 309.

[4] Coupland, *Exploitation*, p. 164.

among the planters. The conditions of this free service were necessarily akin to slavery, and therefore especially open to objection at a time when the British Government was trying to prevent an even more thinly disguised system of importation into the French island of Réunion.[1] At the same time proper rehabilitation of released slaves was a difficult matter. Separation from their tribes was in many ways a worse disaster to them than slavery, a disaster which became apparent only after their release. To house, feed, clothe and nurse them into physical health was only the beginning of the task. Captured usually from among the most backward tribes of all, they had somehow to be educated to survive in the comparatively advanced and individualistic conditions at the coast. Freed slaves presented in miniature what was to recur a generation later as the crucial problem of East African missions. Christianity had not so much to drive out old gods, which were already doomed, as to temper, by industrial and religious education, a social and economic revolution inexorably pressing in from the outside at a rate which threatened to be physically and morally overwhelming. In a sense the issues were clearer at this time than they were ever to be again, since the attacking civilisation was Asian, not European, and since its victims were visibly projected into the middle of it by the British cruisers.

The problem of freed slaves did much to attract missions to East Africa, and even more to interest the British Government in missionary enterprise. The C.M.S. had been running since 1855 a Christian village at Nasik for slaves who were landed at Bombay; and in 1864 the

[1] *AMZ.* 81. 309.

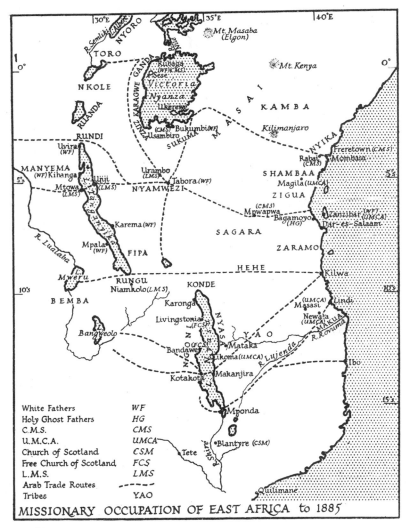

MISSIONARY OCCUPATION OF EAST AFRICA to 1885

White Fathers	WF
Holy Ghost Fathers	HG
C.M.S.	CMS
U.M.C.A.	UMCA
Church of Scotland	CSM
Free Church of Scotland	FCS
L.M.S.	LMS
Arab Trade Routes	- - - - -
Tribes	YAO

B.

first of several Indian-trained Africans were sent as catechists to assist Rebmann at Mombasa.[1] Bishop Ryan tried to do the same at Mauritius, and in 1864 drew the attention of the C.M.S. Committee to the importance of the Seychelles as a base for the ultimate evangelisation of East Africa.[2] Similarly it was the work of the French Congregation of the Holy Ghost among the ex-slaves of Réunion which prompted Bishop Maupoint to visit Zanzibar and to establish a permanent mission there in 1863.[3] When Tozer reached Zanzibar in 1864 with the remnants of the Universities Mission, he immediately accepted an offer of released slaves from the British Consul. Apart from the immediate relief of suffering, this work held an attraction common to all the missions: though the African interior seemed for the moment inaccessible, Zanzibar, Nasik, Mauritius, the Seychelles and, later, Freetown were all to be 'schools of the prophets',[4] from which the cream of their pupils would one day go out to evangelise the tribes from which they had sprung.

Towards the close of the sixties, philanthropic attention became sufficiently disengaged from the trans-Atlantic slave-trade,[5] and sufficiently aware of the East African

---

[1] Stock, *op. cit.*, II, p. 432.

[2] *ibid.*, II, pp. 73–4. A mission to the Seychelles was agreed to by the Committee in 1868. As a result of his suggestion Bishop Ryan was asked to take episcopal charge of the C.M.S. work in East Africa. The Seychelles had a flourishing Roman Catholic mission run by Swiss Capuchins, but these did not extend their field to East Africa until 1922.

[3] G. Goyau, *La Congrégation du St. Esprit*, Paris, 1937, p. 156.

[4] Tozer's *Letters*: to Miss Jackson, 24.ix.64.

[5] The abolition of slavery in the U.S.A. in 1863 was probably the most important factor. As late as 1861 an anti-slavery survey published in *CMI*. 61. 149 contains no reference to East Africa.

situation, to worry the Government to tighten up its restrictive policy in the Indian Ocean. The C.M.S. was prominent in the agitation; and its Lay Secretary, Edward Hutchinson, made himself an acknowledged expert in the whole question of the East Coast slave-trade.[1] The Committee addressed a memorial to the Secretary of State for India in 1869, and encouraged its political friends to press for a Select Committee, which was finally appointed in 1871.[2] Resettlement of freed slaves was naturally an essential part in any plan to liberate more, and Hutchinson, who attended all the sittings of the Select Committee as the C.M.S. witness, indicated that his society would be prepared to help in this connection. When in the following year Sir Bartle Frere was appointed as a special emissary to the Sultan of Zanzibar to negotiate a treaty for the total abolition of the trade by sea, he undertook to advise the C.M.S. as to the most suitable site and system for a settlement.[3] On his way out he visited Pope Pius IX and informed him that the British Government would view with favour a strengthening of the Roman Catholic mission in East Africa.[4] During his stay at Zanzibar, Frere inspected all the missions in the neighbourhood, and in his report[5] recommended that the British Consul should be empowered to

[1] E. Hutchinson, *The Slave Trade of East Africa*, London, 1874.
[2] Actually on the proposal of Mr. Gilpin, a Quaker member; the Committee, however, included two prominent C.M.S. supporters in Mr. Kennaway, the President of the C.M.S., and Mr. Kinnaird. Hansard, 4.vii.71, col. 420.
[3] Stock, *op. cit.*, III, p. 76. A special East Africa Fund was started for this project to which £10,000 was subscribed.
[4] *MC.* 73. 61.
[5] Large sections of this were published in *East Africa as a Field for Missionary Labours*, London, 1874. No subsidies were actually paid till 1884. *CA.* 86. 112.

subsidise them, regardless of denomination or nationality, in proportion to their contribution to the freed slave problem.

Frere's main criticism of the missions as he found them was that the education they provided was too bookish; but he saw one station which appeared to him to be offering a far more competent solution than all the rest. This was the settlement at Bagamoyo, founded in 1868 by the Holy Ghost Fathers from Zanzibar.

To the Catholic mind it was the Church that civilised the 'cultural heritage' of Greece and Rome, and it is the Church which remains the source of all 'true civilisation'. The dichotomy which seems to exist in Europe between the things of the spirit and those of the mind and body is apparent only: if the Church retreated from Europe, Europe would cease to be civilised. In Africa before the European occupation, as earlier in Paraguay and Peru, the Church merely took up again, in so far as it was necessary, those functions which in Europe it had delegated. This position was the easier to maintain in that the Pope exercised a direct control over all missions. Congregations, often on a national basis, were sanctioned to recruit and train missionaries and to watch over their individual welfare; but all heads of missions were centrally appointed, and were responsible in all their official actions to the Prefect of Propaganda. Financial support, though coming from an even wider and often poorer public than that of Protestant missions, was mainly confided to separate organisations—the Society for the Propagation of the Faith being the most important— whose responsibilities began and ended with collecting the

contributions and soliciting the prayers of the home constituency. The influence of public opinion on policy was
therefore negligible, and the priority attached to any particular field of work was a matter for the highest officials only,
since only they could influence the distribution of the
Church's missionary income.[1]

The Vatican had been actively interested in Central
Africa since 1840, but had hitherto concentrated the weight
of its efforts on the Upper Nile valley, under Mgr. Comboni
and his Verona Fathers.[2] The East African outpost had
arisen as a natural extension from the islands in the South
Indian Ocean; and, while the Propaganda was doubtless
aware of the growing importance of Zanzibar, especially
since Speke's explorations, it was content to gain a foothold
and bide its time until the interior became more accessible.
Meantime the freed slaves were a sufficient and a self-
contained task.

The Bagamoyo station at the time of Frere's visit occupied
an estate of about 80 acres on the mainland immediately
opposite Zanzibar. It was run by four priests, eight lay-
brothers, and twelve sisters of the companion order called
'Filles de Marie'. The inmates were 324 freed slaves, of
whom 251 were children; 170 had been handed over by the
British Consul at Zanzibar; of the rest a small number may
have been successful fugitives or slaves abandoned by their
masters, but the majority had been openly bought from

---

[1] cf. J. Schmidlin, *Die Katholischen Missionen in den deutschen Schutzgebieten*,
Hamburg, 1914, p. 11 *sqq.*

[2] J. P. Thoonen, *Black Martyrs*, London, 1941, p. 32. The early history of this
mission falls outside the scope of this volume; *vide infra*, p. 237.

dealers.[1] Though undertaken in good faith, this practice must certainly have been a stimulus to the trade. The principle followed was that 'the negro should learn to be a useful member of society whilst having taught the doctrines of Christianity'. This was effected by a mixture of schooling and manual labour on the mission's plantations, about five and a half hours of each a day, with an additional hour of religious exercises. The pupils were divided into three intellectual grades: the highest was given a literary education, the middle grade was instructed in a skilled trade, while the lowest did nothing but manual labour. Père Horner, the Superior, reckoned that by this method an initial grant of £5 would cover the expenses of an adult recruit until he was self-supporting. Children would cost 5d. a day until they were 12, and the aged and infirm 6d. a day. On these terms he was prepared to take as many freed slaves as the British Government cared to send.[2]

Within about five years of Frere's visit the wider organisation of the Holy Ghost Mission had begun to take shape. Zanzibar was then only the quartermaster's depot, the training-house for novices from Europe and the collecting point for slaves handed over by the British Government. Bagamoyo was the mainland ransoming centre, and the industrial and catechetical training establishment for the whole mission. As soon as the baptised Christians grew up

[1] e.g. MC. 67. 68. After noting that boys of five cost 25 francs and girls 40, Horner continues: 'Si les associés de la Propagation de la Foi voyaient l'abjection et la torture d'où leur sou par semaine retire ces pauvres créatures, ils estimeraient encore mieux le prix de leur aumône; s'ils entendaient les actions de grâce que ces âmes devenues chrétiennes addressent à Dieu pour leurs libérateurs, leur zéle et leur charité n'auraient pas de repos tant qu'il resterait un esclave à racheter.'

[2] Frere, op. cit., p. 48 sqq.

or became self-supporting, they were married off in batches[1] and settled under the charge of a missionary in self-contained Christian villages farther inland, at places where friendly relations had been previously cultivated with the local chiefs. By 1885 five such villages had been founded, spreading more than a hundred miles from Bagamoyo.

'I can recommend no change in the arrangements', wrote Frere, echoing the opinion of every traveller who had experienced the Fathers' hospitality. 'I would recommend it as a model to be followed in any attempt to civilise and evangelise Africa.'[2] Scriptural authority was irrelevant, he argued in an open letter to the Archbishop of Canterbury, since it gave details of missionary work among civilised peoples only. The earliest records of missions to the barbarians of northern Europe showed that the missionary unit corresponded as closely as possible to 'a fully organised Christian community' and was concerned to teach not only religious dogma and morals but 'all the arts of civilised life'.[3]

Frere's argument went only a step further than Livingstone's, but it was a vital step, touching on a deep-rooted difference in attitude between Catholics and Calvinists on the one side and Evangelical Protestants on the other. For

[1] 'Les cérémonies de mariage s'accomplissaient, et pour que rien ne manquât à la fête, on avait soin d'aller tuer au fleuve un hippopotame, qui faisait les frais de la noce.' *Aperçu historique, Congrégation du St. Esprit*, 1936–1, p. 322.

[2] Frere, *op. cit.*, p. 49.

[3] *ibid.*, p. 71. In Frere's draft report on his visits to the mission stations in the vicinity of Mombasa, now in the Zanzibar Museum, there appears the following passage, which was subsequently deleted from the fair copy: 'Mr. Rebmann not allowing preaching or any effort to extend worldly advantages amongst the neighbouring tribes, the result of this Mission has been what I fear would be generally deemed insignificant.' Kindly communicated by Sir J. M. Gray.

where Livingstone had dreamed of bringing about a general penetration of western civilisation as a preliminary to the conversion of individuals to Christianity, Frere was proposing that the Church should associate its primary evangelism with an elaborate system of institutional good works. The Catholic, whose primary object was to induce membership of a Church with consequent access to 'the means of grace' in its Sacraments and its discipline, saw little harm in such material incentives. They were the free gifts of a beneficent Creator to His faithful children. The Calvinist, too, as exemplified by the Basel missionaries in West Africa and the Free Church of Scotland in India, while refusing to accept a sacramental system as the normal medium for the action of the Holy Spirit, seemed prepared to allow the Christian community to become at least a 'bulwark against Satan' by creating a social system and a moral atmosphere in which the Christian character could grow.[1] Like the Catholic, he laid the stress on life after conversion rather than on achieving the supreme moment of 'rebirth' or 'change of heart', which was the main preoccupation of the Evangelical, whether German or English.[2] To these, economic incentives spelt nothing but danger, both to the inquirer

[1] *infra*, p. 58.

[2] Thoonen, *op. cit.*, p. 57. 'Mackay's method, somewhat puzzling to Catholics, is in accordance with the strictly Protestant idea of conversion, the essence of which is a psychological act of trust, or even an emotional crisis, on the part of the candidate. Conversion in the Catholic, missiological sense, consists in the incorporation of the candidate in the visible Church. On the part of the neophyte this requires the desire and the essential dispositions; on the part of the Church and its minister it demands the active acceptance, the "reception", with the necessary sacraments. If this missiological conversion has also to be accompanied by a moral conversion, that is, a change of morals, by the turning away from culpable practices, then this is but an accidental element, a preliminary, the necessity of which depends on circumstances.'

who would be deceived by worldly benefits, and to the missionary who would forget his 'message' as the result of such material distractions. The Evangelical subscriber paid and prayed for 'conversions': 'I am entirely in favour of the Lay Evangelist, the Female Evangelist, the Medical Evangelist, whenever Gospel-preaching is the substantive work; but when it is proposed to have a pious Industrial Superintendent, or an Evangelical tile-manufacturer, or a Low Church breeder of cattle or raiser of turnips, I draw my line.'[1]

A generation later Evangelicals were to discover that the pious superintendents were a necessary part of successful missions in East Africa—so much so, that if laymen were not available, then ordained missionaries must be diverted to do the job. For the moment, however, Frere's open letter was treated with reserve. The German missionary world, arguing without experience, attacked it in their press,[2] and allotted to Livingstone his share of the blame.[3] The C.M.S. loyally took Frere's advice about their new freed slave settlement, which was founded in 1875 and which became the largest of its kind; and yet as late as 1890 the Committee passed a resolution that Freretown was an exceptional case.[4]

---

[1] R. N. Cust, *An Essay on the prevailing methods of evangelising the non-Christian World*, London, 1894, p. 16. Cust was a retired Indian Civil servant, an indefatigable member of the C.M.S. Committee. A man of forthright views, he described himself as having 'had the advantage of being a Ruler of Millions, living among and loving his people and knowing all about their religions and customs'.

[2] *AMZ.* 81. 309: 'Uns ist das Bedenkliche, dass die in Freres Eastern Africa dargelegten Missionspläne, wenn wir sie recht verstehen, das evangelische und biblische Missionsprinzip mit dem römisch-katholischen zu vertauschen drohen, ein Irrtum, das in unsern Tagen, mit der Gewalt einer Epidemie evangelishe Herzen gefangen nimmt.'

[3] *ibid.*, 82. 117.

[4] Cust, *op. cit.*, p. 19.

For a purely practical reason, the High Church Universities Mission was just as shy. Dr. Steere[1] refused to commit his staff to freed slave work for its own sake. He would take in just enough freedmen to assure himself of a nucleus of African catechists and clergy for future work on the mainland, and he would teach a trade to those of his pupils who proved unsuitable for ordination; but that was to be the limit of his industrial work.[2]

There for the moment this vital issue was shelved, to re-emerge after the partition of Africa as 'Missions and Education'. Meanwhile, the freed slave problem had served to attract the Holy Ghost Fathers, to call out the C.M.S. in force and to provide the U.M.C.A. with its opening. On the political side it had led to further interference with the slave-trade and drawn the attention of the British Government to the missions as an auxiliary arm, whose interests could profitably be furthered if they happened to coincide with its own.

*   *   *   *

3

During the fifteen years from 1858 to 1873 in which the missions were slowly gathering their forces at the coast and concentrating their efforts temporarily upon freed slaves, the exploration of East Africa by European travellers was

[1] Tozer had resigned in 1872, leaving Dr. Steere in charge of the mission. Steere was consecrated in 1874 and held the bishopric till his death in 1883.

[2] Heanley, *op. cit.*, p. 109.

proceeding apace. In 1858, the same year in which Livingstone began his exploration of the Zambezi, Burton and Speke set out to find Erhardt's 'Sea of Unyamwezi'. Travelling up the main Arab trade route from Bagamoyo, they reached Lake Tanganyika at Ujiji and spent some months investigating its northern end. On the homeward march Speke left Burton at Tabora and made a quick visit to the southern shores of the Victoria Nyanza. In 1862 Speke returned with Grant to explore this lake, skirting its western shore from south to north, locating the outflow of the Nile at the Ripon Falls, and making homewards through northern Uganda and down the White Nile. At Gondokoro the travellers met Samuel Baker and his courageous wife approaching from the north and directed their attention to the other great basin of the Nile, subsequently named by Baker the Albert Lake. The Bakers completed their journey in 1865; and in the following year Livingstone, having published the narrative of his Zambezi expedition, struck once more into the heart of Africa on his last long journey, which, though little of it lay within the modern political boundaries of East Africa, was close enough to its southern and western periphery to lend additional colour and form to the pictures painted by Speke and Burton.

The effects of these discoveries upon the future of the missionary invasion were considerable. Even the simplest geographical results, the appearance of great lakes upon the hitherto vacant spaces of the map of Africa, had a special fascination for a generation that was just experiencing the new power afforded by steam navigation. It is significant that the placing of steamers upon these inland waterways was to figure in the plans of all five of the British missionary societies which were about to assault the interior of Eastern Africa, and was to be an actual condition of the large benefactions which were to be responsible for setting two of them in motion. From the narratives of the explorers, too, Europe was able to glean its first comprehensive picture of the ethnography and commerce of the whole region, with results which helped greatly to determine the main lines of missionary infiltration. It became clear from the writings of Krapf and Burton that the north-eastern quarter of the hinterland, comprising most of modern Kenya and the northern province of Tanganyika, was the least suited to peaceful penetration, since it was the theatre of the Masai and related Nilo-Hamitic tribes, nomadic, pastoral and predatory, whose country even the armed caravans of the Arabs feared to enter. Farther west, Speke and Baker showed that the line of the Nile from Lake Victoria to Lake Albert formed an ethnic and cultural boundary, to the north of which lived other Nilotic and Nilo-Hamitic races, who, if not as dangerous as the Masai, were as sharply distinguished as these from the rest of the East African peoples, and whose external relations were with the Egyptian slave-traders from Khartoum and not with the Arabs from Zanzibar. South and west of the area dominated by the Masai, and south of the Somerset Nile, the tribes, though infinitely varied in customs and social organisation, had one common feature in that they all spoke grammatically related languages of the great 'Bantu' family, which extends over the whole southern half of Africa from the Equator to the Cape Province, and of which Kiswahili, the language of the east coast, is itself a member. It was the Bantu three-quarters of East Africa, which had been for nearly a century the commercial sphere of the Arab and 'Swahili' traders of the coast, which seemed to be the natural field for missionary penetration; and within this area, the most promising regions were, as the Arabs had already discovered, those lying in the far interior, roughly within the segment of a circle formed by the three great lakes. This fertile and well-watered crescent carried perhaps four-fifths of the total population of the area, and within it lived the peoples who were politically the most advanced, and also the most permanently settled on the land. In its centre were the Nyamwezi, organised in a large number of very small states, but still endowed with the commercial initiative to rival the coastmen in the long-distance carrying trade of East Africa; north and west of them there stretched a line of densely populated, highly organised, monarchical states —Karagwe and Urundi, Ruanda and Ankole, Bunyoro and Buganda—which, though they might be ruled by bloody and barbarous tyrants, contained at least that principle of order, the seeming absence of which in many parts of Africa was so baffling to the European mind.

The final and the most important stimulus of the explorers upon the missionary societies was in their revelation of the extent and character of the Arab trade itself. This stimulus acted in two ways. On the one hand it showed that the interior was not as inaccessible to outsiders as the earlier experiences of Krapf in Kenya and of the U.M.C.A. missionaries on the Lower Shiré had seemed to suggest. Between these two points several well-frequented routes led from the coastal ports across to the lake regions. At Zanzibar and Bagamoyo, porters and caravan leaders could be engaged who knew the roads and were accustomed to the long months of marching. At Tabora, nearly five hundred miles from the coast, there was a small commercial metropolis, where 'the traveller, by means of introductory letters to the doyen of the Arab merchants, can always recruit his stock of country currency—cloth, beads and wire—his requirements of powder and ball, and his supplies of spices, comforts and drugs', though at a price about five times their market value in Zanzibar.[1] Here, the merchant princes lived 'comfortably, often splendidly' in their depots, often for years at a time, 'leaving their factors and slaves to travel about the country and collect the items of traffic'. From Tabora well-known routes radiated, northwards to the Victoria Nyanza and to the kingdoms of Karagwe and Buganda, westwards to Lake Tanganyika, south-westwards to the Rukwa Lake, and due south to the highlands circling Lake Nyasa.[2] Farther south, a still more heavily travelled route led inland from Kilwa through the Yao country towards the centre and south of Lake Nyasa. At Kotakota, half-way up the lake's western shore, there was an Arab settlement second in importance only to that at Tabora, where a family of Swahili 'Jumbes' had made an industry of growing food for caravans and of ferrying slaves in dhows across the lake.[3] Wherever, therefore, a European might wish to settle among the Bantu tribes of East Africa, he could be sure that an Arab had been there before, that the

[1] Burton, *op. cit.*, I, p. 334.   [2] *ibid.*, p. 325.
[3] Johnston to Salisbury, 17.iii.90. F.O. 84. 2051.

people were accustomed to some contact with outsiders, and that some system for obtaining supplies from the coast could be arranged.

The other side of the same picture, and the side which constituted even more of a challenge to missionary enterprise, was the revelation of what this trade implied in the lives of the African inhabitants of the interior. And it was here that Livingstone's often apparently aimless wandering among the byways of the continent were of infinitely greater significance than the rapid and efficient transits of Burton, Speke and Grant along the highroads. To Burton, indeed, the Arabs were the 'truly noble race', whose open-handed hospitality and hearty goodwill showed up 'the niggardness of the savage and selfish African'.[1] Speke and Grant were more perceptive and more compassionate; but it must be remembered that they travelled for the most part among peoples who were thriving on the slave-trade. For to the more enterprising and powerful of the native chieftains, like Mutesa of Buganda or Mirambo of the Nyamwezi, the advent of the Arabs had offered golden opportunities. They raided their weaker neighbours; they handed over their prisoners to the Arabs; they received in exchange the cloth with which to reward their soldiers, and, later, the fire-arms with which to assert still more effectively their hegemony over the disorganised Basoga beyond the Ripon Falls, or over the small and backward tribes living between Unyamwezi and the Tanganyika Lake. Inevitably, through the accident of their route, Burton, Speke and Grant saw more of the prosperity of the oppressors than of the misery of the

[1] Burton, *op. cit.*, I, p. 323.

oppressed. Livingstone's path, by contrast, lay from the first through heart-rending scenes of human callousness and cruelty.

> We passed a woman tied by the neck to a tree and dead. . . . We saw others tied up in a similar manner, and one lying in the path shot or stabbed for she was in a pool of blood. The explanation we got invariably was that the Arab who owned these victims was enraged at losing his money by the slaves becoming unable to march. . . . Today we came upon a man dead from starvation. . . . One of our men wandered and found a number of slaves with slave-sticks on, abandoned by their master from want of food. . . . We passed village after village and gardens, all deserted. . . . A great deal if not all the lawlessness of this quarter is the result of the slave-trade, for the Arabs buy whoever is brought to them, and in a country covered with forest as this is kidnapping can be prosecuted with the greatest ease. . . . The Wahiyao generally are still the most active agents the slave-traders have. The caravan leaders from Kilwa arrive at a Yao village, show the goods they have brought, are treated liberally by the elders and told to wait and enjoy themselves . . . then a foray is made against the Wanyasa who have few or no guns. The Yao who come against them are abundantly supplied with both by their coast guests. Several of the low coast Arabs, who differ in nothing from the Yao, usually accompany the foray and do business on their own account: this is the usual way in which a safari is furnished with slaves.[1]

The Kilwa traders who worked these southerly districts of East Africa were not unique in their atrocities. Later, when wandering through the lands to the west of Lake Tanganyika, where the underlings of the hospitable Arabs of Tabora were about their masters' business, Livingstone,

[1] D. Livingstone, *Last Journals*, London, 1874, I, pp. 56, 62, 64, 66, 78.

even before he had witnessed the frightful and purposeless massacre at Nyangwe which 'sent him staggering back along the path to Ujiji',[1] had formed the impression that the traders were as bloodthirsty as the cannibal Manyema of the district, 'though where the people can fight they are as civil as possible'.[2]

Needless to say, Livingstone was not so naïve as to suppose that it was the Arabs who were alone to blame. Wherever he went he was careful to explain to chiefs and people that the guilt lay as much upon the sellers as the buyers. 'I tell them that if they sell their fellows, they are like the man who holds the victim while the Arab performs the murder.'[3] Though not always satisfied that he had succeeded in arousing a sense of guilt in his audiences, he found that they were nevertheless profoundly impressed by his tales of the loss of life among slaves on their way to the coast.[4] Sometimes he heard that the Arabs themselves did not always return safely from their journeys, and this fact moved him to define with characteristic but telling understatement the terms of his own self-dedication: 'It struck me after Sef had numbered up the losses that the Kilwa people sustained by death in their endeavours to enslave people, that similar losses on the part of those who go to proclaim liberty to the captives, the opening of the prison to them that are bound, to save and elevate, need not be made so very much of as they sometimes are.'[5]

[1] R. Coupland, *Livingstone's Last Journey*, 1947, p. 120.   [3] *ibid.*, I, p. 62.
[2] D. Livingstone, *Last Journals*, II, p. 118.   [4] *ibid.*, I, p. 67.
[5] *ibid.*, I, p. 74.

*　　*　　*　　*

4

Livingstone's death in 1873 among the swamps of Lake Bangweolo opened a new chapter in the history of the missionary occupation. In his life and in his writings he had struck exactly the note which would carry farthest in mid-Victorian England, but much of the life remained mysterious until his death laid bare its secrets. The public burial of his embalmed remains in Westminster Abbey nearly a year later was more than just a fitting climax to the dramatic story of how his faithful porters had carried them 1,500 miles to the East African coast. Seldom, perhaps, has a mere ceremony served so effectively to gather up all the threads of interest which, united, lead to action. The Abbey ticket-holders, the élite and the expert, the explorers and geographers, the churchmen and philanthropists, had long been following his career: now they suddenly found themselves with the support they needed, of the thousands of ordinary people who lined the streets, of Southampton as well as London.[1] A hundred pulpits took up the tale of the missionary-explorer who had died on his knees, invoking in his solitude 'Heaven's rich blessing' upon everyone who would help 'to heal this open sore of the world'. A revolution was set in motion which was to bring a new kind of missionary into Africa and a new and more numerous class of subscribers on to the societies' lists. In missionary circles the talk was no longer of 'perishing heathen', but of Africans 'suffering' and 'neglected'. Soon it was to be of 'open doors'

[1] Introduction to Stanley's *How I found Livingstone*, p. lxxv, 2nd edn., undated.

and 'untouched millions'.[1] The *Daily Telegraph*, which was about to combine with the *New York Herald* to send Stanley on his journey 'Through the Dark Continent' from Zanzibar to the mouth of the Congo, expressed the wider national sentiment and that of the average subscriber in its obituary article: 'The work of England for Africa must henceforth begin in earnest where Livingstone left it off.'[2]

The Scottish Presbyterian Churches were the first to move. The Free Church had indeed contemplated a Central African mission as early as 1861, thanks to the enthusiasm of Dr. James Stewart, later the director of the famous South African mission at Lovedale, who, undeterred by the opposition of the Foreign Missions Committee of the General Assembly, had gathered together a special sub-committee with separate funds, and had himself gone out to meet Livingstone on the Zambezi to prospect for a field of work. Stewart himself had then reported that the difficulties were too great; but in May 1874 he reintroduced the project in the General Assembly, proposing that, as a memorial to Livingstone, an institution, 'of an industrial as well as an educational nature,' should be placed in a carefully chosen and influential place in Central Africa, where it might grow into a town and later into a city, and become a great centre for commerce, civilisation and Christianity. Once again Stewart was left to form a separate Livingstonia sub-committee, but this time, with the aid of a nucleus of sub-stantial Glasgow merchants, the £10,000 required to launch

---

[1] cf. a brilliant study of 'missionary vocation' by Ruth Rouse in *IRM.*, April 1917, p. 17, compiled from the application forms of candidates.
[2] H. M. Stanley, *op. cit.*, Preface to 2nd edn., p. lxxviii.

the scheme was over-subscribed. The plans were thorough. On the advice of Sir Bartle Frere and Horace Waller,[1] the southern end of Lake Nyasa was chosen for the site; and a small steamer was ordered to ply between Mandala, at the head of the Murchison Cataracts, and the lake. E. D. Young, the leader of the Livingstone search party of 1867, who knew the route at first hand, consented to take charge of the expedition. With characteristic insight, Stewart also selected a young doctor-ordinand, Robert Laws, and smoothed the difficulties arising from his membership of the United Presbyterian Church, with consequences pregnant both for the future of Nyasaland and also for the Union of the United and Free Churches, of which Laws himself rose to be the first missionary moderator in 1908. The party left London on the 21st May, 1875, and, having assembled their steamer at the mouth of the Zambezi, dismantled it again at the Murchison rapids and reassembled it on the Upper Shiré, they sailed into Lake Nyasa at dawn on the 11th October, all hands singing the metrical version of the Hundredth Psalm.[2]

The Livingstonia expedition was accompanied by a representative of the Established Church of Scotland, Harry Henderson, who toured the lake with Young and Laws in search of a site for a sister mission, and eventually fixed on a position in the Shiré Highlands to the south of the lake, whither he returned in the following year with a doctor and a party of artisans to establish the settlement of 'Blantyre'.

[1] Lay Superintendent of the first U.M.C.A. expedition and editor of Livingstone's *Last Journals*. A firm believer in 'commerce and Christianity', he became one of the most powerful missionary and anti-slave-trade propagandists.

[2] W. P. Livingstone, *Laws of Livingstonia*, London, 1921, pp. 5–9, 41 and 69.

Henderson, though he had had ten years of pioneering experience in Queensland, was no leader. In December 1876 he addressed to Laws a desperate appeal for help,[1] and after serious misconduct by the lay members of the mission some two years later,[2] Blantyre had practically to be re-founded by Hetherwick and Scott in 1883. But the site selected by Henderson, on his own admission more by good luck than judgment, was a most strategic one for the missionary enterprise of Nyasaland. High and healthy, on the plateau overhanging the Murchison rapids, it commanded the line of water communications and established a British interest at a point from which Portuguese penetration might otherwise have rendered the lake settlements untenable.

There remained the problem of transport on the Lower Shiré and the Zambezi; and when the Free Church sub-committee demurred at the suggestion of a second steamer, its convener, Mr. James Stevenson of Glasgow, founded on his own account the Livingstonia Central African Trading Company, with the dual object of supplying the two missions and of bringing out ivory at a price which would undercut the Arab merchants using slave porters. In 1878 Stevenson sent out the brothers Moir as the first managers, who made their headquarters at Mandala, near Blantyre, and rapidly spread a network of trading-posts as far as Karonga's at the north end of Lake Nyasa. During the twelve years of its independent existence, before it was bought by Rhodes and merged with the British South Africa Company as the African Lakes Corporation, the

---

[1] W. P. Livingstone, *Laws*, 1921, pp. 42 and 105.
[2] *infra*, p. 59.

Livingstonia Company's activities were so much bound up with the missionary societies that its history may be considered a part of theirs.[1]

In the year after Livingstone's death the Universities Mission, too, entered upon an important period of expansion. In 1873 the gentle Tozer was succeeded by Edward Steere, the only other man who had been with the Mission since its retreat from Mount Morambala ten years before. A doctor of laws and a gifted linguist, a theologian, a skilled printer, the architect and building-foreman of Zanzibar Cathedral, a man of stern discipline and unbounded energy, whose twenty years of service in Africa meant permanent separation from his wife and family, Bishop Steere was certainly the most capable leader in the history of the Mission. During an English tour after his consecration in 1874, he added eighteen members to his European staff and gave an impulse to propaganda among the home constituency which doubled the Society's income

---

[1] F. L. M. Moir, *After Livingstone: An African Trade Romance*, London, 1923. Towards the end of its independent existence, the Company became unpopular with both the missions and the British Government, chiefly, it would seem, because it was trying to take upon itself too much responsibility for its very limited capital. Of course the very idea of the brothers Moir and their team exercising the powers of a Chartered Company (as was later suggested) was ludicrous, and their pretensions in that direction disagreeable. H. H. Johnston, who was apt to value business men by the amount of money they were prepared to sink in the extension of the Empire, described the Company's directors as 'a set of miserly uncultured Glasgow merchants and shipbuilders' who wasted most of the interview he had with them 'by angrily discussing how they might turn the Universities Mission out of Monkey Bay and other places on Lake Nyasa, because, they said, it was high time to prevent the further spread of Episcopalianism among the people.' Johnston to Salisbury, 7.x.90. F.O. 84. 2052. Still, the Livingstonia Company has strong claims to have been primarily a philanthropic enterprise. It was agreed that any profits in excess of a 5 per cent dividend should be paid to the Missions; while in actual fact no dividend was paid for eight years. Moir, *op. cit.*

during the six following years.[1] No sooner was he back in Zanzibar than the freed slaves were moved out of the town into a separate establishment at Mbweni and regular schools for free Africans from the mainland set up in their place. In 1875 the first permanent base on the mainland was founded at Magila in the Bondei country, which was destined to become the real centre of the Zanzibar diocese. The following year Steere gathered together the Makua and Nyanja slaves who were in his care with the object of returning them to their homes in the interior. At Masasi, a hundred miles inland from Lindi, the freedmen refused to go any farther, and they were therefore settled in a colony under the care of two missionaries. From here W. P. Johnson in 1879 pushed up the Rovuma to the Yao metropolis at Mataka's; and in 1881 he moved on to start a fifty years' apostolate among the Nyanja peoples living along the eastern shores of Lake Nyasa.[2]

In 1875 the C.M.S. Committee were actively forwarding sober plans for freed slave work at Freretown, when an outside event broke in upon their peace and gave evidence of the new spirit that was stirring among the Evangelicals of the Church of England. On 15th November, 1875, there appeared in the *Daily Telegraph* a letter from Stanley,[3]

[1] 'We shall have to fix the sites of future cities as the monks did in England. . . . First of all we will set up a great central school for the people of one language, and then, whilst preachers go out from it to reach every part of the tribe, we will send up artificers and workmen who will teach the natives all that our civilisation can give them.' Heanley, *op. cit.*, p. 133.

[2] G. H. Wilson, *A History of the Universities Mission to Central Africa*, London, 1936, Chapter IX.

[3] The letter was written in Buganda and entrusted to Linant de Bellefonds, an emissary of Gordon's to King Mutesa, and forwarded by Gordon after the murder of Linant. *Vide* H. B. Thomas in the *Uganda Journal*, July 1934, p. 7.

describing the improvement of political conditions in Buganda since Speke's visit in 1862, and boasting the friendly and enlightened reception by King Mutesa of the Gospel truths which Stanley had imparted to him.[1] Stanley announced that he was leaving behind him one of his servants, a Christian trained by the Universities Mission at Zanzibar,[2] to carry on Mutesa's instruction, and he now challenged the English missionary societies to follow up the work. Left to themselves, the committee would doubtless have discarded Stanley's letter as sensational rather than judicious,[3] but three days after its publication the secretary received an anonymous offer of £5,000 towards a mission to the Nyanza, and before even the issue had been discussed, other money contributions and offers of service started to pour in.

To those members of the committee who failed to discern 'a providential combinátion of circumstances in the recent openings in Equatorial Africa' the idea of such a mission appeared thoroughly romantic. A chain of stations developing slowly inland with Buganda as the ultimate goal would

---

[1] Chief Jamusi Miti, the author of a MS. *History of Buganda*, now in the keeping of the School of Oriental and African Studies, who was about nine years old when Stanley passed through Buganda, entirely bears out Stanley's statements. Sir John Gray, however, is certainly nearer to the truth in pronouncing Stanley to have been 'splendidly duped'. Mutesa, twice visited by the agents of Egypt from the north, and rebuffed in his diplomatic overtures to the Sultan of Zanzibar in the east, was doubtless clutching very deliberately at the straw offered by Stanley in his advocacy of Christian missions from Europe. *Uganda Journal*, January 1934, p. 22; *infra*, pp. 67-9

[2] Dallington Scopion Maftaa, who wrote to Bishop Steere on 23rd April, 1876, asking for 'Swahili prayers and the big black Bible' and for 'slates, board and chalk, that I may teach the Waganda the way of God'. Heanley, *op. cit.*, p. 196: Miti, *op. cit.*, relates that 'Bafutah' afterwards became corrupted by riches and power, and fell away from his former zeal, living as an ordinary Arab resident in Buganda.

[3] Stock, *op. cit.*, III, p. 95.

have been a different proposition, but the terms of the anonymous offer and of the earmarked subscriptions were a Nyanza mission first and supporting stations, if any, later. 'Many wise heads were shaken'[1] on the day of its adoption, after a fierce debate, a week later, and many more must have ached when it came to making plans. Even the direct route from Mombasa involved four months of overland marching, and this was as yet unexplored and known to be occupied by the Masai, the most warlike of all the tribes. On Grant's[2] advice, the much longer route, used by the Arab traders, from Zanzibar through Tabora and Usukuma, was finally selected, while Cameron[3] suggested Mpwapwa as a site for a supporting station. The valedictory instructions delivered to the six members of the first expedition in April 1876 seem frail indeed: mainly concerned with caveats about meddling in native politics, they stressed the importance of Sabbath observance, of daily prayers and restraint of the natural love of sport.[4] And yet—building started at Mpwapwa in September, two members of the party were received by King Mutesa in July 1877, and a reinforcement of three reached Rubaga[5] by the Nile route early the following year.

Two years after his death Livingstone's own society decided to follow him into the East African field. The London

---

[1] Stock, *op. cit.*, III, p. 95.

[2] The companion of Speke on his explorations of 1862–4.

[3] Leader of a second relief expedition for Livingstone in 1873. On hearing of Livingstone's death, Cameron continued his journey right across Africa to Benguela, via Ujiji and Manyema. He became a much-quoted authority on slavery in the interior.

[4] *i.e.* they were not to shoot except for the pot. Stock, *op. cit.*, III, p. 98.

[5] Mutesa's capital, now the site of the principal Roman Catholic cathedral, on the outskirts of modern Kampala.

Missionary Society, theoretically undenominational, in fact drew its support mainly from the Congregationalists, and, as such, represented doctrinally at once the least formal and the most individualistic conception of Christianity. In missionary work it was predisposed to favour intensive methods, since, renouncing so much of the control and discipline which other Churches exercised over their professed adherents, it had farther to lead them before they made the formal profession by baptism. The missionary, being more an individual Christian and less the representative of a Church or system, was expected to spend most of his working life among one tribe or group. It is not therefore surprising, that, when Livingstone had come to advocate the most extensive of all methods, he should have felt unable to continue in its employment. What was surprising was that twenty years later they should undertake a mission separated from the coast by 850 miles of unevangelised territory, the material difficulties of which alone demanded a strength of organisation and a continuity which they of all the societies were least able to supply.

As in the case of the C.M.S. Uganda mission, the decision was prompted by a single large offer, again of £5,000, towards the purchase of a steamer for work on Lake Tanganyika.[1] The first expedition left in 1877 and, travelling by the great central trade-route, reached Ujiji in rapid time. During the next five years stations were opened at Urambo, at Ujiji itself, on Kavala Island and at Mtowa on the west coast of the lake. Yet the mission was both

---

[1] The donor was Robert Arthington of Leeds, who also assisted the Baptists in the Congo.

impractical and unlucky. By the Society's constitution all missionaries served on a basis of absolute equality; and in the event no natural leader was thrown up with the influence to impose a coherent policy on his colleagues. Of the two experienced missionaries who were sent out, Roger Price withdrew and J. B. Thompson died within a year, and Dr. Joseph Mullens, the Secretary of the Society, who himself hurried out to fill the breach, died before reaching the lake. During the first sixteen years eight more men died and fourteen more, becoming unnerved, resigned. Of these who stayed some struggled to keep open the east coast route and the northern stations on the lake; others, who were eventually to prevail, preferred the water route via Lake Nyasa and, as a field of work, the Nyasa–Tanganyika plateau. By 1893 all the original stations had been given up, the steamer had been sold, and the Society had transferred its attention to the British sphere of influence in Northern Rhodesia.[1] Yet from a wider than missionary point of view the attempt was significant. The steamer alone was an important link in Central African communications. Its transport to Lake Tanganyika was undertaken in 1882 by the Livingstonia Company, whose porters carried it in sections along native tracks about eighteen inches wide for the last two hundred miles from Lake Nyasa.[2] This venture led to the commencement by the Company of the Stevenson Road, connecting the two lakes, and so in turn through the Cape-to-Cairo

[1] R. Lovett, *A History of the London Missionary Society*, 2 vols., London, 1899, I, pp. 649–70.
[2] Moir, *op. cit.*, p. 76 *sqq.* The country between the two lakes was first explored by Joseph Thomson in 1877. The road was begun in 1879 when the steamer contract was accepted; but only fifty miles had been completed by 1883.

project in the minds of Rhodes and Johnston to the occupation by the British South Africa Company of north-
eastern Rhodesia.[1] The most remarkable members of the
London Mission during its East African days were two
retired master mariners, E. C. Hore[2] and A. J. Swann,[3]
who successfully navigated Lake Tanganyika for ten years,
the former being a trusted informant of Sir John Kirk, the
British Consul-General at Zanzibar, the latter becoming one
of H. H. Johnston's first assistants when the Nyasaland
administration was founded. One other missionary, Dr.
Southon, is memorable for a residence of four years at the
court of the Nyamwezi chieftain, Mirambo.[4]

*   *   *   *

5

The missionary penetration of Central Africa by Catholic
Europe followed close upon that by Protestant England.
Unlike the Protestant movement, its origins cannot be traced
to the popular acclamation of any explorer hero, nor yet to
any semi-religious hatred of the Arab slave-trade. Moreover,
it was virtually uninfluenced by the Catholic mission already
working near the coast. Even more directly than in the
Protestant movement, however, the forces were set in

[1] *infra*, p. 125.
[2] E. C. Hore. He described his experiences in an extremely readable book called
Tanganyika, London, 1892.
[3] A. J. Swann, *Fighting the Slave-hunters in Central Africa*, London, 1910.
[4] See especially his MSS., *History of the country and people of Unyamwezi*.
Southon to L.M.S., 28.iii.80.

motion by one extraordinary man. The story of Cardinal
Lavigerie is like that of the street scavenger who made a
great fortune out of what other men had thrown away.
Called from a chair at the Sorbonne in 1856 to direct a
mission to the Eastern Churches,[1] he invented, after the
rising of the Druses in 1860, a system of self-supporting
'orphanages', which served both to forward the Catholic
cause and to excite the gratitude of the French state.[2]
Refusing a sure stepping-stone to the purple in the arch-
bishopric of Lyons, he accepted in 1867 that of Algiers.
There, a disastrous famine in the following year provided the
opportunity for more orphanages, and so of missionary work
among Muslims in a form which the French government,
in its own interests, could not afford to forbid.[3] To meet
the emergency Lavigerie founded a new missionary order,
the Société de Notre-Dame d'Afrique or the White Fathers,
which was sanctioned by Pius IX in 1868. For recruits he
turned once more to the humble and meek; he toured
France in search of vocations missed through poverty, and,
as usual, got what he wanted. In 1869 he acquired a huge
estate in the valley of the Chélif, where the orphans were set
to work for their keep under the supervision of lay-brethren.
Lavigerie himself introduced the Muscat grape from Spain,
which yielded the supremely successful 'vin de Carthage'.
As the orphans grew up they were settled in Christian
villages; but Lavigerie's order continued to grow, and by the
end of a decade was in need of a new field for its activities.[4]

[1] L'œuvre des Écoles d'Orient.
[2] G. Goyau, Le Cardinal Lavigerie, Paris, 1925, p. 50.
[3] ibid., p. 85 sq.   [4] ibid., p. 130.

Lavigerie's ambitions for his Church were limitless and he was prepared to use every means to further them. How he persistently used his ecclesiastical position in the interests of French imperialism in Tunisia and won a famous compliment from Gambetta,[1] belongs to another story, but it illustrates a side of him that was also active in Central Africa. In 1877 he drew the attention of Pius IX to King Leopold's African International Association, which was supposed to be co-ordinating the results of exploration, and establishing 'scientific' stations along the line of Cameron's recent march from Zanzibar to Benguela. There had been a Protestant majority at the recent Brussels conference, he urged, and Protestant missions were already launching expeditions.[2] To the Quai d'Orsay he wrote that as a French bishop in Africa he could not remain indifferent to so considerable a task of civilisation, which concerned alike the forces of humanitarianism, of science and of religion: 'J'ai pensé qu'il serait avantageux pour la France d'être représentée, dans ces vastes régions encore mystérieuses, non pas seulement par des pionniers isolés, mais par une corporation qui pourra donner à son action civilisatrice et scientifique la suite, la durée, l'étendue qui la rendent puissante.'[3]

Back at Algiers, Lavigerie worked out detailed plans for a Central African mission. It should aim to be the religious counterpart of the African International Association, working within the same geographical limits, from ten degrees

---

[1] 'L'anticléricalisme, Monseigneur, c'est pour la France, mais ce n'est pas article d'exportation.' *ibid.*, p. 170.

[2] See an interesting letter from Lavigerie in *MC*. 81. 104. 'Il était évident que les protestants, qui avaient pris l'initiative et qui dominaient par le nombre dans le conférence de Bruxelles allaient tenter de s'établir dans ces régions.'

[3] Goyau, *Lavigerie*, p. 149.

north to twenty degrees south of the Equator, and placing its stations within easy reach of those of the lay organisation, so that mutual assistance could be rendered.[1] Self-supporting orphanages were again to be the basis of operations, since the stations could be most quickly and easily populated with ransomed slave children. Brought up in the faith, these could later be settled in self-contained villages, where they could escape from the dangers of a heathen environment, and become at the same time object lessons in the 'vraies lumières d'une civilisation dont l'Evangile est la source et la loi'.[2] These ideas were embodied in a secret memorandum[3] and submitted to Cardinal Franchi, the Prefect of Propaganda, on 24th February, 1878. Two days later it was ratified by a decree of the new Pope, Leo XIII, and Lavigerie was entrusted with its execution. At the same time the Society for the Propagation of the Faith and the Oeuvre de la Sainte Enfance were asked to share the travelling expenses of the missionaries, the costs of the initial building work and of the 'adoption et éducation de jeunes noirs infidèles.'[4]

Lavigerie wasted no time. When Dr. Cust[5] arrived in Algiers two months later to make the not unreasonable request that White Fathers should not at first be sent to

---

[1] Lavigerie in *MC*. 81. 104.   [2] Lavigerie, *Oeuvres Choisies*, I, p. 6.

[3] I have unfortunately not been able to see a copy of this important document. It is clear, however, that Lavigerie was referring to it in the letter to *MC*., referred to above, in which he told the story of the Society's foundation and the moves and motives which inspired it. This is confirmed by Father J. P. Thoonen of the Society of St. Joseph, Mill Hill, who has seen a copy of the memorandum in the library of the Gregorian University at Rome, and who has very kindly read me his notes of lectures which he attended on the subject at the Gregorian University.

[4] *MC*. 81. 126.   [5] R. N. Cust, *supra*, p. 25 n.

compete with the C.M.S. in Buganda, the first expedition was well on the way to Zanzibar and a second was already in preparation. With this latter Lavigerie, having presumably drawn a blank with the French government,[1] and being unsure of the future of the A.I.A., determined to send the nucleus of a private army. Père Charmetant was sent to Brussels to recruit retired papal zouaves to be 'the eventual founders of a Christian Kingdom'. He returned with four Belgians and two Scotsmen, to whom Lavigerie, dressed in pontifical robes, presented the sword and accolade at the altar steps of Algiers cathedral.[2] Meanwhile the first ten White Fathers had left Bagamoyo in June 1878, two months ahead of Lt. Cambier of the A.I.A.[3] They proceeded together as far as Tabora, which was to be the first station. From there five of them under Livinhac turned north-westwards to Bukumbi on the southern shores of Lake Victoria, where they made another base before sending on two of their number to Buganda. From Tabora the other half of the expedition pushed on towards Lake Tanganyika, and Hore reported their arrival at Ujiji in January 1879. They made their headquarters at Kibanga (Lavigerieville) on the peninsula opposite Ujiji, and in 1885 they took over the A.I.A. stations of Karema and Mpala, when King Leopold shifted his attention to the Congo Free State. The military side of the mission, commanded since 1880 by

---

[1] Or was the ill-fated expedition of the Abbé Debaize in 1878, the French government's response to Lavigerie's appeal?

[2] Goyau, *Lavigerie*, p. 153.

[3] The A.I.A. sent out four expeditions between 1878–85. Of nineteen men, six died, six got little farther than the coast: (1) Cambier who built Karema, 1878, (2) Popelin, 1879, (3) Remäkers and Becker, 1880, (4) Sturm and Reichard who built Mpala, 1882.

Captain Joubert, was based at St. Louis, two days' journey from Mpala, where some 200 of the mission's adherents were trained as a defence force.[1]

Thus, when Bismarck published the Imperial Schutzbrief, on 3rd March, 1885, protecting Carl Peters' Society for German Colonisation, some 300 Europeans were already living or had lived on the mainland of East Africa, where in 1856 there had only been Rebmann.[2] Almost all of these new arrivals had been Christian missionaries. Leaving out of account a score or so of explorers and travellers, the exceptions fall into two groups. The Livingstonia Company had exercised a profound influence, but this, it has been shown, was inseparably connected with the missionary interest. The African International Association was not so connected, but of the nineteen representatives which it sent to East Africa only five lived out a three years' term of duty, and their only achievement was the construction of three fortified posts, which were abandoned almost as soon as they had been completed.[3] For practical purposes, then, during the period before the imperialist annexations and during the several years that followed before occupation became effective, the European interests at work in East Africa were the missionary interests of the Churches in France and England.

[1] *AMZ.* 94. 337, quoting White Fathers' bulletin 94. 432.

[2] This figure is probably a slight underestimate. *MC*. 86. 412 gives the number of Holy Ghost missionaries for the period 1860–85 as 112. The same periodical reported the departure of five expeditions of White Fathers between 1878 and 1885, giving numbers in four cases. Sixty would seem the likely total. Lovett's *History of the L.M.S.*, p. 663 *sq.*, says that the L.M.S. sent twenty-nine men. I have not found figures for C.M.S., U.M.C.A., Church of Scotland or Free Church, but it would seem fair to estimate their mainland forces as forty, thirty-five, fifteen and twenty-five respectively. [3] Useful summary in *AMZ.* 94. 337.

Chapter Two

MISSIONARY WORK DURING THE PIONEER PERIOD, 1856–85

I

AS BISHOP STEERE pointed out, the facts of the case hardly justified the popular conception of missionary work as 'sitting under a tree talking to a native'.[1] The missions became a power in the land, and not a spiritual power only. In Buganda, as at Zanzibar, the native political authority was firmly enough established to include the stranger within its protection. Elsewhere even the missionary who set out with a few dozen porters and tried to settle in a native village had to set up what amounted to a small independent state. He was recognised as a kind of chief by the headmen round about, and to a greater or lesser extent the Sultan of Zanzibar and the British or French consul were felt to be behind him, as they were felt to be behind any other head of a caravan manned with porters from the coast.[2] The men he brought with him were under his jurisdiction from the start, and, as time went on, some of the local inhabitants, perhaps political exiles, perhaps fugitive slaves, perhaps tribal misfits, perhaps religious converts, would come and settle on his land. However much he might seek in his

[1] Heanley, *op. cit.*, p. 203

[2] W. P. Johnson, *My African Reminiscences*, London, 1898, p. 126. 'We were in the position of well-to-do squires. . . .'

teaching to support the temporal power already established and to preach to the people in their homes and villages, these men at least would regard him for practical purposes as their chief and look to him for economic support, for law and order, and in the last resort for military defence.

In point of fact, however, only three of the missions, the C.M.S., the L.M.S. and the U.M.C.A., made it a matter of policy to keep their temporal authority down to a minimum; and, even so, the exceptions, the freed slave settlements at Freetown, Mbweni and Masasi, were during the pioneer period at least as important as the rule. These exceptions, together with the stations of the Holy Ghost Fathers, the White Fathers and the Scottish missions, developed into fully-fledged economic and political units, governed and directed by the missionaries, and more or less separated off from the surrounding tribes. These centres did not of course mark the limit of the missionaries' activity, but within them they were able to exercise an altogether different kind of influence from that which was possible outside.

Roman Catholic missionaries at this period seem actually to have preferred the complete temporal as well as spiritual authority which they enjoyed within these mission states to the hazards of working among the free. It has been shown that the Holy Ghost Fathers at Bagomoyo had seen fit to supplement the freedmen handed over to them by the British Government with others bought direct from the dealers. In the same way the White Fathers, except in Buganda, built their stations not only on the main slave-trading routes, but close to the Arab settlements, and gathered the nucleus of each of their communities from this source.[1] The right to govern their protégés proceeded, in the minds of the Fathers, quite logically from the circumstances of their redemption: 'Comme c'est nous qui les avons rachetés de l'esclavage, nous conservons sur eux plein autorité.'[2]

In their schools, life was regulated almost as severely by the mission bell as it was in England by the factory hooter. It summoned the children to prayer at sunrise, to work at 6.30, to religious instruction and rest at 11, to work again from 2.30 till sundown. Having assembled once more at the foot of the altar to thank God for His mercy, they were left to themselves till 9.30, when 'at a signal from the Father, conversation ceased and all sought rest in sleep'. When the pupils grew up and married, each couple was provided with a plot of land and a hut, with two hoes, two iron pots, two mats and material for Sunday suits. For three days a week they continued to work on the mission estate and were paid a small wage in cloth; on the other three they were allowed

---

[1] Two examples will be sufficient to illustrate the Roman Catholic attitude: (1) Guillet to Lavigerie in *MC*. 85. 393, reporting a conversation with Tippu Tib, an Arab slave dealer: 'Quant aux enfants, en Manyema vous trouverez à racheter autant qu'il vous plaira, et pas chers.' (2) Guillet to Lavigerie in *MC*. 82. 490, describing the advantages of the station at Tabora: 'L'avidité du Sheikh [*i.e.* the Arab governor] devenait l'instrument de la miséricorde divine.'

The opposite point of view is perhaps most clearly stated in F.O. 84. 1942. F.O. to Acting-Consul Buchanan, 15.iv.89. 'H.M.G. have always discouraged the redemption of slaves from their owners under any circumstances. The practice is not unknown on the West Coast of Africa, and in 1882 H.M.G. addressed the Portuguese Government on the point in connection with the supply of labour obtained on the mainland for service on the Island of San Thomé. They then argued that the system was practically a form of slave trade, since the process of collecting emigrants directly encouraged native chiefs to make wars and take prisoners whom they disposed of at a profit. . . .'

[2] *MC*. 80. 341.

to cultivate their own land.[1] Free outsiders were allowed to settle on the mission land on condition that they kept the rules in all their rigour and agreed to place themselves under religious instruction: and it is important to note that the system was so far from being regarded as exploitation that, especially under the pressure of inter-tribal warfare, many did so.[2] If a man came alone, he served a probation period, after which the mission bought him a wife and settled him among the married pupils. If a whole group came they were settled in a village by themselves.[3]

Anglican missionaries, faced with the same task in their freed-slave settlements, disliked the system enough to comment more freely upon its implications, but there was little that they could do to modify it. It was almost impossible to explain to the freed slave that he was really free, when in fact any attempt to run away from the station would have involved instant re-enslavement either by Arabs or by Africans of another tribe. Obviously the settlements had to have laws and the laws had to be enforced. One of the first actions reported from Freretown was the organisation of a police force.[4] Maples wrote from Masasi that he was

[1] The above is taken from an account of the White Fathers' stations at Kibanga and Mpala in *MC*. 88. 326 and from a review in *AMZ*. 94. 327 of *Près des Grands Lacs*, a White Fathers' brochure published at Algiers in 1886. *MC*. contains many other accounts, showing insignificant variations.

[2] *e.g. MC*. 87. 112 reports the arrival of 300 at Karema; *MC*. 85. 317 states that at Kibanga a separate village had been set up for these voluntary adherents.

[3] *MC*. 86. 477.

[4] Diary of W. S. Price, 1.x.76. *CMI*. 76. 205. After the retirement of Mr. Price a certain Mr. Streeter, the Lay Superintendent at Freretown, was guilty of outrageous abuse of his powers, which provoked the following comment from Vice-Consul Holmwood in 1881: 'I was not prepared to find that, in addition to long terms of imprisonment, you were also in the habit of inflicting severe floggings . . . without

spending whole days in judicial work[1] and that sometimes he felt more like the governor of a gaol than a missionary.[2] Obviously, too, the missionaries could not charge all the expenses of these large settlements on their subscribers at home, and therefore there had to be work for the mission, just as outside there was work for the native chiefs.[3]

Nor was the defence problem a purely theoretical one. Even within the comparatively well-ordered dominions of the Sultan there was constant danger of armed conflict between the freed-slave settlements of the C.M.S. and the United Free Methodists and the slave-owning Arabs of Mombasa. The Arabs naturally felt that their authority over their own legally held slaves, and so ultimately their means of livelihood, was being threatened by the proximity of these stations, which inevitably attracted deserters from the locality, rendered desperate by the fear of detection and

---

judicial investigation and in the majority of cases without recording or even hearing evidence. The ocular proof of the severity of these floggings . . . shocked both Captain Byles and myself, and I must tell you that in cases where the slaves of Arabs apply to our Agency at Zanzibar showing such traces of ill-treatment, the Sultan is at once asked to free them, on the grounds that persons inflicting such injuries are unfit to be entrusted with the charge of human lives.' Holmwood to Streeter, Mombasa, 6.vii.81. Inclosure 2 in Kirk to Granville No. 289 of 1881. (KP).

[1] 8.v.81. Chauncy Maples: *Letters and Journals*, London, 1897, p. 146

[2] *ibid.*, p. 121. 'The punishment for lighter offences is the taking away of the food allowance; for heavier offences they are tied up and thrashed; for the most grievous sins of all they will in future be expelled.' August 1877, *ibid.*, p. 100. But in a letter to Waller from Newala of 29.vii.83, Maples wrote: 'The Bishop had given us a rule "Don't send anyone away. You can no more get rid of your people than a king can get rid of his subjects", and indeed if we had sent them away it would have been to send them back into slavery, for every outlaw in these parts as a matter of course has a slave-stick clapped on his neck.' *Waller Papers*, III.

[3] Maples, *op cit.*, p. 100. 'All receive a daily allowance of meal or beans; in return they work for us three days a week.'

punishment. Outbreaks might perhaps have been avoided had the missionaries been either able or willing to turn away these fugitives, as successive consuls at Zanzibar advised them to do.[1] But the C.M.S. Committee, though supporting the Consul in principle, always excused its agents when they overrode the law by accepting fugitives who had been ill-treated;[2] and there is no doubt that the missionaries interpreted this conscience-clause in the most liberal spirit, that they were ignorant of many, and shut their eyes to many more, of the illegal accretions to their stations.[3] The Mombasa Arabs had early taken a vow to make soup of the missionaries' livers, and in Ramadhan, 1880, Freretown was actually attacked, the Lay Superintendent giving his advice in Cromwell's words: 'Trust in God and keep your powder

[1] *e.g.* Kirk to Granville, 9.x.80 (KP): 'The present difficulty at Mombasa arose out of the reception given at the mission stations (both C.M.S. and Methodist) to fugitive slaves, and while on the one hand the missionaries feared a combined attack on the part of the townspeople, the owners of the slaves on their part felt they were in personal danger of a general slave-rising instigated by . . . the missionaries. . . . It became practically impossible for any master singly to recover a slave who had once been received, as for instance at Rabai there were about 200, all well-armed with poisoned arrows or guns, ready to defend their companions without the order of the missionary. . . . Demonstrations were made by the slave-owners for the purpose of doing in a body what they found it dangerous to attempt alone.' In reply to the above the C.M.S. (Hutchinson to Granville, 14.i.81) claimed that the armed bands referred to were not in fact inhabitants of the mission station, but fugitive slaves from the neighbouring Giriama tribe formed into a settlement of their own.

[2] 'From time to time men ran away who had half their feet burnt off by slow fires; others who had been hung up for a day in the sun by their heels or wrists; others again, who after having their backs cut open by the cruel whip or being cut from shoulders to waist with knives, had salt or red pepper rubbed into their wounds, and were then tied spread-eagle fashion in the burning sun.' Hutchinson to Granville, *loc. cit.*

[3] The first full-scale inquiry held in 1888 by Mr. George Mackenzie of the Imperial British East Africa Company revealed that 1,421 runaway slaves were being harboured at the four freed-slave stations near Mombasa, of whom 933 were found at Rabai. Euan Smith to Salisbury, 20.xi.88. F.O. 84. 1908.

dry',[1] and admitting at the subsequent inquiry that he had had in his possession a white flag 'with the word "Freedom" plainly visible upon it in Swahili characters', the unfurling of which was to have been the signal for all the Mombasa slaves to rise against their masters.[2]

In the interior, too, there were perils of wars, though less from the local inhabitants than from more distant raiders. The lake regions of Central Africa, from the Zambezi to the Sukuma country to the south of Lake Victoria, had been since the eighteen-forties in a state of unusual turmoil as a result of the incursion of the Ngoni Zulus. These people, having left the neighbourhood of the present Swaziland about 1825, had raided their way northwards, adding to their numbers as they went, and had crossed the Zambezi at the time of a solar eclipse in 1835. By 1848 they had reached the Fipa country to the south-east of Lake Tanganyika, and here their leader Zwangendaba died. A dispersion followed. The main body, turning south-west, established during the fifties and sixties two strong principalities, under Mpezeni and Mombera, in the fertile grazing country to the west of Lake Nyasa.[3] These Ngoni were the unruly neighbours of the Livingstonia Mission when it moved from Cape Maclear to Bandawe in 1881; and the missionaries found the

---

[1] *CMI.* 1880 quoted in *AMZ.* 81. 309.

[2] Hutchinson to Granville, 14.i.81, states that the C.M.S. understood in 1876 that periodical support, and demonstrative visits by warships and by the Consul, would be provided to assist the freed-slave settlements in slave-owning districts. No such assistance had in fact been provided, and the missionaries were therefore justified in taking steps to defend themselves if necessary.

[3] W. A. Elmslie, *Among the Wild Ngoni*, London, 1901, Chs. I and II; Margaret Read, 'Tradition and Prestige among the Ngoni', *A.* 36. 453; D. G. Lancaster, 'Tentative Chronology of the Ngoni', *JRAI.*, xlvii (1937), p. 77.

remnants of the aboriginal tribes, the Chewa, the Tonga and the Tumbuka, perched in the caves and clefts of the mountains or hidden among the swamps by the water's edge.[1] The arrival of Europeans, dispensing cloth and other wealth among these 'slave' populations, naturally excited the cupidity of the Ngoni warriors; and it was only through the courage of Dr. Laws in visiting Mombera and his foresight in appointing Dr. Elmslie as a sort of diplomatic representative to this chieftain for several years before permission was given to teach among his subjects, that disaster was averted.[2] Even so, the lives of the missionaries hung in the balance for several weeks in 1887, when the Ngoni peremptorily demanded the removal of the central station from Bandawe to their own capital, while the miserable Tonga, aware of their danger, blockaded the Europeans into their station and cut off their access to the lake.[3]

After Zwangendaba's death the eastern shore of Lake Nyasa had been possessed by another group of the Ngoni, often known as the Magwangwara, who raided as far afield as the Indian Ocean,[4] and who in 1882 sacked and burnt Masasi, though the inhabitants had received warning in time to escape.[5] It was among the tributary peoples of the Gwangwara that the U.M.C.A. in 1881 started their Nyasa

[1] Elmslie, op. cit., p. 78 sq.

[2] And to the presence on his staff of a South African assistant, William Koyi, who could make himself understood in the Zulu tongue.

[3] The cause of this trouble was the jealousy of a brother of Mombera's named Mtwaro, and the matter was eventually settled by promising to establish a station in his village also. ibid., Chapter XI.

[4] Read, op. cit.; S. S. Murray, A Handbook of Nyasaland, 1932, p. 61 sqq.

[5] Wilson, op. cit., p. 56 sq.

mission; and their presence was responsible for the choice as a base of the stony island of Likoma, to which the future native catechists could be brought for instruction, and from which the missionaries could visit the lake-side villages by steamer.[1] Yet another group of the same Ngoni, the Watuta or Maviti, raided the east coast of Lake Tanganyika and, together with the powerful slave-raiding Bemba of north-eastern Rhodesia, laid waste the Nyasa–Tanganyika plateau, keeping the L.M.S. missionaries within stockaded villages till 1904.[2] Local attacks and punitive raids seem to have been a regular feature of the White Fathers' missions to the west of Lake Tanganyika, whither the fourth and last division of the Ngoni had made their way under Ntabeni; but detailed evidence of Captain Joubert's activities in this region is unfortunately scanty.

The temporal power of the Scottish missions based on Livingstonia and Blantyre arose chiefly from their policy of introducing material civilisation side by side with Christianity. Where the Roman Catholics developed estates and plantations in order to support their protégés, the Presbyterians developed them as things desirable in themselves and acquired protégés in order to cultivate them. At Blantyre this trend was from the first more clearly marked

---

[1] cf. Johnston to Salisbury, 17.iii.90. F.O. 84. 2051.

[2] Returning from England in 1883, E. C. Hore found that most of the Alungu at the south end of Lake Tanganyika had been wiped out, and the remainder were suffering from acute famine, after Bemba raids. *Tanganyika*, p. 232: 'I looked for the many well-to-do villages of my old acquaintances, the prosperous and lively Walungu: of some of them all vestige was gone, the sites overgrown with jungle, of others nothing remained but the blackened ruins.' In a letter to the L.M.S., of 14.ix.83, he reported that slaves were being traded to an Arab named Kabunda, who had his headquarters on the Lofu River. cf., Johnston to Salisbury, *supra*, 17.iii.90.

than at the Free Church stations on Lake Nyasa. The weak Mang'anja population of the Shiré Highlands had been decimated by two slave-raiding tribes, the Yao and the southern Ngoni; and it was perhaps inevitable that a large proportion of the mission's recruits were either fugitives or slaves, who had more than once to be defended by force against their irate pursuers. But it was above all the clumsiness and, one must add, the brutality, of their attempts to exercise criminal jurisdiction in cases of theft, rape and murder which distinguished the Church of Scotland missionaries from their more humane and circumspect Free Church compatriots. True, the Blantyre missionaries had received explicit, though utterly illegal, instructions to found a republic and to exercise jurisdiction;[1] but it is unlikely that any mission in East Africa at this time in practice escaped the exercise of some such powers.[2] Nevertheless, something of a sensation was rightly caused in England when a traveller called Chirnside, who had visited the station in 1879, revealed in a pamphlet that the missionaries had ordered floggings so severe that one of the victims had subsequently died, and that a death sentence had been carried out with the aid of a native firing-squad with an incompetence too horrible to describe.[3] At Livingstonia,

[1] These instructions had emanated from Dr. MacRae, the Convener of the Church of Scotland Committee, but apparently not from the Committee itself. W. P. Livingstone, *Laws*, p. 135.

[2] *e.g.* the L.M.S., which was probably the most strictly evangelistic of all the missions, found it necessary as late as 1904 to pass a resolution that no missionary should be involved either directly or indirectly in the flogging of adult natives for offences of any kind. *ibid.*, p. 174.

[3] Chirnside's allegation that the Blantyre missionaries had not reported their proceedings to Scotland was evidently untrue, for W. P. Livingstone, *Laws*, p. 172–3,

by contrast, Dr. Laws tried always to adopt native law in so far as it was applicable, always consulted a native jury before inflicting punishment, and ruthlessly resorted to expulsion in the more serious cases.[1] After moving the mission to Bandawe he refused to accept any more fugitive slaves on any pretext whatever, and always tried to refer miscreants to their own chiefs.[2]

At all these stations, which might be collectively classified as 'residential', the missions were able to bring about their most spectacular achievements in economic and social progress. In them a limited number of Africans, a few

shows that the authorities of the Established Church had consulted the Free Church Committee on their own initiative, and had sent definite instructions to the Rev. Duff Macdonald that his position must 'be understood as excluding the power and jurisdiction known as self-government'. On the publication of Chirnside's pamphlet, however, a Commission of Inquiry was conducted by Dr. Rankin on behalf of the General Assembly, assisted by Consul O'Neill from Mozambique, whose two dispatches to Lord Granville of 18.xi.80 and 5.xii.80 in F.O. 84. 1565 have recently been exhaustively studied by Dr. A. J. Hanna in a Ph.D. thesis for London University entitled *The History of Nyasaland and North-Eastern Rhodesia, 1875–95*, p. 158 *sqq.* The Commission substantiated the main charges made by Chirnside, of two excessively brutal floggings which had been ordered by the lay missionaries for suspected theft, and of one execution for suspected murder, which had been carried out with the consent of Macdonald, the only clergyman in the Mission. In the last case at least the semblance of a trial had been held, the missionaries sitting in judgment with the headmen of the mission villages; and though the evidence was not such as would have convinced an English court of justice, the bona fides of the missionaries was not questioned, and it was reported that the confidence of the natives had not been impaired by their proceedings. Macdonald, the clergyman, Macklin, the doctor, and two of the artisan missionaries were dismissed from their posts; but the two last remained in the country. One of them, Fenwick, becoming a private trader, was subsequently murdered; the other, Buchanan, became a much respected coffee-planter in the Shiré Highlands and in 1888 was even appointed Acting-Consul. Sources: Hanna, *op. cit.*, and *AMZ.* 82. 421, quoting *Church of Scotland Record*, 81. 382 and *Independent*, 24.iii.81.

[1] W. P. Livingstone, *Laws*, p. 136–7.
[2] *ibid.*, p. 186.

thousands at the outside,[1] lived in freedom from famine and from the constant threat of war and slavery. Many of them learned to read and write their own languages, some learned Swahili, a very few, English or French. All had access to some kind of medical attention. Some were taught skilled trades, smithing or carpentry, masonry or brick-baking, printing or tailoring. All acquired some new tool which made life easier. Digging-sticks were replaced by iron hoes, sometimes even by the plough. Saws came to the aid of axes, metal cooking-pots to the aid of earthenware. With settled agriculture, houses became more permanent and more comfortable. Doors and windows made their first appearance, together with the simplest kind of furniture. Clothing became more plentiful and more hygienic, if not more becoming, and soap made its début in East African life.

The outward appearance of these enclaves always impressed the traveller by contrast with the 'non-residential' stations, which were sometimes hardly less squalid and unkempt than the native villages around. Frere's comments on Bagamoyo have already been quoted. Johnston in 1890 remarked that Blantyre had fully come up to his 'expectations

---

[1] Numbers are difficult to gauge, but some examples may be interesting: (i) Livingstonia in 1880 had 600 residents; 141 men, 202 women, 247 children. Some of the latter were boarding-school pupils and therefore temporary—*Laws of Livingstonia*, p. 179. (ii) Kibanga (Lavigerieville) had 700 in 1888—*MC*. 88. 326. These consisted of the central schools, three 'villages' of grown-up pupils, and twelve villages of refugees. (iii) Mpala, another White Fathers' station, seems to have been differently organised with a small boarding school of forty pupils, two 'absolutely dependent' villages with eighty-eight families, while Captain Joubert claimed some kind of less absolute authority over the vast number of 20,000 spread over a wide territory round about—*MC*. 90. 520. (iv) Freretown numbers had reached about 1,000 when Hannington arrived in 1885—Stock, *op. cit.*, III, 409. The vast majority were slaves captured at sea and their descendants.

as a pleasing English Arcadia set in the middle of harsh African savagery. It is a place of roses and geraniums, pink-cheeked English children, large-uddered cattle and laying hens, riding-horses and lawn tennis. . . .'[1] Direktor Merensky of the Berlin Mission, passing through in the following year, noted in more detail the material achievements of the mission after sixteen years of work. There were European houses, schools and a church. Well-engineered and beaten roads connected the station with Katunga on the Lower and Matope on the Upper Shiré, and with the outstations at Domasi and Magomero. Bridges of wood and stone spanned the water-courses. South African ox-waggons and carts were in daily use. Irrigated plantations of coffee, tea, sugar and tobacco stretched in all directions as far as the eye could see. Native carpenters were erecting a veranda unsupervised; masons were building a girls' school out of bricks burnt on the spot. The mission press was turning out a monthly news-paper in English and Yao.[2] At Livingstonia, Johnston counted over 400 scholars in the school and saw a workshop and a printing-press, which was perpetually turning out primers and translations of the Scriptures, tales and easy lessons in geography and natural history, in Nyanja, Tonga, Ngoni, Nyakusa and Nkonde. There were brakes of pine-apples, orchards of oranges and limes, and tidy plantations of local vegetables. But he reserved the fullest measure of his praise for the personality of Dr. Laws himself:

This man, with his fifteen years of whole-hearted devotion to Nyasa-land, and his energy of doing good which has made him learn to make

---

[1] Johnston to Salisbury, 17.iii.90. F.O. 84. 2051.   [2] *AMZ*. 92. 52.

bricks himself in order that he may teach others, which has led him to become a practical carpenter, joiner, printer, photographer, farrier, boat-builder, engineer and druggist, so that he might induct his once savage people into all these arts and trades, which has made him study medicine and surgery to heal the bodies, and sufficient theology to instruct the minds of these Africans, about whom he never speaks with silly sentiment and gush, but whose faults, failings and capabilities he appraises with calm common sense—Dr. Laws with these qualities of truly Christian self-devotion should justly be regarded as the greatest man who has yet appeared in Nyasaland.[1]

On Lake Tanganyika the White Fathers' station at Kibanga could in 1890 boast of plantations extending 'à perte de vue', of rice and manioc, maize and sweet potato, oil-palms and bananas, sugar-canes and European vegetables.[2] Teaching that work was an expiation according to the divine law, the Fathers may sometimes have been hard task-masters; but in their little kingdoms they produced a state of material prosperity unknown in the war-ridden lands around. 'Il fait bon vivre chez les Blancs' was said to be the motive of the voluntary settlers whom they attracted.[3]

'One method of mission work', wrote Bishop Steere, 'is to take the natives into tutelage, to make them live by order and work when and as they are bidden. This produces fine plantations, good cultivation, well-kept houses and a most respectful demeanour.'[4] It also produced the vast majority of the early converts. The inhabitants of these stations had all been uprooted, often since childhood, from the tribal

[1] Johnston to Salisbury, *loc. cit.*, F.O. 84. 2051.
[2] Mgr. Bridoux in *MC*. 90. 489.
[3] *MC*. 88. 326.
[4] Heanley, *op. cit.*, p. 387.

solidarity which alone could give meaning to the ancient beliefs. Within the enclaves there was no social ostracism to be endured for Christ's sake. There was no sorcerer to threaten with all too material injury the intending back-slider from his vested interest. The ancestral spirits, whose power was purely local, could not pursue the delinquent to wreak their vengeance. There were no sexual initiation rites and no ceremonial debauches to inflame the passions beyond their normal vigour. Instead, there was a new social solidarity calculated to support the ethical doctrines of Christianity. Monogamy, the greatest stumbling-block, was a condition of residence, and polygyny in the new economic conditions lost much of its significance as the only means to wealth and power. In the new society the man was trained to do his share of the daily labour, leaving the woman free to assume her central position in the Christian family. In the more spacious huts it was possible for the children to sleep at home instead of in the communal dormitories of the old order. Above all, a steady course of religious instruction, lasting over several years, pointed the path to baptism and the fuller spiritual discipline of the Church.

Notwithstanding their initial success, most missionaries were forced to admit after a generation of experiment that these 'centres of Christianity and civilisation' were unsatisfactory places, whether the inhabitants were freed slaves or whether they were free men who had merely changed their political allegiance. The missionary, called to be the ruler of ne'er-do-wells and malcontents, could produce results that were outwardly fair; but too often his activities were a hindrance and not a help to the evangelisation of the country in general.[1] His pupils, lacking all the family ties and inherited traditions of free African society, were regarded as more foreign than the European himself, while the missionary's political relation to them inevitably brought him into collision with the native rulers. Only at Livingstonia, where ethnic circumstances combined with the diplomatic genius of Dr. Laws made it possible for the central institution to be from the first merely the nucleus of a wide network of evangelistic stations, can the residential mission be accounted an unqualified success. But in defence of Dr. Laws's less fortunate and perhaps less gifted contemporaries it must be remembered that they were not, as many recent critics have suggested, attacking an ideally functioning tribal system, but mopping up in the name of humanity that system's septic overflow, to which Livingstone and others had so forcibly drawn attention. They can, in fact, be forgiven for opening oases in the tribal desert rather than running springs which would flow out and irrigate the whole.

---

[1] 'Upon the whole I think the presence of the returned slave community retarded rather than assisted the work among the tribes. I say upon the whole, for I am willing to admit that in a few matters belonging rather to material progress than to moral, to the cause of civilisation rather than Christianity, the community exercised a beneficial influence and proved auxiliary. Our great difficulty . . . at Masasi . . . was this. We had to take care of a number of worthless people who not only were not Christians but whose conduct was so bad that there was scarcely any hope of their ever becoming Christians: meanwhile their misdoings, quarrels and excesses of all kinds took up an untold amount of time as day after day I had to listen to their disputes and mete out satisfaction to the parties injured by them. . . .' Maples to Waller from Newala, 29.vii.83. *Waller Papers*, III. cf. Gertrude Ward, *Life of Bishop Smythies*, London, 1890, p. 170.

*   *   *   *

2

Outside their own political dominions the missionaries were able during the pioneer period to do little more in a religious way than to sow the seed in hope. Many of the impediments were only too obvious. A mission station could become temporarily untenable as the result of a severe famine,[1] a succession quarrel following the death of a chief,[2] the approach of a raiding tribe,[3] or even the cutting of communications by an upheaval hundreds of miles away.[4] Permanent installations were useless as long as the migrations involved in shifting cultivation might leave the original site isolated after a few years.[5] The diversity of languages was a severe handicap when a dozen missionaries might be attempting to cover an area in which as many dialects were spoken.[6] The sparseness of the population, the continual absence of the men in warfare or hunting, the great gulf fixed between the life of the women and the men, the full employment of even the young children, all contributed to the difficulties of making any but the most superficial

[1] Clark to C.M.S. from Mpwapwa, 10.xi.76 and 10.xii.76.

[2] *e.g.* the empire of Mirambo broke up after his death in 1884 and the whole region fell into extreme disorder. The White Fathers had temporarily to withdraw their mission from Tabora.

[3] The area east of Lake Nyasa became very dangerous in the late seventies and early eighties owing to the incursion of the Gwangwara. W. P. Johnson's early attempts to settle at Mataka's had to be abandoned for this reason.

[4] The communications of the L.M.S. were often threatened by Mirambo's clashes with the Arabs 200 miles away.

[5] *e.g.* Masasi found itself isolated after a very few years, the people having moved to the neighbourhood of Newala.

[6] Last to C.M.S. from Mpwapwa, 2.vi.79.

impression.[1] Still, the missionary's impact upon free tribal life was in the long run his most important activity, whether he was a whole-time missionary preacher and teacher, like Lourdel or Mackay in Uganda, or Johnson on the Rovuma, or whether he was a missionary prince acting sometimes in an extra-territorial capacity, like Laws in Nyasaland or Père Horner in Ukami.

The first condition of ultimate success was to secure the goodwill of the chief; and, fortunately for the missionary, the chief had many reasons to compete for his presence if not for his doctrine.[2] To the powerful and well-informed ruler, like Mutesa of Buganda or the Nyamwezi chief Mirambo, the fact that he was a European was of supreme interest. Both these rulers had had enough contact with the outside world to know that the friendship of a new class of foreigners was worth cultivating as a diplomatic counterweight to the class they knew already. Mirambo had long passed the stage of amicable co-operation with the Arabs who travelled and traded in his dominions. He coveted their wealth and feared their growing power. Obviously it was in his interest to establish through the missionaries good relations with the British Consul who was known to exercise such influence at the court of Zanzibar.[3] Mutesa had an even more urgent reason to seek new allies, not in this case against the traders from the east coast, but against the advance of Egyptian imperialism from the north. Baker's first journey to Lake Albert in 1863–4 had brought the White Nile slave-traders

---

[1] Southon to L.M.S. from Urambo, 1.xi.79.
[2] The case of Mombera and his brother Mtwaro has already been quoted, *supra*, p. 57.
[3] *infra*, p. 84-6.

to the borders of Bunyoro, the Bantu kingdom lying immediately to the north and west of Buganda; and on the death of Kamrasi, the former ruler of that country, the Egyptians had sold their services to both sides in the succession quarrel which followed.[1] A party of them had visited Mutesa in 1869 or 1870. They had slunk away as soon as they had understood that trade, and not the razzia, was the rule in Buganda;[2] but two years later had come the news that Baker had returned, this time at the head of Egyptian troops, that he was building forts in the Acholi country north of the Somerset Nile, and that he had even raised the Egyptian flag outside Masindi the capital of Bunyoro. Baker had been forced by the Banyoro to retreat; but in 1873 he had been succeeded by Gordon, who had built more forts and had sent emissaries to Buganda, first, in 1874, Chaillé Long, then Linant de Bellefonds whose visit had coincided with that of Stanley, finally, in 1876, a company of troops under an Egyptian officer, Nuer Aga, who had instructions to erect a fort in the north of Mutesa's own kingdom. Mutesa did not need to be told that Baker and Gordon had been commissioned by the Khedive Ismail to put down the slave-trade and to annex the Nile sources to the Egyptian crown. The forts and the soldiers spoke for themselves, as did the fact that these Arabs from the north travelled without the trade goods which were the passport of the Zanzibaris. In 1875 the contrast between Stanley, the private traveller, and Linant, the Khedival envoy, had been unmistakable.[3] No wonder that Mutesa had shown himself

---

[1] Baker, *Ismailia*, II, p. 178.   [2] *ibid.*, II, pp. 98–9.
[3] H. M. Stanley, *Through the Dark Continent*, London, 1899, edn. I, p. 161.

such an apt disciple of Stanley's Christian teaching; no wonder that he had grasped so eagerly at the offer of resident teachers of the new faith, which, whatever it might mean, had been so carefully opposed by Stanley to the Islam of the Egyptians.[1]

In the smaller chiefdoms the wealth of the missionaries themselves made them an economic asset. All of them were employers of labour and therefore dispensers of calico and trade goods. For the erection of their stations, even the simpler ones, they required the assistance of hundreds of Africans, and for their daily existence they needed food and firewood, cooks and gardeners and many other services. The transport of their supplies alone became quite an industry. Hore employed 1,000 porters to carry an open steel boat overland to Ujiji in 1882;[2] a figure of two or three hundred was quite common for the routine caravan, bringing up tinned food and missionaries' chattels, European building materials and barter goods.[3] In this capacity the missionaries probably dealt their most effective blow at the slave-trade, for they supplied in wages the imports which had previously been bought for slaves, and which had come to be regarded by the chiefs as necessities of life and power.[4] Certainly, as the

[1] A complete account of the Egyptian intervention would be out of place in this study. For the full story the reader is referred to Coupland, *Exploitation*, pp. 271–300 and to two important articles by Sir J. M. Gray, 'Mutesa of Buganda', *Uganda Journal*, January 1934, p. 22, and 'Sir John Kirk and Mutesa', *ibid.*, March 1951, p. 1.

[2] Hore, *op. cit.*, p. 199.

[3] *e.g.* a routine caravan to Mpwapwa, only 200 miles inland, carried 150 loads, more than half of which was barter cloth. Last to C.M.S. from Zanzibar, 3.iii.79. The first two expeditions of the White Fathers employed 450 and 600 respectively. *MC.* 79. 582.

[4] *e.g.* Smythies in a sermon in 1887: 'Wherever we have settled for long the slave trade is coming to an end. People are able to get cloth . . . without buying, selling or

pioneer period wore on the Arabs were driven to seek their
victims farther and farther west, while at Ujiji, one of the
largest of their commercial centres, the price of cloth fell by
more than half during the first ten years of the missionary
occupation.[1]

There were many smaller ways in which the missionary
could increase his prestige with chief and people. In the
field of magic he could outdo the most competent of the
native witch-doctors. He had at his command a whole
variety of miracles, from making water effervesce by the
addition of Fruit Salts to performing a surgical operation. By using an anaesthetic he gained the reputation of
being able to kill people and then restore them to life.[2]
He might be able to mend a gun or a musical-box, to build
a boat or upholster a chair.[3] If there was a famine at one end
of Lake Tanganyika, he could bring food and seed from the
other by steamer.[4] In a land where the exchange of presents
was a customary part of any transaction, a judiciously chosen
gift, like a brass bedstead or an ornamental uniform,[5] could
bring him into high favour. As a wealthy and distinguished
stranger his advice was sought on all kinds of political and
judicial questions. Succession claims were brought to him

catching each other. Before we came people did not dare to go to the coast; now they
regularly go and earn money by fetching loads for us, and the roads are safe and
open.' Ward, *Smythies*, p. 101.

[1] Hore, *op. cit.*, p. 71.

[2] W. P. Livingstone, *Laws*, p. 140.

[3] Mackay built a boat and mended guns for Mutesa; the chair and the musical-box
were by Southon at Urambo. Southern to L.M.S., 2.xi.79.

[4] Hore, *op. cit.*, p. 232 *sqq.*

[5] The brass bedstead was chosen by the L.M.S. directors from the Army and
Navy Stores; the uniform was given to Mutesa by Lavigerie.

for arbitration. He was the appointed go-between in many acts of diplomacy.[1]

This initial popularity did not last for ever. The novel skills of the missionary, which at first were hailed as the beginning of an age of wonders, were discovered in time to have their limits. It slowly dawned upon the chief that the white men would not be content for ever to act as his unpaid mechanics, enhancing his own prestige and attending to his material comfort.

Let one live in the land beyond the term of novelty of display and profusion of hospitality; let him express a horror of the barbarity of the practices he sees . . . let him lift up his voice in condemnation of treachery, of lies, of lust, and of cruelty and murder—then the spell is broken, and the character of the people comes out in its true light. Instead of hospitality he finds hatred; instead of food he finds himself face to face with famine; instead of being received, as he expected, as a welcome benefactor of the people, as a teacher of truth and a leader in the way of light, a lover of law and love, he is denounced as a spy, as a bringer in of foreign customs, and especially as a breaker down of the national institutions and religion.[2]

Still, the period of favour had probably been long enough for some individuals to have attached themselves to the missionaries with a loyalty strong enough to ignore the general reaction. Some of the small boys who had come to stare at the foreigner's strange methods of building, who had learned to pass him some tool when he was at work, who had peeped at him with awe when he settled down to read his book, who had asked him the simple, open questions

---

[1] Ward, *Smythies*, p. 31 *sqq.*
[2] *Mackay of Uganda*, by his sister, London, 1891, p. 217.

of childhood and had pondered his unusual and exciting replies, some of these continued to visit him after he had become the object of suspicion or indifference, to listen to his talk, perhaps to spell out the familiar words of their own language from his mysterious letters. Where parental interest was slight, they might make their homes at the mission for months at a time. It would become their resort in sickness, their refuge in the time of persecution. Or again, some young men, not yet irrevocably entangled in the coils of polygamy or witchcraft, who had perhaps been deputed by the chief to fetch and carry for the strangers during the period of official hospitality, who had become in time their trusted helpers and informants, would stay on to help their foreign friends to reduce the language to writing, to render into their own speech, fresh and full of meaning, the wonderful phrases of the Scriptures, and so at last would be brought to pray and worship as Christians.[1] Gradually a school would develop, small, irregularly attended, hampered at every turn

[1] cf. Mackay from Kagei, Usukuma, 9.vii.78: 'When they see the turning lathe at work, or find me melting down the fat of an ox and turning out beautiful candles, their wonder knows no bounds. Of an incongruous mass of bars of iron and brass and bolts, they could not guess the use of, they have seen me fit together one and another complete steam engine, and various other things which looked so marvellous, that again and again I have heard the remark that white men came from heaven. Then I teach this and that more intelligent fellow the use of various things, and try to impress upon all a truth I find them very slow to believe—that they themselves can easily learn to know everything that white men know. I tell them that we were once naked savages like themselves, and carried bows and arrows and spears; but when God began to teach us, we became civilised. . . . Round comes Sunday, when tools are dropped, and the reason asked, 'Why?' I have my Bible and tell them that it is God's book . . . and many I find eager to learn to read that they may know the book which I say God Himself wrote for men. . . . At all times I find myself surrounded by a host of little boys, eager to help me in anything . . . I cannot think the day far distant when I shall see my daily school for these children, and watch them grow in wisdom and understanding, and in the fear of God. Such a class I dream I see the

by fearful fathers and conservative grandmothers, but which would gather in time a nucleus of mainly resident adherents.[1] Though numbers were much smaller, the free missions, like the mission-states, achieved their first real converts by separating Africans from their tribal environment. Unlike the mission states, the free missions did not find the results unsatisfactory, for the separation was seldom complete. Many pupils fell away before the end of their training, and returned to their families with something of the white man's influence upon them. Of those who stayed, few broke altogether with their relations, and all maintained a nominal allegiance to their old chiefs. These first adherents amounted by 1885 to mere handfuls, numbered usually by dozens and scores; but they were to acquire a very great significance in the second generation of missionary work.

*   *   *   *

3

Of these 'free' missions, those in Buganda were the outstanding prototypes. Mutesa was the jealous monarch of a highly centralised feudal kingdom with somewhere between

nucleus of a training college, which shall furnish manifold seeds of life in place of the units which we white men must ever be in Africa. Of these some will be trained for the work of the ministry, and the day arrive when a Msukuma will be bishop of Unyamwezi, and a Muganda primate of all Nyanza.' *ibid.*, pp. 72–3.

[1] See an article by Father Barnes in *CA.* 02. 62. After the initial swing-over from day schools, there was a period when the boarding school amounted to almost 'total adoption'. This was gradually relaxed. Baxter to C.M.S. from Mpwapwa, 13.v.79, reports requests to 'settle and join our mission people'. All the evidence implies that every mission station was obliged to adopt for a period a nucleus of residential adherents.

one and two million subjects, and there could be no question of founding either mission states or regular boarding schools within his dominions, or even within the neighbouring principalities which were within the reach of his powerful armies and his fleets of war canoes.[1] The missionaries had to settle at his capital and to follow the example of visiting Arabs, and also of the great vassal-chiefs, by dancing attendance at court. This had one consequence which was fortunately unique in East Africa, in that it brought Catholic and Evangelical missionaries into close contact with one another.[2] The results of sectional rivalry were to be dire in the future; and from the earliest days unedifying scenes took place at the court, where the missionaries of Christ accused one another of lying, and denounced each other's doctrine with a rigour attributable only to the grossest ignorance of each other's language and religious traditions.[3] But it is a remarkable fact that Christianity,

[1] Mackay from 'C.M.S. Eleanor', Victoria Nyanza, 21.i.84: 'We would naturally like to settle where we choose, and carry on our work quietly and without demonstration; but that is perfectly impossible. . . . Mutesa is greedy to have all the white men at his capital.'

[2] Protestant domination of the Brussels Conference was the leading theme of Cardinal Lavigerie's Mémoire Sécret to the Prefect of Propaganda in 1878. Thoonen's notes *vide supra*, p. 47 n. The comment of the C.M.S. on the Roman Catholic occupation of Uganda was as follows: 'Plainly the lesson to be deduced is that, casting aside the maundering cant which labours to maintain that Rome is a portion of genuine Christianity, she should be recognised in her true aspect as its avowed and persistent antagonist.' *CMI.* 80. 156.

[3] A. Nicq, *La Vie du Vénérable Père Siméon Lourdel*, Paris, 1896, pp. 191–206. Père Lourdel wrote to Mackay on his arrival asking for his support with the king; but Mackay rather did his best to discredit him, saying that Catholics worshipped a woman called Mary. Lourdel was astounded to find that the passages of Scripture read by Mackay at court dealt, one with Solomon and his thousand wives, the other with the Apocalypse. He denounced Mackay's Bible as 'a book of lies'. cf. Stock, *op. cit.*, III, p. 105.

so far from becoming the laughing-stock of Buganda, achieved there one of its most rapid conquests. Both the missions confirmed Stanley's view that political conditions were unusually favourable.[1] At Rubaga, the capital, which stretched for six miles in front of the royal enclosure and for two miles on either side of it, there were gathered together the town houses of the great provincial chiefs and of some hundreds of lesser chiefs, all with their wives and retainers. This town-dwelling aristocracy formed a leisured class, largely emancipated from the religious ties and social observances of ordinary tribal life. Especially was this true of the innermost circle, consisting of the officers of the body-guard, and of the young pages drawn from the best families, who received their education in the royal household.[2] Within this group there were already some who were accustomed to looking outwards, beyond the immediate circle of Bantu states which formed the cosmos of their compatriots, some who were familiar with the more catholic conception of religion introduced by the Muhammedan traders, some who had developed a capacity for independent thought and a sense of individual responsibility which were fundamental to the Christian scheme of sin and redemption.

Mutesa, it has been shown, had a special reason for promoting the satisfaction of the missionaries, and he threw himself into the part of a Christian inquirer with all the verve of a great actor. The first C.M.S. party had scarcely reached

---

[1] Livinhac in *MC*. 81. 230: 'L'organisation politique de l'Ouganda peut être d'un grand secours; au dessous du Kabaka, monarque absolu, se trouvent les chefs des grandes familles [Mohamis], puis les nobles du second rang, puis les serfs. Donc: l'évangélisation par seigneuries.'

[2] John Roscoe, *The Baganda*, London, 1911, Chapter VII.

the southern shores of the Nyanza when they received letters from Mutesa, composed for him by Stanley's ex-servant Maftaa, in which he begged 'My Dear Friend Wite Men' to 'come quickly . . . because this king is very fond of you'. On their arrival at Rubaga they received an ovation. The relative strength of Britain and Egypt was the subject of the first conference; but on their second Sunday, Wilson and Shergold Smith were invited to conduct divine service before the king and his great chiefs, Maftaa interpreting, and were amazed to hear 'hearty Amens' from the distinguished congregation at the conclusion of each prayer.[1] During the next three years—while the Egyptian danger was still uppermost in Mutesa's mind—reading and religious disputation became the fashionable pastimes of the court, the king himself leading the discussions and handing out the reading sheets.[2] The delusion of the missionaries deepened steadily. Mackay, on his arrival in 1878, rejoiced at being able to carry on the good work which Stanley had begun. He lectured an Arab trader at the palace on the evils of slave-dealing, and the practice was promptly forbidden—at least in public. 'I believe', he wrote, 'the reading of the life of our Lord is not without effect. Today the king remarked to his people "Isa (Jesus) was there ever anyone like him?" ' A year later Mackay was still in hopes: 'Mutesa acknowledged that he believed in our Lord as the Son of God from all eternity and as the only future Judge of the world. . . . He seems to take pleasure in discussion however.' But the spell was soon to break. In 1879 Gordon evacuated the southernmost of the Egyptian forts, at Mruli and Foweira on the

---

[1] Stock, *op. cit.*, III, p. 100 *sq.*   [2] *CMI.* 80. 680.

Somerset Nile. In December of that year the king fell sick, and the national gods were called on as of old. Mackay's protests were ignored. He was informed by the chief minister that the business of missionaries was to make guns, caps and powder, 'guns innumerable as grass'. The oracle recommended human sacrifice as a remedy for the king's illness; and hundreds of innocent people were accordingly seized and butchered. 'Mutesa', wrote Mackay in February 1880, 'is a pagan—a heathen—out and out.' As long as the king lived the missions were free from violence; but the royal Sunday school ceased; and when in 1884 Mackay summed up his experiences of Mutesa's last four years, it was in a sombre tone: 'It requires the most careful diplomatic skill so to humour the court of Uganda that we may have toleration there at all.'[1]

The years of royal disfavour, however, proved to be the period of real progress. A month before the king's illness references to private teaching began to appear regularly in Mackay's journal.

All day occupied with readers at various stages. Some I hear in the house, while others I take to the workshop and teach them while I am busy at the vice. . . . We find our work growing in our hands. . . . Hosts of people come to us every day for instruction—chiefly in reading of course; and, as we put portions of the scriptures into their hands, as soon as they get over the first difficulties of reading, we have very frequent means of instructing them in the truths of eternity.

During the massacres of February 1880 the C.M.S. missionaries were concerned for the safety of Duta, the son of one

---

[1] Mackay, *op. cit.*, pp. 104–5, 131, 166, 183, 247.

of the great county chiefs, 'a lad who has been much with us for instruction', a lad who was destined to be the foremost of the first generation of African clergymen in the Angh an Church of Uganda. Later that year Lourdel baptised the first of his converts into the Roman Church. In the next, Mackay received a request for baptism from his 'old faithful pupil and assistant' Sembera, the serf of a minor chief now living far from the capital, whose zeal had been such that he had taught his master to read also. He was received into the Church with four others in March 1882. The number of inquirers continued to swell. Some in their enthusiasm went to 'read' at both the missions. Of the sincerity of these early Baganda Christians there can be no doubt. They had won their way to a faith which was sharply opposed to many of the most deeply rooted customs of their people; and in 1886 many of them were to stand the test of a martyrdom as terrible as any in Christian history.[1]

*   *   *   *

4

Outside the closed communities of freedmen and refugees and the only slightly less segregated circles of free adherents, the pioneer missionaries played some part as prophets, if not yet as priests. All of them from time to time left their stations and tramped, perhaps for two or three weeks at a time, through the villages of the surrounding districts, to

[1] Mackay, *op. cit.*, pp. 139, 141, 193, 229.

prospect for future sites, but also to announce for the first time and in the simplest way the gospel of man's redemption. They found that, having mastered their first few words of Kiswahili, the lingua franca introduced by the Arabs, they could be sure of finding an interpreter and an attentive audience.[1] Their message, too, awoke some echo from the more dimly apprehended background of Bantu religions, all of which recognised the existence of a single and personal, if somewhat disinterested, Creator, and taught belief in a shadowy form of life after death.[2] Livingstone, with his vast experience, felt able to pronounce that the Bantu had a conception of sin as offence against their fellow men, whether living or departed, and that their idea of 'moral evil' differed in no way from his own.[3] That the Son of God had appeared among men was a perfectly acceptable proposition: that He had appeared among white men did much to explain their superior powers; that He had been put to death by them was no stumbling-block, as it was to the Muslim;[4] that He had left His words in His Book was especially impressive to a people prone to believe in divination and to whom the art of reading appeared the greatest of human mysteries.

Needless to say, these 'tournées évangéliques', as the French Fathers used to call them, brought no very immediate or practical consequences. Occasionally some

---

[1] Clark to C.M.S. from Mpwapwa, 10.xi.76.
[2] D. Livingstone, *The Zambezi Expedition*, p. 521.   [3] *ibid.*, p. 521.
[4] The Muhammedan conception of God as 'Power', to whose will man must 'submit' or else be ground into the dust, is irreconcilable with the Christian belief that God could so respect the free will which He has created in man as even to suffer under it, and not crush it, when directed against Himself. Islam recognises Jesus as a Prophet, and, for that reason, teaches that He was not put to death, but carried up to Heaven like Elijah.

outstanding attention to the sick or the blind might result in a baptism 'in articulo mortis' or in some individual detaching himself from his village and coming to live at the mission. These exceptions, however, merely proved the rule that the solidarity of inherited belief and custom was such that no individual could become a Christian while remaining a full member of his tribal community. Nevertheless some less tangible influence was exerted which can perhaps be best summed up as impact on fear. Livingstone described in telling terms the fundamental characteristic of life in a state of nature: 'People awaking in fright utter the most unearthly yells, and they are joined in them by all who sleep near. The first imagines himself seized by a wild beast, the rest roar because they hear him doing it: this indicates the extreme of helpless terror.'[1] Most nights, said W. P. Johnson, one would hear the drums going, and generally they were being beaten to exorcise the spirits. 'I would first talk to the people of the good Providence we believed in, and then try to help them with some sedative medicine.'[2] Many other devices were used in the same good cause. Livingstone, discovering that in one district iron-work was the basis of a sorcerer's prestige, gave public lectures in the art of smelting.[3] Bishop Smythies and Archdeacon Woodward climbed the 'spirit mountain' behind Magila in full view of the watching populace.[4] Père Horner at Mandera made a point of adopting the intended victims of superstitious infanticide and proving that they could be raised to healthy manhood.[5] Laws fought a long battle against the poison ordeal among

---

[1] D. Livingstone, *Last Journals*, II, p. 19.   [2] Johnson, *op. cit.*, p. 44.
[3] Chamberlin, *op. cit.*, p. 81.   [4] Wilson, *op. cit.*, p. 77.   [5] *MC*. 84. 506.

the Ngoni, and used his medical art to prove that disease and death could have other causes than the malice of one's enemies.[1] All these men would probably have been surprised to hear that a later generation would accuse them of attacking innocent superstitions and of substituting one fear for another. Their own assessment would certainly have been more old-fashioned:

> The old Dragon under ground,
> In straiter limits bound
>   Not half so far casts his usurped sway.

* * * *

5

During the short period of their activity so far described, the missionaries, together with their supporters at home, became a powerful force attracting attention in Europe to East Africa. Inevitably the deployment of so many Englishmen over a territory which was still so slightly known and so full of hazards was a matter of concern to the British Government and especially to the Consul-General at Zanzibar. Within the Sultan's dominions, along the coastal belt from Cape Delgado to Lamu, they operated under his licence and enjoyed full consular protection. Every cargo of slaves intercepted by the British warships brought him into contact with their settlements; and from 1884 it was his duty to administer the government subsidies recommended

---

[1] W. P. Livingstone, *Laws*, p. 94.

D

in the Frere report.[1] But it was especially the troubles
between the missions and the Arabs at Mombasa which
called for his constant attention and swelled his correspondence with England. Though never guilty of the disagreeable sarcasm of Lister and his subordinates at the Foreign
Office, Sir John Kirk came no closer to appreciating the
difficulties of the missionaries than they came to appreciating
his own. 'Slavery', wrote Kirk after the trouble of 1880, 'is
doomed . . . but it will be disastrous if this is attempted to
be brought about by the unauthorised and irresponsible
action of private parties.'[2] According to his view it was the
duty of officialdom to press the Zanzibar government to a
closer and closer limitation of the slave-trade, until the
institution of slavery itself died a natural death, and the
duty of the missions was on the one hand to care for those
slaves who had been liberated through their owners'
infringement of the treaties, while on the other hand
scrupulously respecting the legal status of slavery within the
Sultan's dominions.[3] Had this been the view of the C.M.S.
Committee, or even of Sir Bartle Frere who advised them,
their settlements would have been placed on the Seychelles
or in some equally safe position where no political complica-
tions would have arisen. In fact, however, Freretown had

[1] Lister to Kirk, 24.iii.86. F.O. 84. 1771. C.M.S. and U.M.C.A. to receive £5
per slave handed over w.e.f., 1.vi.84. Initial payments were £1,545 to the C.M.S.
and £120 to U.M.C.A.
[2] Kirk to Granville, 9.x.80 (KP).
[3] *ibid.*, 'I considered it no business of ours to help the masters in any way to recover
their slaves, and I stated publicly that I regarded slavery as dying out and that by
legitimate means I should do my best to bring about its extinction. . . . I told the
missionaries that in case of civil war they would find themselves opposed not to the
Mombasa mob, but by the Sultan's regular forces and armed ships.'

been deliberately sited to be a thorn in the side not only of the mainland slave-trade, but of the whole institution of domestic slavery as practised at Mombasa. That a steadily growing settlement of freedmen would become a cause of resentment among the slave-owners and of dissatisfaction and desertion by their slaves must have been foreseen by the planners, who clearly expected a more partisan support for their agents by the British Consul than in the event they received.[1]

Farther inland the missionaries travelled at their own risk, but Kirk still watched their progress with interest and sometimes with anxiety. The conduct of missionaries in the interior was always liable to have repercussions at the coast or even on a wider diplomatic field. Commenting on the Blantyre atrocities, Kirk wrote: 'The Portuguese authorities meantime look on in amazement, waiting to see what the upshot of this will be, perhaps hoping that further disturbances may call for active interference.'[2] The moving of large caravans over long distances in the interior often drove the best men to desperate measures. No less a man than Mackay, the evangelist of Buganda, was capable of shooting at and wounding four deserting porters and of disregarding Kirk's summons on the grounds that his action had been a legitimate way of dealing with mutiny.[3] Missionaries, like other travellers, were liable to implicate their governments

[1] Hutchinson (C.M.S.) to Granville, 14.i.81. Enclosure 1 in No. 194 of 1881 (KP).

[2] Kirk to Granville, 1.vi.80 (KP).

[3] Kirk to Derby, 1.iv.78 (KP) and 8.vi.78, reporting that compensation having been paid to the wounded men, the charge against Mackay had been withdrawn and that the Sultan of Unyanyembe had been informed in this sense.

by flying their national flags,[1] or even by posing as the official representatives of the Queen.[2] In judging these examples of misconduct which came before him, and which perhaps occupied a disproportionate amount of his correspondence on missionary matters, Kirk showed himself well able to make all the necessary allowances for the influence of the climate and of fear, and for the many situations in which the absence of public opinion and an established standard of morals led men to do deeds less than Christian and sometimes less than civilised. The long and careful reports which he received from missionaries all over the interior, which were forwarded by him to the Foreign Office, and which remain the best sources for the general history of East Africa during these years, are evidence of his willingness to help and to profit by missionary enterprise.

There remained one basic difference in attitude between Kirk and the missions in the interior which was the same in essence as that which existed on the coast. Kirk regarded the political penetration of East Africa by Great Britain as something which must be based on Zanzibar. Whether the Government eventually declared a protectorate, or whether a British company gained a concession carrying governmental powers, or whether Britain decided to rely on her diplomatic influence alone to protect her interests, Kirk, like Hardinge a decade later, visualised a full utilisation

[1] Hore got into trouble with the Arabs, and later with Kirk for flying the British flag at Ujiji in 1878. Hore, *op. cit.*, p. 95.

[2] Mackay to Kirk from Buganda, 30.i.86. F.O. 84. 1773 (not clear in what enclosed): 'O'Flaherty . . . was particularly upset at your letter [to the King] affirming that we were not political agents, as he had previously most imprudently given the King to understand that he was sent here by the Queen. . . . By nationality and temperament he proved too rash in language and in action for usefulness here.'

of Arab influence in the interior. Zanzibaris would be the non-commissioned officers of the European administration in a land of savages. The missionaries, on the other hand, though they were not yet in open conflict with the Arabs, naturally regarded them as the root of most of the social evils which Christianity had come to destroy. Whenever, therefore, Arab and native forces came into open collision, the missionaries and the Consul took opposite sides. When in about 1878 the Arabs settled at Tabora (Unyanyembe) grew disaffected towards the Sultan, Kirk decided that it would be wise to cultivate the friendship of Mirambo[1] and to convince him 'through the influence of the missionaries settled with him, that the only way of securing a paramount influence in the country was to give security to traders and travellers.'[2] Yet when, two years later, Mirambo grew strong enough to defy the Arabs and when at the same time an ally of Mirambo's murdered two members of a Belgian expedition in Mpimbwe, Kirk abruptly threw up this policy with the unfounded insinuation that doubtless Mirambo had received bad advice.[3] 'The value of British-Indian capital that is now employed in the hand of Arabs is immense', wrote Kirk to Dr. Southon, apparently oblivious of the fact that a great part of that capital was employed in the prosecution of the slave-trade. 'It will be for you to consider how far it is possible for you to maintain the mission with Mirambo; but . . . before deciding to do so, you should fully consider the dangers that may arise in the course of a native war in which the sympathy and support of the

[1] Kirk to Derby, 3.v.78. No. 448 (KP).   [2] Kirk to Granville, 20.viii.80 (KP).
[3] *ibid.*

civilised world will be against Mirambo and his allies.'[1] To Granville, Kirk reported that the Arabs would now have to fight for their existence if they meant to retain the trade of the region. The Sultan was therefore preparing a force to occupy a first advance line near Mpwapwa and so 'for the first time assert a distinct claim . . . to the sovereignty over Central Africa'.[2] Kirk, as it proved, had taken unnecessary alarm. Six months later he was evidently on good terms with Dr. Southon and once more confident of being able to influence Mirambo through him.[3] But the incident is important as illustrating the advancement of a claim by Zanzibar with Kirk's full encouragement, which in the following decade was to drive missionaries throughout Central Africa into the imperialist camp.

There is little evidence that during the years 1875-85 any of the missions were consciously trying to draw their governments 'into Central Africa in their wake'.[4] Individual indiscretions apart, the only pressure brought to bear upon the British Government was for new diplomatic connections —at Mombasa and on Lake Nyasa. Both the C.M.S., who asked for vice-consular status to be given to their Lay Superintendent at Freretown,[5] and the Free Church, which requested a similar position for Dr. Laws,[6] were aware that any exercise of civil jurisdiction was technically an offence against the Foreign Jurisdiction Act and could be legalised

[1] Kirk to the L.M.S. Agent at Urambo, 12.viii.80. Copy enclosed in above.
[2] Kirk to Granville, 24.viii.80. No. 450 (KP).
[3] Kirk to Granville, 8.iii.81. No. 226 (KP).
[4] Hanna, *op. cit.*, p. 135.
[5] Kirk to Derby, 7.vi.76. No. 587 (KP).
[6] W. P. Livingstone, *Laws*, p. 43.

only by this means.[1] On Lake Nyasa there was a further reason. Obstruction by the Portuguese authorities on the Zambezi had aroused the fears of the Free Church mission as early as 1877; but Dr. Stewart had made it very clear to Elton, the British Consul at Mozambique, that 'on the point of any recommendations home about protection on the Lake: there is only one reason for that, and it is not the natives. . . . It is if our Portuguese friends are to claim all that we have done, 10–12 years hence'.[2]

In 1877 the C.M.S. submitted a memorial to the Foreign Secretary urging that the Khedive should be restrained from annexing Buganda, and they explicitly suggested that King Mutesa was entitled 'to an assurance from Egypt that the independence of his kingdom and sovereignty will be respected, and the neutrality of, and free trade on, Lake Victoria be secured'.[3] The Government, for its part, treated every form of pressure with persistent caution. The subject of Mutesa's independence was pressed in Cairo, because it coincided with the already expressed views of Kirk, that the Nile lakes had long been within the commercial orbit of Zanzibar, where Britain was able to exercise more effective

[1] Sir Bartle Frere, now Governor at Cape Town, took the view that all missionaries working beyond the reach of European influence should be endowed with some kind of vice-consular authority, since it was both necessary and desirable that they should accumulate political adherents. See an interesting report of his conversations with the C.M.S. East African Missionary. J. C. Price at Cape Town: Price to C.M.S., 28.viii.79.

[2] Stewart to Elton, 15.iv.77, enclosed in Elton to Derby, 28.v.77. F.O. 84. 1479. I am indebted to A. J. Hanna, *op. cit.*, for this reference, but disagree with his interpretation of it. By 'protection' Stewart clearly meant what was later to be distinguished from 'protectorate' as 'sphere of influence'.

[3] C.M.S. Memorial to the Earl of Derby, March 1877, cited by Sir J. M. Gray in 'Sir John Kirk and Mutesa', *Uganda Journal*, March 1951, p. 8.

influence against the slave-trade than in Egypt. The
requests by the C.M.S. and the Free Church for consular
status for their missionaries were refused; and even when the
Blantyre atrocities were made the subject of a motion in the
House of Commons, the Government would not be drawn
into active interference.[1] Still, the mere presence of the
missionaries was not without its effect on the conduct of
foreign affairs. Their reports on the slave-trade made clear
the necessity for diplomatic representation, not only at the
coast, but in the interior. In 1880 Kirk himself suggested
that Hore should be given an official appointment at Ujiji,[2]
and in 1883 a whole-time consul was posted to Lake Nyasa.
More important still, there grew up at the Foreign Office in
London a generation of officials—men like Sir Villiers Lister,
Sir Percy Anderson, Sir Julian Pauncefote, Sir Edward
Hertslet and Sir Clement Hill—who were well versed in the
affairs of Central Africa, and who, when the time for partition came, were able to point, not merely to blank spaces on
the map intersected by the itineraries of a few explorers, but
to the existence of British interests to be safeguarded and
British lives to be protected.

Alongside the officials there was already a small but

---

[1] On 2nd July, 1880, Dr. Cameron, the Member for Glasgow, moved 'that a
humble address be presented . . . praying Her Majesty to take measures to prevent
British subjects not commissioned by Her from assuming rights of criminal jurisdiction over the natives of uncivilised countries, and perpetrating upon them acts of
war. . . .' Sir Charles Dilke replied that though the Government agreed with the
sentiments of the motion, and though they had ample powers to deal with such cases
under the Foreign Jurisdiction Act, they preferred not to act until the Commission
appointed by the Church of Scotland had reported. Hansard, 2.viii.80, col. 1424.
No official action was in fact ever taken.

[2] The proposal was turned down, not by the Foreign Office, but by the L.M.S.
directors. Kirk to Hore, 23.iii.80. L.M.S. papers.

informed public which watched the progress of the missions with attention, and which was to become in time a powerful influence in the affairs of East Africa—Church dignitaries, lay committee-men of the missionary organisations, members of the Anti-Slavery Society, explorers, scientists and, above all, business men with philanthropic interests, who believed in the doctrine of 'legitimate trade', and who were prepared in its interest to risk capital which could have been more gainfully employed elsewhere. Foremost in this last group, which occupied that interesting borderland between philanthropy and high finance, were Sir Thomas Fowell Buxton, the grandson of the abolitionist, and Sir William Mackinnon, the pious founder of the great eastern trading firm of Mackinnon and Mackenzie. Buxton was high in the counsels of the C.M.S. and the Anti-Slavery Society; and he was one of the inner group which inspired the pressure brought by those organisations to keep Gordon and the Egyptians out of Uganda.[1] At the same time he had been engaged with Mackinnon in a private venture, to build a road from Dar-es-Salaam to Lake Nyasa in the hope of developing legitimate trade. There followed in 1877 a much wider scheme whereby, at the invitation of Sultan Barghash, a company headed by Mackinnon and Buxton was to take over and develop the whole of the mainland dominions of Zanzibar under a seventy years' concession. It was even suggested to Gordon that he should leave the service of the Khedive and take charge instead of the projected company's operations in East Africa.[2] In the event the negotiations

[1] Sir J. M. Gray, *loc. cit.*, *Uganda Journal*, March 1951, p. 8.
[2] Gordon to Waller, 17.i.77. *Waller Papers*, II.

dragged on for two years and then lapsed. The reasons for their failure are still obscure. It was asserted by Mackinnon's supporters that the Foreign Office failed to give the necessary assurances of assistance; from the limited evidence available, however, it seems more likely that the promoters themselves failed to raise in the City the very large amount of capital needed for the undertaking.[1] A decade later, when the Germans were already ensconced in the southern half of the Sultan's dominions, a new concession was to be signed, of which Mackinnon and his associates were to be once more the doubtful beneficiaries. The Imperial British East Africa Company, as it was then to be called, was to prove financially quite inadequate to its task; but its operations were to play a vital part in consolidating British interests in East Africa during the period of partition, and in committing the British Government to direct intervention. Needless to say, neither the missionaries in the field nor the societies on which they depended were, as such, directly responsible for these developments, but it is probable that, had it not been for the stimulus of the missionary occupation, Buxton and Mackinnon would not have acted as they did.

In the scientific sphere, too, the pioneer missionaries attracted the notice of the experts in Europe. In geography they added important contributions to the work of the professional explorers. In many districts it was they who first left the beaten tracks and trade routes to trace the rivers, chart the lakes, climb the mountains, measure the temperatures and calculate the rainfall. The whole of the

---

[1] cf. Coupland, *Exploitation*, pp. 300–18.

Rovuma district was first opened up by missionaries of the U.M.C.A. Maples explored the north of what is now Portuguese East Africa:[1] Steere and Johnson carried on the work eastwards to Lake Nyasa.[2] Lake Nyasa itself was first circumnavigated by Stewart and Laws of the Free Church Mission, who discovered its northern half and who visited the Ngoni chieftains behind its western coast.[3] All these contributions were recognised by Fellowships of the Royal Geographical Society, and many more attracted attention. Hore of the L.M.S. completed Cameron's work in charting Lake Tanganyika and confirmed its outlet into the Lukuga River.[4] Mackay of the C.M.S. traced the Wami River and built a new road from Saadani to Mpwapwa. Horner explored much of Ukami, Ukaguru and Uzigua. The White Fathers were the first to travel in Urundi.[5] Less sensational, but scientifically no less important, was the missionaries' pioneer work in African languages. Steere and Laws, both fine scholars, spent precious hours in the study and the printing office, preparing grammars and dictionaries and

[1] *Proceedings of the Royal Geographical Society*, 1880, p. 337. Maples, 'Masasi and the Rovuma district', *ibid.*, 1882, p. 79. 'Makualand and the district between the Rovuma and the Luli'.

[2] Johnson, 'Journals in the Yao Country and the discovery of the Lujenda sources', *ibid.*, 1882, p. 480. 'Seven years' travels in the region East of Lake Nyasa', *ibid.*, 1884, p. 512.

[3] E. D. Young, 'Sojourn at Lake Nyasa', *ibid*, 1876–7, p. 225. Stewart, 'Lake Nyasa and the Water Route to the Great Lakes', *ibid.*, 1881, p. 257. Stewart, 'The Second Navigation of Lake Nyasa', *ibid.*, 1879, p. 289. Laws, 'The West Side of Lake Nyasa', *ibid.*, 1879, p. 305. Stewart, 'West Nyasa and the Country between Nyasa and Tanganyika', *ibid.*, 1880, p. 428. Stewart, 'Survey of the East Coast of Lake Nyasa', *ibid.*, 1883, p. 689.

[4] Cameron, 'Examination of the Southern half of Lake Tanganyika', *Journal of R.G.S.*, 1875, p. 184. Hore, 'Lake Tanganyika', *Proc. R.G.S.*, 1882, p. 1.

[5] *AMZ*. 89. 140.

New Testament translations in Swahili and Nyanja. Others made beginnings in Ganda and Yao, Tonga and Gogo, Nyamwezi, and many other less important dialects. Presses were set up at Zanzibar, Livingstonia and Blantyre, while in England the British and Foreign Bible Society and the Society for Promoting Christian Knowledge struggled to keep pace with the literary needs of the Protestant missions. As a result of all these activities, though no imperialist desires were consciously stimulated, new information about East Africa started to percolate through the academic world and into the educational system, finding its way into school atlases as well as into the learned periodicals. In the press, nurserymen advertised African grasses, and an enterprising furnisher marketed firescreens 'embossed with handsome tropical beetles'.[1] From all these growing interests, both erudite and frivolous, the advocates of a forward policy in Africa were to draw much of their popular support.

Finally it must be remembered that the missionary societies at home employed powerful propaganda departments to raise their incomes: and through these the East African missionaries exercised a direct influence upon the ordinary church-going public. Their letters were widely circulated in the missionary magazines: Rubaga and Mpwapwa were household words in many an English home. When they came to England on furlough, they spoke on public platforms up and down the country. If spiritual action was their object, material aid was their immediate need; and in framing their appeals they naturally tended to

---

[1] Both these items were advertised in illustrated brochures discovered between the pages of *CMI.* for the years 1886–7.

dwell rather upon intentions than upon achievements, and to bolster the humble facts with grandiose if acceptable suggestions that the genial tide of western progress was flowing in, even among 'the neglected children of Ham'. Naturally, too, the reaction of the audiences did not always correspond exactly to the ideas of the speakers. If the missionaries on 'deputation' did not ask either for armies or administrators, they did spread the feeling that European influence could only be an unqualified blessing to the African. They built up those sentiments of duty and responsibility to which Kipling was so effectively to appeal in 1899, when the partition of Africa was an accomplished fact.

> Take up the White Man's Burden—
>   Send forth the best ye breed—
> Go bind your sons to exile
>   To serve your captives' need;
> To wait in heavy harness
>   On fluttered folk and wild—
> Your new-caught sullen peoples,
>   Half-devil and half-child.[1]

[1] It would be tedious to quote specific sources for these generalisations. They are based on sermons quoted in Heanley, *op. cit.*, and in Ward, *Smythies*, and also from the accounts of speeches at anniversary meetings in *CA.* and the *CMI.*

Chapter Three

THE MISSIONS AND THE EUROPEAN
OCCUPATION, 1885–95

I

THE GERMAN INRUPTION into East Africa in 1885[1]
started a train of events which converted the missions into
an important vehicle of militant imperialism in Europe,
with consequences which vitally affected their future
standing in Africa. This fact is outwardly surprising, since
in Germany itself the awakening of missionary interest was a
by-product rather than a cause of the imperialist movement.
The promoters of German colonialism were mostly rich
Hamburg merchants, who neither sought nor commanded
the support of the predominantly Pietist and socially inferior missionary groups.[2] The much-quoted Fabri[3] was, it
is true, a director of the Calvinistic Barmen Mission; but
both he and his society were strongly criticised by the
Lutheran-Evangelical majority,[4] who were already fully

---

[1] I take for convenience the date of the publication of the Imperial Schutzbrief.

[2] Mirbt, 'Die Bedeutung des Pietismus für die Heidenmission', *AMZ.* 99. 145.

[3] Author of a celebrated pamphlet, *Bedarf Deutschland Kolonieen?*, Gotha,
1879. It is quoted by M. E. Townsend in *The Rise and Fall of the German Colonial
Empire*, and by P. T. Moon in *Imperialism and World Politics*, rightly as an example
of imperialist arguments, but wrongly as an example of the German missionary
viewpoint.

[4] See especially *AMZ.* 92. 441.

occupied in South Africa, India, China, Australia and New Zealand and had no special desire for new fields of work or for the superintendence of a German government. They were even less favourably impressed when Carl Peters and other leaders of the colonial group started a series of attacks upon their policy and methods, saying that they should 'stop working for England', that they should 'be incorporated into the German colonial movement' and work 'in the German-national spirit', and, above all, that they should 'teach the natives to work'.[1] Later, when the Government had taken over the administration from the German East Africa Company, they were slowly to change their attitude; but the only immediate Protestant response to the early colonial moves in East Africa was the foundation of two new societies by groups more imperialist than missionary, which were for some time to come more remarkable for their committees at home than for their work abroad.

The 'evangelisch-lutherische Missionsgesellschaft für Ostafrika in Bayern' was founded in 1885, and two missionaries were sent out early the following year. But funds were difficult to raise in competition with the already established Leipzig society;[2] and it was typical of the somewhat hysterical origin of the venture that the first station was built at Jimba, near Kisulutini, which subsequently turned out to be in the British sphere of influence.[3] Moreover, the missionaries discovered that the outlying groups of the Kamba tribe, to which they had been directed, had decamped from the neighbourhood a few months before their arrival, leaving only a small pocket of Swahili-speaking coast

[1] *ibid.*, p. 443 *sqq.*　　　[2] *infra*, pp. 166–7.　　　[3] *AMZ.* 87. 87.

natives with no wide racial connections.[1] The other imperialist foundation, the 'Deutschostafrikanische Missionsgesellschaft zu Berlin', commonly known as Berlin III, was at first scarcely more successful. The influence of Carl Peters was apparent in its avowed aim to educate the natives to work on the German plantations; and it aroused the criticism of the older societies by spending missionary funds on a hospital for Europeans at Zanzibar.[2] Berlin III followed exactly the line of the colonial occupation, starting at Dar-es-Salaam and spreading into the unpromising Islamised province of Usaramo; and its missionaries, as Germans, were attacked in the Arab rebellion against the German East Africa Company in 1888.

In East Africa, the missions already established at the coast were at first actively hostile to the Germans. The Company's agents were notoriously tactless with the Arabs and brutal to the Africans.[3] Naturally, too, the Protestant

---

[1] *AMZ.* 87. 89.   [2] *ibid.*, 91. 169.

[3] A contemporary contrast between German and British methods by Mgr. de Courmont, the head of the Holy Ghost Mission, is perhaps worth quoting: 'Les agents allemands, déjà peu sympathiques aux indigènes s'installent dans les ports concédés, annoncent par publication solenelle l'état de choses nouveau, déployent partout leur pavillon, parlent de leurs juges, de leurs gouverneurs, de leurs impôts, de leurs règlements. La population assiste, d'abord surprise, mais peu à peu le mécontentement grandit, s'étend, éclate. . . . Pendant que les officiers allemands gagnent des victoires, les agents anglais font des affaires. A la fin de septembre 1888, Mackenzie qui a fait en Perse un séjour de quinze ans et qui connait son monde orientale, débarque à Zanzibar, et après s'être muni des lettres nécessaires au sultan, parcourt la côte sous le pavillon de Sa Hautesse. Il vient, répondant aux instances de Said, pour essayer de ramener le commerce et la prospérité dans ces ports déserts, et faire profiter tout le monde des bienfaits qui seront répandus. Pas un mot de pavillon nouveau, ni de taxes ni de règlements, ni de déplacement de fonctionnaires, ni de juges, ni de rien. Seulement en souvenir d'amitié le gouverneur reçoit un cadeau, les anciens reçoivent des cadeaux, les gens influents reçoivent des cadeaux, et tout le monde dit "Vive Mackenzie!"' *MC.* 90. 437.

missions disliked the idea of working under a foreign government, especially since Peters' personal morals were distasteful to them, and since he openly expressed the opinion that non-German missions should not be tolerated in German territory.[1] Inevitably, wrote Smythies, acts of violence and oppression committed by one set of white men must react upon the standing of the other in the eyes of the natives. Christianity would be degraded and the lives of the missionaries endangered.[2] In particular the advent of a new government would falsify their relations with the native chiefs, whose power they had supported in their teaching.[3] In the event many of these fears proved unfounded. In the rebellion of 1888 the ringleader, Bushiri, showed by his unfailing courtesy to the old-established missions that the coastal Arabs could distinguish between one European and another, while among the native tribes the missionary in fact tended to gain prestige by his services as mediator rather than lose it by association with the European overlord. Nevertheless, it is an interesting fact that at the very moment when missions were beginning to advocate imperialism, they were also busy decrying its first manifestation.

* * * *

2

The most important effect of the German invasion upon their work was never recognised as such by the missions,

---

[1] *AMZ.* 92. 441.   [2] Letters quoted in Ward, *Smythies*, p. 133 *sqq.*
[3] Smythies to *The Times*, 4.v.81.

because this result took place, not at the coast where the German officials were landing, but in the far interior regions round the Great Lakes, and because it affected their relations, not with the Africans, but with the Arabs.

As long as they had remained the only intruders in Central Africa, the Arabs had made no attempt to set up empires of their own. Some of them, and perhaps, as Johnston suggested, the majority of those who came by birth from the olive-complexioned Arabic-speaking aristocracy of the coast and from southern Arabia, were merchant adventurers, whose ambitions, like those of the Indian nabobs, were to amass their fortunes quickly and then retire to estates at Muscat or Zanzibar.[1] Others, starting usually as the employees of the former type, had become in the course of a generation or so colonists with a fixed place of residence in the interior and small desire to return to the coast. Others again, while doubtless making a part of their livelihood as middlemen in trade and as agents of the great merchants of the caravan-routes, had found local fame and fortune as scribes and skilled craftsmen at the courts of native potentates, who had sometimes honoured them with land as well as slaves. But these colonists would seem, until very nearly the date of the German inruption, to have been the smaller fry. The general significance of the Arab penetration had

[1] Johnston to Salisbury, 17.iii.90. F.O. 84. 2051. (cf. A. M. Mackay in *CMI*. 89. 20.) 'All such men as Tipu-Tipu (Upper Congo), Mlozi, Msalema, Bwana Omari (Konde), and Jumbe of Kota Kota are Swahili Arabs, born on the African coast, and scarcely any of them are able to talk Arabic. . . . On the other hand Mohammed bin Khalfan, Kabunda, Sherif Majid and several leading Arabs who pass backwards and forwards through Nyasaland are white or olive-complexioned, come from Arabia to trade in Africa, and return thither when they have amassed a modest competence, chiefly in the ivory trade nowadays, but formerly in the traffic in slaves.'

been commercial rather than imperialistic. Nothing struck Baker more forcibly than the contrast between the good prices paid by the Zanzibar traders and the naked rapine of the Khartoumers.[1] Even in the south, where the tribes were weak and where the Kilwa traders could have placed themselves by a few well-organised expeditions in a position to seize without payment all that they required, Livingstone found it almost impossible to buy food because the people were so well supplied by the Arabs with all that they needed.[2]

The entry of the missions, it has been shown, brought the beginnings of a rival economic system. Mirambo, already strong enough to defy the Arabs, could afford to lay aside his slave-raiding and exist on the profits of caravan porterage.[3] Many of the small chiefs, particularly in the Rovuma basin and round Lake Nyasa, no longer needed to deal in slaves if there was a mission in the neighbourhood. But before 1884 the rivalry led to no open clashes. If the Arabs knew that the missions were hostile to the trade, they also knew that they were connected with the Consul at Zanzibar, and that the Sultan, whom they acknowledged as their overlord, was out-wardly supporting the British campaign against slavery. They therefore avoided the mission districts and pressed

[1] 'The Arab envoys of Abou Saood had been treated like dogs by the great Mtese of Buganda, and they had slunk back abashed, and were only too glad to be allowed to depart. They declared that such a country would not suit their business: the people were too strong for them; and the traders from Zanzibar purchased their ivory from Mtese with cotton stuffs, silks, guns, and powder, brass-coil bracelets, beads, etc. The beads were exchanged by equal weight for ivory. . . . While fair dealing is the rule south of the equator, piracy and ruin are the rule of the north.' Baker, *Ismailia*, II, pp. 98–9.
[2] D. Livingstone, *Last Journals*, pp. 56–7, etc.
[3] Southon to L.M.S., 28.iii.80.

farther to the west, where their methods, it is true, were less savoury. The blockade of the coast, moreover, especially after the Frere Treaty of 1873, had reversed the relative importance of slaves and ivory, at least as articles of export; and the latter was obtained for the most part from the neighbourhood of the Upper Congo, by methods not dissimilar to those used for procuring 'red rubber' during the administration of King Leopold. 'It is well known', Kirk had reported in 1877, 'that Manyema slaves never reach Zanzibar. The wonder therefore comes to be why the slave-hunting spoken of by Dr. Livingstone is carried on.'[1] Ten years later Stanley solved the mystery. 'Slave-raiding becomes innocence when compared with ivory-raiding.' Bands of some 300 to 600 Manyema, 'armed with Enfield carbines and officered by Zanzibari Arabs and Swahili', were ranging over the whole of the forest country west of the Upper Congo, destroying the villages, capturing the women and children, and holding them as hostages to be exchanged for ivory.[2] In their search for ivory the Arabs had by 1884 almost reached the west coast of Africa; but, though whole regions were devastated, there was still no tendency to stay and govern. All these territories, moreover, lay far beyond the missionaries' ken, and did little to change the relations between Europeans and Arabs within their field of contact, to the east of the Great Lakes. Here the

[1] Kirk to Derby, 15.iii.77. (KP), 1877–8, No. 75.

[2] Stanley's Report on the Emin Relief Expedition. Enclosed in Euan Smith to Salisbury, 28.xii.89. F.O. 84. 1982. 'What Ugarowwa had done within his elected circle, Kilonga Longa has performed with no less skill . . . and the same cruel, murderous policy was being pursued within dozens of other circles into which the region as far south as Uregoa, north to the Uelle, East to longitude 20° 30′ and west to the Congo was parcelled out.'

missionaries, for their part, knew better than to quarrel with the Arabs. The White Fathers reported that their relations with the slavers were excellent, for they bought up the sick and wounded slaves who would otherwise have been unmarketable.[1] Protestant missions relied on the friendship of the Arabs for many services, for hospitality, for storage and for transport. Travel was always safer where the Arabs had been before, and among the dominant tribes which had benefited from the Arab commerce, the missionaries often found their most intelligent supporters. Socially, there was always something of a fellow-feeling between the European and the Arab in the centre of Africa. In private life the great slave-traders could be genial companions and were sometimes not unamenable to a theological discussion over their coffee and sherbet.[2]

Between 1884 and 1888, however, the attitude of the Arabs towards the missionaries changed abruptly all over Central Africa. What were the connecting threads in this web and in particular what part, if any, in the weaving of it was played by Seyyid Barghash at Zanzibar, will probably never be known. Its origins cannot have been exclusively due to the Germans, since the first moves at Ujiji took place six months before Carl Peters landed at Zanzibar.[3] In Buganda at least, it was probably strengthened by the Mahdi's rising, which affected the adjoining kingdom of Kabarega in Bunyoro.[4] One strand at least seems to have

[1] Numerous references exist, *e.g.* Père Guillet from Tabora in *MC*. 82. 488; Père Charbonnier from Ujiji in *MC*. 85. 272; Guillet again in *MC*. 85. 393, etc.

[2] cf. Swann, *op. cit.*, p. 170 *sqq.*

[3] *infra*, pp. 109–10; Peters landed in November 1884.

[4] This influence, tempting as it is in point of date, should not be over-emphasised. Lavigerie withdrew the White Fathers from Uganda from November 1882 till

had its origin in the Egyptian attempt to invade East Africa in 1875.[1] Another would seem to have emanated as early as 1880 from the policy of Sir John Kirk.[2] It is certain, however, that the movement, even if already planned in outline, received a powerful stimulus from the German intrusion, which defined the whole course of its later development. Kirk, sympathetic with Barghash and mainly pre-occupied with events near the coast, reported only an increase in the volume of the slave-trade. O'Neill, the Consul at Mozambique, noticed the same thing.[3] Salisbury in a letter to Sir Edward Malet at Berlin, commented on the concatenation of disturbances 'from Lake Nyasa in the south

July 1885 (*M C*. 83. 328); but this was a precautionary measure, based on information from the Verona Fathers in the Sudan (see R. Wingate, *Mahdiism and the Sudan*, Chapters I and II).

[1] Kirk to Derby, 19.ii.77, enclosing Steere to U.M.C.A. Committee, 27.vii.76: 'The Turks and Egyptians have by no means abandoned their desire to get possession of this coast. . . [stating] . . . that they are coming to relieve them of the oppression of the English and to protect them in the enjoyment of their slaves. . . . Already the effect of their appearance has shown itself in a change of tone among the coast Mohammedans, all of whom belong to the Turkish sect and not that of the ruling Arabs. They meet us now everywhere in a spirit of defiance and hatred, which is altogether new.'

[2] *supra*, pp. 84–5. Kirk profoundly disagreed with his government's estimate of the importance of East Africa. He knew that with the Sultan of Zanzibar British interests would always receive first consideration; but he also knew that as long as the Sultan's dominion over the mainland remained in doubt there was a danger of Britain being forestalled by any foreign power which cared to bypass Zanzibar. After the failure of the Mackinnon Concession, therefore, he did everything to persuade Barghash to consolidate and extend his mainland possessions, possibly not realising, possibly not caring, that in the far interior this could only be effected, immediately, by an extension of the power of the Arab slavers. How far Kirk's encouragement went, it is impossible to say and it is natural to suppose that he would have taken care to cover his tracks. Certainly Kirk's known friendship with Tippu Tib was a puzzle to the L.M.S. missionaries. See especially Hore to L.M.S., 28.xi.86.

[3] *Accounts and Papers*, 1887–8, LXXIV, p. 49.

to Suakin in the north'.[1] Missionaries throughout this region, isolated and without access to broad-based intelligence, noticed two things of profound significance: that the Arabs were now aiming at political power, and that they were seeking to drive out the European.

*   *   *   *

3

In Buganda the transition was accentuated by the death of King Mutesa in October 1884. The new king, Mwanga, was a boy, who fell easily under the influence of the Arabs at Rubaga. They plied him with alarmist accounts of Joseph Thomson's travels in Kenya,[2] and early the following year there arrived, as if to confirm them, the news of Peters's treaty-making activities farther south. Immediately Mwanga sought to restrain his people from consorting with the missionaries; and on 31st January three young followers of the C.M.S. paid for their association with their lives.[3] From the Arabs (according to the accounts of both the missions) the king also learned the practice of sodomy; and during the year 1885 the thwarting of his passions by his Christian pages became a further source of friction with the missions.[4] In July Mackay set up a Native Church Council to carry on in case of disaster to the Europeans. In September more

[1] *ibid.*, p. 97. Salisbury to Malet, 5.xi.88.

[2] Stock, *op. cit.*, III, p. 411. For Thomson's journey see Coupland, *Exploitation*, pp. 368–70.

[3] Stock, *op. cit.*, III, p. 411.

[4] *ibid.*, p. 414, Thoonen, *op. cit.*, pp. 132, 278, who is certainly right in claiming it as the chief factor, rather than the Germans, in 1886. Why else was Mwanga's fury directed against mere children?

Arabs arrived with news of the German annexations in Usagara; and less than a month later James Hannington, the first C.M.S. Bishop in East Africa, was murdered on the borders of Busoga by Mwanga's command.[1] The murder of the English missionaries at Rubaga was seriously discussed at the court; but, warned by a Christian princess, they saved their lives by following the native custom of sending a present to the king, to show that they harboured no ill-will.[2]

The dispatch of reinforcements was clearly out of the question; but for two years more the existing missionaries stayed on under perilous conditions. Further clashes took place between the king and his Christian subjects, both Catholic and Protestant, and a prominent Catholic chief was put to death in November 1885 for reproaching him with the murder of Hannington.[3] In May 1886 the sexual issue led to a showdown. The king summoned the pages and demanded to know which of them were 'readers'.[4] More than thirty stepped forward, and on deliberately refusing to recant, were burned alive in one great funeral pyre at Namungongo, sixteen miles from Kampala.[5] Eye-witness accounts collected later told sincerely of the sustained bravery and of the conscious desire for martyrdom

---

[1] F.O. 84. 1772. Kirk to Salisbury, 1.i.86, encloses Mackay to Kirk dated Uganda, 27.x.85, warning Kirk of Hannington's danger, news of German atrocities having reached Rubaga. 'The English Consul is well known here. We shall look to you to aid us as you think fit.'

[2] R. P. Ashe, *Chronicles of Uganda*, London, 1894, p. 78.

[3] See the carefully documented account in Thoonen, p. 132.

[4] *i.e.* learning to read at the missions: catechumens.

[5] Thoonen, *op. cit.*, p. 168; and Stock, *op. cit.*, III, 415. In 1920 twenty-two Catholic martyrs were beatified by Pope Benedict XV in the Vatican Basilica. The ceremony

shown by some of the victims. There were others, too, who suffered torture and death in and around the capital; and a wave of persecution swept over the land, carrying with it, however, fresh seeds of the new religion which were to sprout and flourish after it had passed. Catechumens came to the missions by night for instruction and baptism; while those who were under suspicion as readers fled to the country districts and spread the faith among their relatives.[1]

During these two years, however, the Christians also became a political party—or rather two political parties—in scarcely veiled opposition to the Arab party at the court, the leaders being for the most part the officers of the royal bodyguard (Batongole), who along with the persecuted pages had formed the cream of the early converts.[2] By 1888 Catholics and Protestants were each capable of putting a thousand armed men in the field, the Muslims only about 300.[3] The king wavered helplessly between the rival factions, trying to incite Catholics against Protestants and Muhammedans against both. Finally, in September 1888, he planned to lead a pagan revival and to exterminate all the foreigners, together with their leading supporters among the Baganda, by enticing them on to a small island in the lake and there leaving them to starve. The naïve plot was discovered; and the three monotheistic parties temporarily united to seize

was attended by Denis Kamyuka, who had himself as a boy walked the martyrs' road to Namungongo, but who had been reprieved at the last moment on account of his extreme youth.

[1] Livinhac in *MC*. 88. 556. 'L'œuvre de Dieu se poursuit sans bruit et dans l'ombre.'

[2] Mackay to Euan Smith from Usambiro, 19.iii.89. Enclosed in Euan Smith to Salisbury from Aden, 26.xi.89. F.O. 84. 1981.

[3] Nicq, *op. cit.*, p. 504.

power. Mwanga was deposed in favour of a younger brother Kiwewa. Freedom of conscience was declared and the principal offices shared out among the victors, a Roman Catholic Christian becoming prime minister.[1]

The news of the great persecution of May 1886 had reached Zanzibar at the end of September,[2] and Holmwood, the Acting-Consul-General, had immediately addressed a strong letter to Mwanga,[3] demanding the missionaries' release, which, backed by another from the Sultan he had entrusted to Suliman bin Zeher, an Arab trader from Buganda who was personally known to the Sultan and who was said by him to be entirely reliable.[4] Suliman had reached Buganda in April 1887,[5] and though he had deliberately mis-interpreted Holmwood's letter to the king,[6] Mackay had been allowed to depart to the south end of the lake in June, leaving Gordon and Walker at the C.M.S. mission and Lourdel and Frère Charles Stuart at the Catholic mission.[7] These facts are relevant to the *coup d'état* which was effected by the Muhammedan party less than a month after they had deposed Mwanga in September 1888 with the aid of the Christian Baganda. Persuading Kiwewa that the

[1] Nicq, *op. cit.*, p. 504; Ashe, p. 95–107.

[2] Holmwood to F.O. 23.ix.86. F.O. 84. 1775.

[3] On which T. V. Lister at the F.O. made the following note: 'Mr. Holmwood understands savages much better than I do, but I cannot help feeling that if I were the bloodthirsty tyrant of an inaccessible country, I should kill the missionaries on the receipt of such a letter as he has addressed to the King of Uganda.' Dispatch Holmwood to Iddesleigh. Same date.

[4] Holmwood to Iddesleigh, 27.ix.86. F.O. 84. 1775.

[5] Mackay to Holmwood from Buganda, 19.iv.87. Enclosed in Holmwood to Salisbury, 15.vii.87. F.O. 84. 1853.

[6] Mackay to Holmwood from Buganda, 29.v.87. Enclosed in Macdonald to Salisbury, 25.x.87. F.O. 84. 1854.

[7] Mackay to Holmwood from Msalala, 10.viii.87. Enclosed in above.

Christians intended to depose him, the Arab party one morning secretly filled the royal enclosure with their armed slaves, and, after accusations made in open court, fired upon the unarmed Christian chiefs and drove them from the capital. The European missionaries were arrested, their stations plundered by the slaves of the Arabs, and their lives were for some days in danger, before they were eventually allowed to make their escape by boat to the southern end of the lake.[1] 'This movement', wrote Mackay, 'was not one made by the Baganda themselves. . . . Even Kiwewa sent a private message to Père Lourdel that the plundering and expulsion of the Europeans was no work of his: that he was helpless in the hands of the Arabs.' The Muslims sought to consolidate their victory by imposing their religion. There were forcible circumcisions; and when Kiwewa himself refused to submit to the rite he was replaced by a younger brother, Kalema, the Arabs styling him 'the Little Seyyid' and themselves 'the guardians of the Kabaka', and the former custom of all sitting in court being changed to standing, 'which, they say, is the custom in Zanzibar'.[2]

The 'ringleader and acknowledged chief' of the Buganda Arabs throughout the events of 1887–8 was, according to Mackay, none other than the Suliman bin Zeher, the trusted friend of Seyyid Barghash, who had been selected as the bearer of Consul Holmwood's letter to Mwanga, and who called

[1] Authorities: Ashe, *op. cit.*, pp. 111–21; E. C. Gordon in *CMI*. 89. 149; Livinhac in *MC*. 89. 153. This enforced society seems to have temporarily improved the relations of the French and English missionaries. They wrote home mutually charitable accounts of the trip, during which their boat was capsized by a hippopotamus.

[2] Mackay to Euan Smith from Usambiro, 19.iii.87. Enclosed in Euan Smith to Salisbury from Aden, 26.xi.89. F.O. 84. 1981.

himself the Sultan's accredited agent. Nor had his hostility ended with the expulsion of the Europeans from Buganda.

Since coming to Magu, Suliman bin Zeher schemed to get us turned out of this place (Usambiro). He and Kipanda (alias Said bin Sef) have sent a message to Kwoma, the overlord of this district (Uzinja), telling him that since he is tributary to Buganda (which he is not in reality), and that country is theirs (the Arabs'), he must drive the English out of this place and the French out of Western Busambiro, where they have recently formed a station. Kwoma, however, refused. Accordingly Suliman bin Zeher and Said bin Sef have together written a letter to the King of Buganda begging an army and a fleet of canoes from him to expel all Europeans from the whole shores of the Nyanza.[1]

Three months later Mackay found that the general impression among his Zanzibari carpenters and labourers at Usambiro was that not only the events in the interior, but also the insurrection of the Arabs under Bushiri against the Germans at the coast, had been privately instigated by the Sultan of Zanzibar, whose outward collaboration with the European powers was merely a deceptive stratagem.[2]

*   *   *   *

[1] Mackay to Euan Smith, 19.iii.87: 'Besides Suliman bin Zeher, who has been the ringleader and acknowledged chief among the Arabs in Buganda during the late insurrection, the following are the names of the principal Arabs against whom we make the charge of instigating the Baganda to overthrow the Mission: Said bin Jumeah, Salim bin Mahmoud, Hamis Behlul, Salim bin Saleh, Salehe [Mgazija], Khalfan, son of Said bin Sef of Magu, Said bin Hamisi [Yalel], Said bin Hamed [el Mauli]. The last two are, I believe, friendly, but took no steps that I am aware of to oppose the other Arabs in their plot to destroy the Mission.'

[2] Mackay to Euan Smith from Usambiro, 10.vii.89, enclosed in above. In view of these letters, the fact that Suliman bin Zeher was heavily fined by Sultan Barghash on his return to Zanzibar, must not be taken as proving the Sultan's innocence.

4

The course of events during the years 1884–8 is less easy to trace in the regions around Lake Tanganyika and south to Lake Nyasa than in Buganda. There was no great native kingdom, no capital like Rubaga, attracting both the missionaries and the Arabs, where all the principal events were enacted and where the rival parties could watch each other's daily moves. In so far as there was any centre closer to the scene of action than Zanzibar, it was at Ujiji where Tippu Tib and Rumaliza, the two great slaving partners, had their headquarters, and whence their underlings radiated westwards into Manyema and eastwards along the road through Tabora to the coast.[1] But the L.M.S. missionaries abandoned their station at Ujiji in 1884, after which their impressions were gathered during widely spaced and fleeting visits. Still, the outline which emerges from their reports, if sketchy, is clearer in its essential features than the more detailed picture of Buganda.

Early in 1884 Tippu Tib hinted to Hore that he had a new plan for 'putting things right' round the lake. Hore reported the interview in a cryptic fashion; but in a confused sentence, obviously intended as much for Kirk as for the L.M.S. directors, he concluded: 'If I could think that there was any extensive demand for slaves at Zanzibar or accessible regions beyond, I should say look out for an energetic attempt at a revival of the slave-trade or else a large extension of the Sultan's influence and dominion in the interior.'[2] At the

---

[1] Swann, *op. cit.*, p. 86.   [2] Hore to L.M.S., 23.iv.84.

end of the year D. P. Jones, another L.M.S. missionary, was
more definite. 'The Arabs', he said, 'have been commissioned
by the Sultan of Zanzibar to take possession of all the
countries round the lake.'[1] In general the missionaries found
it impossible to see this movement behind the acts of violence
which it involved and which they automatically classified as
slave-raiding. At the end of 1884 Rumaliza was reported to
be 'slaving' round the north end of the lake[2] while Tippu
Tib was 'devastating' Ulungu in the south.[3] Hore, in a rare
moment of detachment, depicted events in a truer light:
Tippu Tib was doing what any European power would
have to do, only his methods were more frightful. At the
moment he was doing it for the Sultan; but he would
probably be prepared to do it for any European power which
would pay him more. Was this the reason why Kirk was
cultivating his friendship?[4] If Kirk ever answered this
point, Hore never forwarded the letter to the L.M.S.; but
in August 1885 Kirk did address a strange appeal to the
L.M.S. directors to keep on with the Tanganyika mission.
The lake region was just coming into prominence. The
present difficulties would be overcome.[5] Were these just
gratuitous words of encouragement? Or was Kirk, too,
aware that the Sultan's subjects were consolidating a new
dominion behind the German sphere of influence, and
hoping that the presence of a British missionary society
might one day help him to secure its recognition?[6]

[1] D. P. Jones to L.M.S., 2.xii.84.   [2] *ibid.*   [3] A. J. Swann to L.M.S., 1.i.85.
[4] Hore to L.M.S., 28.xi.85.   [5] Kirk to L.M.S., 3.viii.85.
[6] It must be remembered that at this time no westward limit of the German
sphere had yet been fixed. The whole future of the territory depended very largely
on what was to be recognised as the dominions of the Sultan on the African mainland.

The White Fathers were slower to realise what was afoot. Living in their closed and well-defended communities they were not at first attacked. In some ways the results of Rumaliza's preliminary campaigns suited them well, for hundreds of refugees placed themselves under their protection, and joined them in their way of life.[1] As in Buganda however, the movement, as it developed, grew hostile to the Europeans. At the end of 1886 Père Charbonnier reported that the mission was no longer on such friendly terms with the Arabs as it had been before. Rumaliza had subjugated all the native chiefs round the northern end of the lake and was now carrying the war into Ruanda. The station at Masansa had had to be abandoned.[2] In the course of 1887 the White Fathers in Ufige and Uvira fell back on Kibanga, and in December, Kibanga itself was attacked.[3]

Tippu Tib, who was the acknowledged leader of the Arabs on Lake Tanganyika and farther west, himself played a curiously double game. At the end of 1886, when plans for the relief of Emin Pasha were under discussion in London, Holmwood telegraphed to Lord Iddesleigh from Zanzibar that 'Tipputip, who is here and places himself at your Lordship's disposal', had received a letter from his agent at Stanley Falls dated 1st September, reporting a fight between the Congo Association and his people. The agent had written that if again attacked, the Arabs, who were said to command 50,000 guns in that region would 'raise a religious war to drive the Europeans from the Congo'.[4]

---

[1] *Vide supra*, p. 53.   [2] *MC.* 87. 328.
[3] *AMZ.* 94. 337, quoting White Fathers' *Bulletin.*
[4] Holmwood to Iddesleigh, 24.xii.86. F.O. 84. 1776.

In March 1887, Stanley, as the head of the Emin Relief Expedition, signed an agreement on behalf of King Leopold with Tippu Tib,[1] recognising the latter's authority as far west as Stanley Falls and engaging him as the Congo Association's governor at a salary of £30 a month. Travelling up-country from the coast in 1887–8, Swann found the Arabs all along the route in a dangerous mood. At Ujiji there was not the usual welcome. Tippu Tib received him behind closed doors and explained that, as a result of the German occupation, his subordinates were getting out of control.[2] A few months later, news of the initial success of the Bushiri rising spread inland like wildfire. Mgr. Bridoux and a party of White Fathers were arrested at Tabora and saved from massacre only by the personal intervention of Rumaliza, who charged a large fee for his service.[3] The nearby station at Kipalapala, at the junction of the roads to Uganda and Lake Tanganyika had to be evacuated.[4] Moreover the threat spread to the south and west. There was trouble at Karema[5] and even Joubert's headquarters near Mpala was reported to be in danger.[6] The L.M.S. station at Niamkolo in Ulungu was never attacked, but Kabunda, a powerful subordinate of Tippu Tib's, who had been settled for some years in the neighbourhood of the Lofu River as a buyer of slaves from the powerful Bemba

[1] Holmwood to Salisbury, 3.iii.87. F.O. 84. 1852. Sir Percy Anderson at the Foreign Office commented: 'The missionaries naturally distrust this slave-dealer. But his assistance is vital to Stanley and he undertakes to put down the slave-trade in his district.'

[2] Swann, *op. cit.*, p. 168 *sqq.*

[3] Mgr. Bridoux in *MC*. 90. 549.

[4] *MC*. 89. 619.   [5] *ibid.*, 90. 550.

[6] *AMZ*. 94. 337 quoting White Fathers' *Bulletin*.

tribe, suddenly set himself up as Sultan of Ulungu,[1] and the station, like those of the Roman Catholics, was flooded with helpless refugees.[2] As time went on, the threat of penury and starvation succeeded that of open violence, for during the second half of 1888 and the whole of 1889 the missions on Lake Tanganyika were completely cut off from communications with the outside world.[3]

South of Ulungu, on Lake Nyasa and the plateau separating it from Lake Tanganyika, the key-points were held by a different group of Arabs, who used originally to acquire their slaves by the commercial method from the Ngoni and Gwangwara chieftains.[4] Their collecting centres were at Mponda's, where the Shiré flowed out of Lake Nyasa, and at Kota Kota, where Jumbe operated a ferry across the middle of the lake to Makanjira's on the eastern shore.[5] From there the slaves were marched by a north-easterly route to Lindi and Kilwa. The arrival in the late seventies and early eighties of the Scottish and Universities' Missions with

[1] F. D. Lugard, *The Rise of Our East African Empire*, 2 vols., London, 1893, I, p. 53.

[2] Swann, *op. cit.*, p. 190.

[3] Lovett, *op. cit.*, I, p. 663 *sqq.* Johnston's comment on Kabunda in 1890 is illuminating: 'From what I heard from the A.L.C.'s people at the north end of Lake Nyasa, I was led to believe that he was ruthless ravager of the regions around the south end of Tanganyika; but the L.M.S. agents at Niamkolo . . . seemed to regard him as a somewhat superior man to the usual trading Arab. He had quarrelled and fought a good many times with native chiefs in the past, but whatever wrongs had been committed were now repaired and forgotten, and Kabunda was looked up to by the Ulungu chiefs as their most potent protector against the raids of the Wawemba. . . . He threw the whole weight of his authority into the furtherance of my projects and thus enabled me to come to terms with the powerful Itawa Arabs and the old native chief of Itawa, Muriro, as also with Tshungu, the supreme chief of the Ulungu and Tshitimba his subordinate.'

[4] S. S. Murray, *A Handbook of Nyasaland*, London, 1932, p. 38.

[5] Swann, *op. cit.*, p. 87 *sq.*

their steamers, and especially of the Livingstonia Company,
with its rival interest in ivory, had been a grave embarrassment to the Arabs, who knew that their ways were being
observed. Maintaining only their headquarters, they had
gradually left off slaving round the lake itself, and had
opened up a new hunting ground of their own farther to the
west between Lakes Mweru and Bangweolo, and, as the
Free Church mission and the Company penetrated northwards up the lake to Bandawe and Mt. Waller and Karonga's,
they had started to use a new line of communications to the
coast, passing still farther to the north over the Nyasa–
Tanganyika plateau. The pioneer of this route was an Arab
Coastman called Mlozi.

In this region as elsewhere the German occupation of the
coast had repercussions upon the Arabs. Like Tippu Tib
farther north, Mlozi started to aim at territorial sovereignty.
He subdued the Konde tribe and proclaimed himself their
Sultan.[1] In 1886 he established a fortified point twelve
miles north of Karonga's and astride the Stevenson Road to
Lake Tanganyika. In 1887 Dr. Laws heard that he had

[1] 'Prominent among a little band of these black half-caste Arabs who had con-
ceived the scheme of founding a Swahili state at the north end of Lake Nyasa were
Mlozi, Kopakopa, Msalema and Bwana Omari. They were aided in their projects by
Salim bin Nasur and other Arabs of the Senga country. Quarrels were picked up
with some of the leading Konde chiefs, and the armed slaves of the Arabs—perhaps
adherents would be a better word, as the association of many of these natives with the
Arabs was a purely voluntary one, entered into in the hope of plunder—these fierce
Wa-Henga, Wa-Wemba and Wa-rugaruga from Unyamwezi were launched against
village after village in the Nkonde country, of which they burnt the houses, killed the
male inhabitants and carried off the women and children to be distributed as slaves.
In fact Mlozi and his friends were conquering the country in the usual Arab fashion,
and so sure did they feel of the outcome of their undertaking that Mlozi already
styled himself Sultan of Konde and invited recognition of this title from the A.L.C.'s
agent at Karonga.' Johnston to Salisbury, 17.iii.90. F.O. 84. 2051.

entered into an alliance with the Ngoni chief, Mombera, to spread his authority right down the western coast of Lake Nyasa and to sweep the land clear of all Europeans.[1] The first open clash came in November 1887 when Mlozi attacked the Livingstonia Company's trading post at Karonga's,[2] forcing the resident agent to withdraw to a more easily defended position. There was an immediate reaction by the Arabs' Yao allies on the south-east coast of the lake. When Johnson of the U.M.C.A. and Buchanan, the acting-consul, landed at Makanjira's on a friendly visit in February 1888, they were arrested, stripped naked and held to ransom.[3]

Whoever and wherever the real authors of these movements may be, wrote Consul O'Neill of Mozambique, it is at Zanzibar that their chief actors reside: thence the sinews of war have been furnished: and only at that place therefore can the evil be really nipped. At whose instigation and with what objects have the swarms of Arabs that have poured in Central Africa during the past three years left that place?[4]

Thus in four years the position of the missions in the interior, from Buganda in the north to Lake Nyasa in the south had been radically changed. Before 1884 their entry and settlement had hardly anywhere been challenged. Their caravans had moved freely up and down the Arab trade routes. A bare half-dozen out of more than three hundred had been murdered; and, without exception, these mishaps

[1] W. P. Livingstone, *Laws*, p. 238.
[2] Lugard, *op. cit.*, I, p. 53–4.
[3] Murray, *op. cit.*, p. 43; W. P. Livingstone, *Laws*, p. 243.
[4] Consul O'Neill to Salisbury, 3.ii.88. F.O. 84. 1901.

had been' suffered at the hands of Africans to whom they were strangers, as a result of ignorant fear in one case, of European misbehaviour in three others.[1] By 1888 the missions were everywhere threatened, in many places driven out, not by the Africans among whom they had settled, but by commercial freebooters from Zanzibar and Oman who were making a last desperate bid to keep their dominion in East Africa. That the issue was presented in the form of a crisis, and not as a crescendo of massacre and slavery, growing steadily in proportion to the import of fire-arms by the Arabs, was important in that it provoked an equally sharp reaction by the missionaries. That the crisis had been precipitated by the German occupation, they scarcely realised; nor was this fact relevant to their main contention, that the choice for Africa was not Europe or independence, but Europe or Zanzibar.

[1] Shergold Smith and O'Neill, of the C.M.S., were murdered in Ukerewe in December 1877 by Chief Lukonge of Ukerewe, who connected them with an Arab trader, Songoro, who had built a dhow with timber supplied by Lukonge and who tried to launch it and sail away without paying for the timber; vide Stock, op. cit., III, p. 104. Père Deniaud, a White Father, was murdered in 1881 in Urundi, while trying to recover by force a 'racheté' who had run away; vide Griffiths to L.M.S., 29.v.81, also a slightly different account in MC. 81. 532. Fenwick, a layman lately dismissed from the Blantyre mission, was also murdered through his bad behaviour.

For the murder of Penrose, a C.M.S. missionary, at the end of 1878, see Kirk to Salisbury, 28.ii.79 and 7.iv.79 (KP, Nos. 59 and 88). Some porters employed by the French explorer, the Abbé Debaize, had seized two men of the village of Nyungu, who were carrying tusks of ivory, and killed them for stealing it. The Chief Jiwe la Singa ordered his people to take blood revenge on the next European caravan.

*   *   *   *

5

In 1888 Cardinal Lavigerie, then at the zenith of his power, threw the whole weight of his influence into the imperialist scale. In a letter to the Directors of the Society for the Propagation of the Faith he marshalled the main facts about the African slave-trade. Quoting Schweinfurth and Nachtigal, Stanley and Cameron, as well as the estimates of his own missionaries, he concluded that Africa was being depopulated at the rate of 400,000 human beings a year. He described the horrors of the trade in all its stages, in the initial massacres, on the thousand-mile march to the coast, in the dhows, in the harems of Asia. He referred to the age-long connection between Islam and slavery. He cited Leo XIII's recent Encyclical to the Brazilian bishops, calling upon all men of influence whether in Church or State to join in suppressing the hateful traffic.[1] 'C'est sans contredit', he concluded, 'aux gouvernements de l'Europe que l'obligation de sauver l'Afrique est tout d'abord imposée.'[2]

At Whitsun he led a joint delegation of Africans and White Fathers to the Pope to solicit his help. 'Mgr. Lavigerie,' replied Leo, 'we depend upon you.' Thus commissioned, the Cardinal started on a nine-months' tour of western Europe to preach a nineteenth-century crusade. In Paris in July he

[1] The Encyclical, written to mark the abolition of slavery in Brazil, is the 'In plurimis' of 5th May, 1888. It is printed in *Acta Sanctae Sedis*, xx, p. 545. 'Utinam omnes, quicumque imperio et potestate antecedunt, vel jure gentium et humanitatis Sancta esse volunt, vel religionis Catholicae incrementis ex animo student, ubique omnes, hortantibus rogantibus Nobis, ad ejusmodi mercaturam qua nulla inhonesta magis et scalerata, comprimendam, prohibendam, extinguendam enixe conspirent.

[2] Lavigerie's letter is printed in instalments beginning at *M C.* 88. 457.

formally abandoned the old policy of ransoming individual slaves: it had turned out a useless concession to brute force. Instead, he called for the formation of a new Military Order,[1] a well-armed force of 500 volunteers, who would destroy the brigands in their lairs. In London his theme was just as perfectly tempered to the mood of his audience. He retold the tale of Wilberforce and of Livingstone, and left it to his sponsor, Lord Granville, to petition the Government to take the appropriate action. In Brussels in August he adapted the parable of the wheat and the tares, with King Leopold as the sower and Islam as the enemy.[2] Leopold was enchanted, and sent Père Charmetant post-haste to Rome to propose to Leo XIII that 'a pontifical colony' should be set up in Central Africa, an offer which was politely declined.[3] Germany Lavigerie avoided, in deference to the known anti-clericalism of the Chancellor; but a written memorandum resulted in the foundation of a German anti-slavery group, the 'Verein deutscher Katholiken', whose imperialist influence was so salutary that it drew an acknowledgment from Bismarck to the Pope.[4]

The success of Lavigerie's crusade was due chiefly to his genius for so framing his efforts to 'excite the anger of the world',[5] that this anger could operate through the ordinary nationalist channels. He was recognised by European statesmen as an outstanding authority on Africa, and his

---

[1] 'Pourquoi, jeunes gens chrétiens des divers pays de l'Europe, ne ressusciteriez-vous pas, dans les contrées barbares de l'Afrique, ces nobles entreprises de nos pères?' Goyau, *Lavigerie*, p. 213.

[2] *ibid.*, pp. 212–16.   [3] *ibid.*, p. 224.   [4] *ibid.*, pp. 218, 223.

[5] *ibid.*, p. 215. At Brussels: 'Pour sauver l'Afrique intérieure il faut soulever la colère du monde.'

insistence upon the slave-trade provided them with a convenient set of terms in which to discuss their own more particular imperialist designs. Once, however, this genius led him into a serious miscalculation. Early in 1889 he heard that Cardoso had annexed the Shiré Highlands for Portugal. Welcoming what he called a 'généreuse initiative' by a Catholic power, he arranged with the Portuguese President to found a mission in Nyasaland. Five White Fathers were solemnly dedicated at Algiers, and the ceremony closed with the Portuguese national anthem.[1] A year later his mission had to be withdrawn 'because of certain difficulties', not to appear again till 1902.[2]

*   *   *   *

6

The Protestant missions, supported by national Churches, had no such dilemmas about where to lodge their appeals. By 1888 Dr. Laws, for one, had no doubts on the imperialist score. 'These dark clouds', he wrote on receiving the news from Karonga's, 'may be the precursors of a great blessing'.[3] The Government had done well to appoint consuls: it ought now to back them up with such a force as would prevent them from becoming 'the butt of any slave-dealing red-handed murderer'.[4] Consul Hawes himself evidently took a more pacific view of his duties, for he decided, after a brief visit to the scene of action, that the Livingstonia Company was in no position to tackle the Arabs, and, recommending

[1] *MC*. 89. 313.   [2] Murray, *op. cit.*, p. 397.
[3] W. P. Livingstone, *Laws*, p. 234.   [4] *CA*. 88. 46.

them to make peace and if necessary to abandon Karonga's, he proceeded to England on leave.[1] The Company's agents, however, determined to fight. Retreating to the hills above Karonga's, Monteith Fotheringham and Nicoll trained a large force of Wankonde who had fled to them for protection, and European 'officers' were recruited by the brothers Moir in Natal.[2] O'Neill, the Consul at Mozambique, who had previously asked for leave of absence in order to join the force in his private capacity, in April, sent up Captain F. D. Lugard, then on leave from the Norfolk Regiment, who took command of the whole expedition. With the aid of this force the Company was just able to maintain its position at Karonga, though no systematic reduction of the Arab strongholds was possible.[3] Most of the volunteers drifted away before the end of 1888; but in October 1889 Johnston was able to report that 'the Arabs of North Nyasaland have had a most severe lesson. They have lost nearly all their property in ivory which they had amassed, their prestige and credit with the natives is gone, and I do not think that they will attempt to tackle us again, at any rate not for several years.'[4] Throughout the war Dr. Laws's station at Bandawe served as the advanced base, and Dr. Cross of the Free Church mission served with the forces for most of the period. As late as June 1889 both the Presbyterian missions remained adamantly in support of the Company's offensive policy. Only the Universities Mission, which had

---

[1] Hawes to Salisbury, 16.i.88. F.O. 84. 1883.

[2] Hawes to Salisbury, 10.ii.88, *ibid.*, and Johnston to Salisbury, 17.iii.90. F.O. 84. 2051.

[3] Lugard, *op. cit.*, 1, pp. 53–153.

[4] Johnston to Salisbury, 17.iii.90. F.O. 84. 2051.

lent its steamer to Consul Hawes during the first emergency, showed any obvious desire for peace to be made with the Arabs.[1]

The news of Mlozi's attacks reached England in January 1888, and in February the Member for Glasgow asked in the House of Commons whether the Government was aware that the Livingstonia Company, 'if empowered by Charter to enter into alliance with friendly tribes and assisted by Government', was prepared to equip and maintain an armed police force and to place a gunboat on Lake Nyasa.[2] Lord Salisbury, however, was not interested in the Arab war as such ; and it was ony when Alexander Hetherwick returned from Blantyre in March, bearing news of the impending departure of a Portuguese 'scientific expedition' under Serpa Pinto to the Shiré Highlands, that the pressure of the missions' supporters at home began to assume a decisive importance.[3] In April representatives of the Scottish Missions, the Universities Mission and the Livingstonia Company met in conference in London with interested Members of Parliament, and subsequently a deputation waited on Lord Salisbury to ask for 'measures to secure the safety of British subjects and interests in Nyasaland'. Salisbury in reply laid down three points of policy, which, though apparently cautious, in the event settled the future of Nyasaland. The Government would on no account send an armed expedition to Lake Nyasa; but the Company and the missions had a perfect right and liberty to defend

[1] Buchanan to Salisbury, with enclosures from Dr. Laws, D. C. Scott, and Bishop Maples, 4.vii.89. F.O. 84. 1942.
[2] Hansard, 28.ii.88. 1648.
[3] W. P. Livingstone, *A Prince of Missionaries*, London, 1931, p. 49.

themselves, and provision would be made for the importation of arms. The Government would further insist on the free navigation of the Zambezi. And, finally, it would on no account assent to any annexations by Portugal north of the confluence of the Shiré and the Ruo rivers.[1] Regarding the Arab war, Salisbury repeated in the House of Lords on July 6th that it was:

one of those tasks which must be and will be carried through by the individual Europeans who have undertaken it. . . . We are certain that we shall only injure instead of promoting those great civilised and missionary efforts if we were to convert them into a cause of war . . . with all the scum of humanity which is found over that vast territory which is governed principally by Arabs of the sort with whom we have dealt in the Soudan, who combine the greatest cruelty with a spirit of fanaticism. We must leave the gradual dispersal of this terrible army of wickedness to the gradual advance of civilisation and Christianity.[2]

Meanwhile the Directors of the Livingstonia Company and the General Assemblies of the Church of Scotland and the Free Church had started a campaign to publicise the facts. Slavery was a slogan of proven power with the British public; while the claims of the Portuguese, in view of their known backwardness in anti-slavery measures and, especially, of their blocking tactics on the Zambezi line of communications, formed from the first another side of the agitation. They enlisted the aid of Horace Waller, now in his old age the outstanding British authority on slavery questions, and also that of Henry Drummond, the celebrated author of

---

[1] W. P. Livingstone, *Laws*, pp. 244–5.   [2] Hansard, 6.vii.88, col. 0537.

The Natural Law in the Spiritual World, who had visited Lake Nyasa in 1883. Extracts from the reports of Dr. Laws were sent to the press. Alexander Hetherwick addressed meetings all over Scotland. In August 1888 a committee was formed in Glasgow to raise and administer money for the 'Nyasa Anti-Slavery and Defence Fund', and though the missions as such did not contribute, the bulk of their subscribers probably did so as individuals. Arms and ammunition were purchased and dispatched, including a small mountain gun, which arrived early in 1889, the Government having to exercise pressure to get it through the Portuguese custom-house at Quilimane.[1]

In the spring of 1889 there occurred two completely secular events which disposed the Government to consider more seriously the possibility of a Central African protectorate. First, Dr. D. J. Rankin discovered the Chinde mouth of the Zambezi, which made it possible for the first time to pass up-country without landing on Portuguese territory, and so in turn, to insist in practice on the free navigation of the Zambezi.[2] Next, in March, Cecil Rhodes, then in London seeking a charter for the British South Africa Company, offered to contribute £10,000 a year towards the cost of administration if the Government would establish a protectorate. This offer was, in the short run, the most decisive link in the whole chain of negotiations, for it enabled the Conservative Cabinet to act without applying to Parliament for money, and so without exposing themselves to the fiery

[1] Moir, *op. cit.*, p. 139. W. P. Livingstone, *Laws*, p. 242.

[2] The other mouth previously used was the Kwakwa, which was not navigable for steamers. Goods had to be unloaded from the sea-going vessel, carried four miles and then reloaded into the river-vessel.

denunciations of the Liberals, who had been nursing a special grievance against imperial expansion ever since the Conservatives had joined with their own Radical extremists in voting them out of office for the mishandling of the Gordon Relief expedition in 1885. In January 1889, H. H. Johnston had been appointed to the Mozambique Consulate, with comparatively cautious instructions to proceed up the Zambezi and report on the extent of Portuguese rule in the interior. Beyond this sphere he was authorised to make treaties of friendship with the native chiefs which, while not committing his government to protective duties, would give them legal priority over any future claimant.[1] In March, when his luggage was already packed and at the docks, he was suddenly recalled to the Foreign Office and dispatched instead to Lisbon, to work out the basis of a final agreement with the Portuguese government on spheres of influence in South Central Africa.[2]

The missionary supporters, however, had still one very important part to play. Harry Johnston was, even at this stage of his career, one of the greatest personalities of his

[1] F.O. to Johnston, 13.ii.89 and 30.iii.89. F.O. 84. 1968.

[2] Johnston's own testimony, made to Rhodes on the occasion of a serious misunderstanding in 1893, is perhaps the most eloquent: 'At that time affairs in what is now called British Central Africa were rather at a deadlock. The Foreign Office and the Colonial Office then and now entertained very much the same ideas that you and I held about the necessity of extending the British Empire within reasonable limits over countries not yet taken up by European Powers, to provide new markets for our manufactures and afford further scope for British enterprise. But the permanent officials of the Treasury held opinions . . . exactly the reverse and hold them still. . . . It seemed to me as though this offer on your part changed the situation at once. . . . Within a week of its being made new instructions were drawn up for me at the Foreign Office, and an entirely new scheme of policy developed, of which the direct result has been the establishment of British supremacy over British Central Africa.' Johnston to Rhodes, 8.x.93. F.O. 2. 55.

time, the originator, according to his own claim, of the Cape-to-Cairo dream, which was to exercise so profound an influence on British policy during the next fifteen years, and the devotee, according to his own admission, of only one religion: the extension of the British Empire.[1] Of the full instructions which he took to Lisbon there is no written record, but a letter which he wrote to Sir Villiers Lister at the Foreign Office leaves little doubt but that he overstepped them.

The uttermost concession I have been able to get from Gomes involves not only the cession of the Shiré but even of part of the western shore of Nyasa, of course under the most favourable terms for the commercial and evangelical interests there. But in return we get what to *my* thinking is so important, an uninterrupted though narrow belt of British influence from the Zambezi to the main sphere of activity of the African Lakes Company on Nyasa and Tanganyika, together with a considerable portion of the western and northern littoral of Nyasa recognised as British. Roughly we may say that Portugal sacrifices her idea of a band across Africa and we in exchange give up Blantyre and the surrounding region to the Portuguese.[2]

[1] Johnston to Rhodes, 8.xi.93. F.O. 2. 55 claims that he introduced Rhodes to the Cape-to-Cairo idea at their first meeting in 1889, whereupon Rhodes gave him a cheque to cover the expenses of prolonging his treaty-making journey of 1889–90 as far as the north end of Lake Tanganyika.

[2] H. H. Johnston to Sir Villiers Lister from Lisbon (5.iv.89. F.O. 84. 1969) adds that Blantyre and district depend for access on transit through definitely Portuguese territory. 'But with regard to the regions north of the middle Zambezi—such as the Barotse country—and the western part of Nyasa and the south end of Tanganyika, where the African Lakes Company is mainly established, all this belt of country is more and more attaching itself to British South Africa and seeking its base of supplies in that direction rather than on the East Coast, from which it is and will for a long time be cut off by this uprising of the Arab element. I cannot bear the idea of our making the Zambezi a hard and fast limit to British enterprise in Southern Africa and of wilfully and almost carelessly chucking away our last chance of securing to

The weight attached by Lord Salisbury to the mobilisation of religious opinion in support of his dealings with the Portuguese Government may be gauged by the elaborately staged manoeuvres of the next six months. He did not turn down Johnston's agreement at once, but instead summoned the Scottish interests to London, showed them the Anglo-Portuguese boundary which Johnston proposed to draw, and enlarged upon the strength of Chauvinist opinion in Portugal. He even allowed Johnston to visit Scotland and attempt to persuade the missionary committees and the Directors of the Company to accede to the terms of the agreement. From the Church of Scotland Foreign Missions Committee Johnston met with a blank refusal even to discuss his terms, which was relayed by the convener to Lord Balfour of Burleigh.

Next day Lord Balfour sat down beside the Prime Minister in the House of Lords. 'My Lord,' he said, 'my Scottish friends don't like the Portuguese terms'. 'Neither do I', was the reply. 'I don't want your Scottish friends to accept them. I want the Portuguese to know that I, too, have a strong public opinion behind me, and I am sending their Government a warning that they must not go too far.'[1]

The hint was duly taken and four bulky volumes of memorials, signed by 11,000 ministers and elders of the Church of Scotland, survive as evidence of the Scottish protest against the inruption of the Portuguese into the land of Dr. Livingstone.

our grand-children an open way between Tanganyika and the South African colonies, which may some day serve as a link between Egypt and the Cape. . . . I do earnestly hope that Lord Salisbury will approve of what I have done and back me up.'
[1] W. P. Livingstone, *A Prince of Missionaries*, pp. 48–52.

In June Johnston left for Africa, armed with powers to declare a protectorate over Blantyre and the Shiré Highlands if the Portuguese should cross the Ruo frontier. On his way up-country he encountered Serpa Pinto in the neighbourhood of the present Port Herald, who on learning of his instructions returned to Mozambique to consult his superiors. Meantime, however, his subordinate, Lt. Coutinho, crossed the Ruo and made preparations to occupy Blantyre. On August 19th, accordingly, Acting-Consul Buchanan declared a protectorate over the Makololo country and the Shiré Hills. Johnston himself pressed northwards to acquire the legal titles to the remainder of Nyasaland and north-eastern Rhodesia; and on his return, early in 1890, opened a dispatch from the Foreign Office, which enabled him to communicate to the missionaries the welcome news that 'in consequence of the representations of Her Majesty's Government . . . the Government of Portugal have taken the following engagements. Portugal will not endeavour to settle any territorial questions by acts of force, and will give instructions to the authorities in the Province of Mozambique that no such acts will be committed against the British settlements in the Shiré or Nyasa districts. . . .'[1]

First-hand contact with the missions, which he gained on his journey, caused Johnston radically to revise the estimate of 'evangelical and commercial interests' which he had held when he was in Lisbon. In a memorandum to the British South Africa Company on the administration of Nyasaland

---

[1] F.O. to Johnston, 4.ii.90. F.O. 84. 2050. Johnston's report on his journey which has been extensively quoted in this chapter and the last, is contained in his dispatch to Salisbury of 17.iii.90. F.O. 84. 2051.

he stated unequivocally that the 'chief hold which we have over these regions comes from the quite extraordinary work done by these four missionary societies'.[1] Hitherto the Lakes Company had been too much fettered from want of funds, and consequently from lack of men, to vie with the missionary societies in influence over the natives. Missionaries, he recommended, should be encouraged to the uttermost. They alone could afford to reside in unprofitable places until they became profitable. 'The missionary is really gaining your experience for you without any cost to yourself. . . . They strengthen our hold over the country, they spread the use of the English language, they induct the natives into the best kind of civilisation, and, in fact, each Mission Station is an essay in colonisation.'[2]

*   *   *   *

7

The missionary occupation of Nyasaland provided both the historical justification and the immediate pretext for the British annexation. At a critical moment in the negotiations, moreover, one section of the missionary constituency in Scotland prevented the sacrifice of the Shiré Highlands to Portugal in exchange for the passive acceptance by that country of a British Rhodesia. Thanks to the wealth and the generosity of Cecil Rhodes, however, the acquisition of

[1] *i.e.* the Church of Scotland Mission, the Free Church Mission, the Universities Mission and the London Missionary Society.
[2] H. H. Johnston to the B.S.A.C., 17.vii.90. Copy in F.O. 84. 2052.

Nyasaland remained for some years an almost clandestine act of diplomacy. It made no immediate appearance among the Government's financial estimates; and even the Radicals, who might have been expected to oppose it on juridical and humanitarian grounds, in fact concentrated their attention on the activities of the British South Africa Company farther south. In contrast, the declaration of a protectorate in Uganda marked a turning-point in Great Britain's African policy. The financial exhaustion of the Imperial British East Africa Company after little more than five years of activity forced upon a Liberal Cabinet and an unprepared parliamentary and public opinion, not only the question of national responsibility for the acts of chartered companies, but with it the wider one of Britain's part in the scramble for new markets and sources of raw materials. Every step in this path was keenly debated; and the missionary interest, though possibly of less ultimate importance than it had been in Nyasaland, became in consequence far more openly involved in the secular issue. Among their contemporaries, the Uganda missionaries were touted by Jingoists and derided by Little Englanders as pawns in a game which was only half their own; and it is therefore the more necessary, through a clear understanding of the events which led up to the crisis, to rescue them from the half-informed denigrations of one side and from the hypocritical heroics of the other.

The imperial issue had presented itself to Mackay in Buganda as early as 1885. Just at the time when rumours of German annexations at the coast had resulted in the murder of Bishop Hannington in Busoga, Mackay had received letters from Emin Bey, Gordon's Lieutenant-Governor in the equatorial province, reporting that he had retreated southwards from the Mahdi's forces and had established himself with his Sudanese troops at Wadelai, on the northern frontier of Bunyoro. He begged Mackay to inform his correspondents, that through them the Egyptian Government might learn of his predicament.[1] At once Mackay wrote to Kirk: 'The future of the Victoria Lake will depend very much upon the relations between this country and England. . . . You say truly "Better the Germans than the French". But better the English than either. You can well afford to let the Germans steam into the swamps of the Makata valley. There are finer uplands inland.'[2] Hearing four months later of German explorations in the Kenya Highlands he became more insistent. 'Who can tell what plans may be conceived by Fischer and Emin when they think of Berlin? England has undoubtedly, through your efforts, a prior claim to rescue the East African Lake region.'[3] Then, to Mackay's surprise, in July 1886, a month after the Buganda persecutions, Emin himself started to unfold in a series of private letters a scheme for the occupation of Central Africa, which, if it had ever fallen into the hands of Cecil Rhodes, might have changed the whole course of the scramble for Africa. 'To your question am I prepared to aid in the annexation of this country by England,

---

[1] Emin to Mackay, 16.xi.84, quoted in Stanley Report; Euan Smith to Salisbury, 28.xii.89. F.O. 84. 1962.

[2] Mackay to Kirk, 8.xii.85 and 22.xii.85, enclosed in Kirk to F.O., 12.iii.86. F.O. 84. 1773.

[3] Mackay to Kirk, 14.v.86. Enclosed in Holmwood to F.O., 23.ix.86. F.O. 84. 1775. In actual fact Fischer never reached Emin. See Coupland, *Exploitation*, p. 353.

I answer frankly "Yes". If England intends to occupy these lands and to civilise them, I am ready to hand over the government into the hands of England, and I believe that thereby I should be doing a service to mankind and lending an advance to civilisation.'[1] No blessing, said Emin, could ever come from the Egyptian government; and nor did he like the 'perspective Dr. Junker opens me', of the annexation of his province by the German East Africa Company. In a letter dated 1st October, 1886, he amplified his proposals in all their magnificent simplicity.

I never had the pretension of a great military expedition being sent to relieve us. All that I request is some paltry caravans of ammunition and arms be started from Mombasa to Mount Masaba . . . from whence I am able to fetch it; that some intelligent officers be sent with whom I may confer or to whom eventually I would hand over the government of the country if my services be not requested. Once strengthened in this manner the organization of *the British Protectorate* as a fait accompli is very easily done, and no one has any reason to protest, the responsibility resting mainly with me. . . . No fuss must be made. Your Consul-General in Egypt informs our Government that some small caravans are to be started for supplying us with arms and other things, and all is said.

A strong government here established, the pretensions of King Mwanga would quickly come to an end. By opening the road to the south (Lake Albert via Usungora to Tanganyika) another very valuable step should have been done to secure the realising of your dreams: from the Zambezi to the Bahr el Ghazal![2]

[1] Emin to Mackay from Wadelai, 6.vii.86, enclosed in Mackay to Kirk from Buganda, 24.viii.86, enclosed in Holmwood to Iddesleigh, 18.x.86. F.O. 84. 1775.
[2] Emin to Mackay from Wadelai, 1.x.86. Enclosed in Holmwood to Salisbury, 9.iv.87. F.O. 84. 1852.

'Now by the Providence of God', wrote Mackay in his covering letter to Kirk, 'Emin's peculiar position, if taken advantage of, will give England at once a firm base of operations in the very heart of the Continent, by which not slave-dhows but slave-raids can be in time effectively put an end to.'[1]

But Emin's conception, evidently stimulated and evoked by Mackay's letters to him, now lost, reached England at least two years too early to meet with an imaginative response from British statesmen. The earlier letters did indeed go before the Cabinet in November 1886; but, as Kirk who saw them at the Foreign Office commented: 'From these papers I understand the only question is how to communicate with Emin Bey and enable him to retire.'[2] Lord Salisbury wrote from Balmoral that an armed expedition was quite out of the question. 'It simply means war with Uganda conducted out of British resources . . . I think the Germans ought to be placed in possession of our information. It is really their business if Emin is a German.'[3] The British Government contented itself with securing a subscription of £10,000 from the Egyptian Treasury for the privately organised relief expedition, which, travelling under Stanley by the unexplored Congo route, reached Lake Albert nearly two years later, to find Emin, without ammunition and so devoid of prestige, 'a poor prisoner in the hands of his own mutinous soldiers',[4] so disillusioned, moreover,

---

[1] Mackay to Kirk from Buganda, 26.xii.86. Enclosed in above.

[2] Minute by Kirk on Holmwood to Iddesleigh, 23.ix.86. F.O. 84. 1775.

[3] Minute added to minute by Kirk on Holmwood to Iddesleigh, 23.ix.86. F.O. 84. 1775.

[4] Stanley's report on the Emin Expedition. Enclosed in Euan Smith to Salisbury, 28.xii.89. F.O. 84. 1982.

with the performance of Gordon's countrymen in the land
he had longed to save from the slave-trade, that he ended his
career in German service as the Resident of Bukoba Province
and probably scheming the overthrow of British power in
Uganda.[1]

Meantime in Buganda events dragged out their slow
course, and Mackay watched with increasing exasperation
the growth of Arab power.[2] During 1887 and 1888 it
seemed to him as though the European occupation was
destined to be confined to the coastal regions for many years
to come; and he appealed in his letters for at least an em-
bargo on the traffic in arms which alone was turning a
numerically insignificant minority into the real arbiters of
African fortunes. A few petty merchants in Birmingham,
Belgium and Zanzibar were doing more to retard progress
in Africa than all the peaceful agencies combined were able
to do in promoting it.[3] He had the full support of Consul-
General Euan Smith in a plan which he next put forward
for allowing individual native chiefs to purchase a limited
supply of arms every year on condition of good behaviour,
and so forcing them to realise their dependence on England
and Germany rather than upon the individual Arab middleman.[4] But after the Muhammedan *coup d'état* of October

[1] *e.g.* the incident described by Bishop A. R. Tucker in *Eighteen Years in Uganda
and East Africa*, London, 1911, p. 40.

[2] *supra*, pp. 103–8.

[3] Mackay to Holmwood from Buganda, 19.iv.87. Enclosed in Holmwood to
Salisbury, 15.vii.87. F.O. 84. 1853.

[4] Mackay to Euan Smith from Usambiro, 18.v.88. Enclosed with covering dispatch Euan Smith to Salisbury, 28.vi.88. F.O. 84. 1907. Salisbury's comment is
interesting if specious: 'A combined movement for the exclusion of arms and ammunition from Africa ought not to be entered into without careful examination.
The Slave Trade which is reaching such gigantic proportions is said to consist of the

1888, which drove the missionaries out of Buganda and threatened them even in their refuge on the southern shores of Lake Victoria, he realised that it was too late for half-measures: 'These events render the question now paramount: Is Arab or European power henceforth to prevail in Central Africa?'[1]

*   *   *   *

8

By the beginning of 1889, however, two new factors had entered into the situation, which were radically to affect the future of Buganda and were to draw both the C.M.S. missionaries and the White Fathers deep into the political affairs of the country. First, news reached the missionaries at the southern end of Lake Victoria that the Imperial British East Africa Company had received a Royal Charter, and that the British and German governments had agreed

operations of a comparatively small number of Arabs on vast multitudes of an inferior race. It is probable that these Arabs are already armed. . . . If so our humane efforts to prohibit the importation of arms will have the effect of disarming not them but their victims. They are irresistible notwithstanding their inferiority in numbers, because they are exclusively in possession of arms, the same superiority which enabled Cortes and Pizarro to conquer in America. If we restrict the importation of arms, we perpetuate their superiority and consequently their power for evil. When we concluded the Sand River Convention we thought we had done a very humane and sagacious thing. But its main effect has been to enable the Boers, numbering only 40,000, to trample on and enslave some 800,000 blacks. If you read the accounts of their encroachments in Bechuanaland it is their inferiority in arms which makes the natives so helpless.' Salisbury, 1st August.

[1] *CMI.* 89. 149.

upon a boundary between their respective 'spheres of influence', running from the Indian Ocean to the eastern
shores of Lake Victoria, but no farther.[1] Thenceforward,
Mackay's 'paramount question' transformed itself in the
minds of both sets of missionaries into that of whether
British or German influence was ultimately to prevail in
Uganda. In the events which followed the Anglicans
naturally strove to promote the interests of the British
company; the White Fathers, in the absence of a Catholic
power, favoured the German cause in preference to what
they assumed would become a liaison between a British
administration and a Protestant mission. Next, it became
apparent that the Baganda themselves were not going to
submit quietly to the *coup d'état* which had placed Kalema
on the throne and the Arab faction in control of the state.
Naturally, the forces of resistance centred round the African
Christians of both denominations, who had gathered, some
in the neighbouring kingdom of Ankole, and some on the
southern shores of the lake, whither it was known that both
the European missionaries and Mwanga, the deposed king,
had already made their escape. Already, in December 1888,
Mwanga had presented himself in a mood of deep penitence
at the White Fathers' station at Bukumbi, and had been
given refuge. In the following April came a joint deputation
of Protestant and Catholic Baganda from Ankole, proposing
a campaign to restore Mwanga to his throne. Mackay, from
his neighbouring station at Busambiro, refused any assistance,
but the Catholic missionaries lent their aid, as did Charles

[1] Agreed in London on 1st November, 1886. P. L. McDermott, *I.B.E.A.*, London,
1893, p. 7.

Stokes, a former lay missionary of the C.M.S., who was now engaged in trade on his own account.[1]

Accordingly, on 29th April Mwanga set sail in Stokes's boat for Buddu, the southernmost county of Buganda, where he was soon joined by some thousands of the local inhabitants, as well as by 800 Christian refugees from Bukumbi, who were mostly of the Catholic persuasion. The legitimist troops were unorganised; and they were soon driven off the mainland by the forces of Kalema, which had been armed by the Arabs with breech-loading rifles. Mwanga, however, succeeded in rallying to his cause the inhabitants of the Sese Islands, lying off the Buddu coast, who controlled a large proportion of the canoe transport of the lake; and with their aid he was able to take up a position on the little island of Bulingugwe in the Murchison Gulf, only about eight miles from the capital. From here he invited the missionaries of both denominations to join him; and in June he also addressed an appeal for help to Mr. F. J. Jackson, the leader of the Imperial British East Africa Company's caravan which was thought to be approaching Kavirondo. Stokes, meanwhile, had departed to fetch more ammunition from Bukumbi, whence he returned at the end of August. In September the Christian refugees in Ankole, under the Protestant leader Apolo Kagwa, attacked Buganda from the south-west, and, aided by Mwanga's forces from Bulingugwe, retook the capital on

[1] In the following account of the Muslim–Christian war, which is necessarily much condensed, I am heavily indebted to Sir J. M. Gray's masterly paper in the *Uganda Journal*, March 1950, pp. 23–49, which is based not only on an exhaustive search of the contemporary published literature but also on valuable material from the Zanzibar archives and on the accounts of eye-witnesses.

5th October. On the 11th Mwanga returned in triumph; Kagwa became prime minister; and Catholics and Protestants formed an uneasy alliance and divided the offices of state between them.

Kalema and the Arab party, however, were not yet finally defeated. Withdrawing to the north-west, they secured the alliance of King Kabarega of Bunyoro; and in November they were able to return and drive the Christians back to the islands. A day or so before their flight, there arrived from Jackson a reply to the appeal sent in June, which he had only received on his arrival at Mumia's on the 7th November. Together with Mwanga's letter, long out of date, Jackson had received news of the better turn taken by events in October, and as he had had explicit orders not to go to Uganda—for the Company with its limited resources had no wish to be entangled in unprofitable adventures—he asked for confirmation of the need for help. He also made it clear that he would require, in exchange for his help, not only material compensation which Mwanga had already offered in his appeal of June, but also a treaty. Mwanga's first reply, dispatched on 25th November, was evasive on the question of the treaty, and Jackson accordingly decided to pursue the Company's interests by setting out upon a three-months' expedition towards Mount Elgon in search of ivory. Before he left, however, he sent Mwanga a flag, acceptance of which would on the one hand oblige the Company to assist him and on the other hand oblige him to enter into a treaty with the Company. Meanwhile, Mwanga back on the islands was hard-pressed and, on the advice of the Catholic missionaries as well as the Anglicans, addressed a further appeal to Jackson on 1st December accepting his terms without reservations. This letter did not reach Jackson until he returned to Mumia's in the following March.

The Christian legitimist cause, however, once more rallied without help from the outside. A naval victory over the Arabs had brought to Mwanga, by way of ransom, a large store of arms and ammunition. His scattered forces were reorganized. A solemn alliance was drawn up between the Catholic group and the Protestant group, and early in February 1890 the Arab–Muslim forces were decisively routed at Bulwanyi. Kalema and the remnants of his army fled to Bunyoro; Mwanga once more entered his capital.

A fortnight after the Christian victory there occurred an event which did much to widen the rift between the Catholic and the Protestant parties. It will be remembered that England and Germany had not yet agreed on a boundary between their spheres of influence to the west of Lake Victoria. On 4th February Carl Peters marched into Jackson's base camp at Mumia's and read Jackson's correspondence, including Mwanga's letter of 1st December. On 24th February he was in Mengo offering a treaty with the German Company which in the circumstances had much to recommend it. The Arab party, though temporarily beaten back to Bunyoro, was still dangerous. No help had materialised from Jackson; and the French missionaries regarded Mwanga, on that account, as absolved from his acceptance of the British Company's protection. Acting on their advice, therefore, the king and the Catholic chiefs signed the treaty immediately: the Protestant chiefs only with the greatest reluctance, and after some days of loudly expressed indignation. Peters, apprised of the approach of the British Company's force, suddenly withdrew to the south of the lake, to be replaced in April by an extremely angry Mr. Jackson, armed with 180 Snider rifles and proposing a treaty which even the Anglican missionaries agreed to be onerous. Backed by Father Lourdel, Mwanga refused to accept the proffered conditions; whereupon Jackson returned to the coast to consult his superiors, leaving his lieutenant, Gedge, and as many soldiers as he could spare.

All these treaty-making incursions were in the event invalidated by the Anglo-German Agreement signed in Berlin on 1st July, 1890, which settled the first parallel of southern latitude as the boundary between the British and German spheres of influence on Lake Victoria and to the west of it. For the relations of the missions to each other and to the political power, however, they were all-important. During the course of 1890 the British Company's flag became the outward symbol of Protestantism: the Catholic crucifix became the badge of royalist opposition to British power; while northwards, in Bunyoro, the Muslim party gathered their strength for a new invasion, establishing communication with the Arabs on Lake Tanganyika by a new land route passing to the west of Buddu by which they received large quantities of arms and ammunition. The Catholic party, too, was still importing armaments through the agency of Mr. Charles Stokes. Alfred Tucker, the new Anglican Bishop who arrived in Buganda in December, while rejoicing at the size of his Christmas congregation, was astounded to find that the Christians carried their rifles even to church. 'Uganda', he said, 'was like a volcano on the verge of an eruption.'[1]

A fortnight before Tucker's arrival Captain F. D. Lugard had entered Buganda to replace Jackson as the accredited agent of the I.B.E.A. Company, bearing the somewhat facile instructions to maintain order while showing the strictest impartiality between the religious factions.

*   *   *   *

9

It is certain that, in sending Lugard to Uganda,[2] the Directors of the Company were serving the call of patriotism in defiance of their own economic interests.[3] It may also be true, as they claimed, that, had they refused to do so, no other national agency would have come forward and that Uganda would have been lost, immediately to the forces of

---

[1] Tucker, *op. cit.*, I, p. 42.

[2] In the following account of the 'religious wars', I have used (i) the Catholic version in G. Leblond, *Le Père Auguste Achte*, Paris, 1904; (ii) the Protestant version in R. P. Ashe, *op. cit.*, 1894; (iii) the Company's version in F. D. Lugard, *op. cit.*, 1893, and in P. McDermott, *I.B.E.A.*, London, 1893. I have also used the correspondence relating to Sir Gerald Portal's mission to Uganda, contained in F.O. 2. 60, and in particular, of the report of Captain J. R. L. Macdonald on his inquiry into the charges made by the White Fathers against the I.B.E.A. Company's agents, which is enclosed in Portal to Rosebery of 7.iv.93, *ibid*. Though Macdonald's conclusions, and in particular his strictures on Lugard's absence in Toro and Bunyoro in 1891, sometimes go further than the evidence warrants, the evidence itself seems to have been fairly taken, and it brings to light much that does not appear in the published sources.

[3] The evidence of pressure by public opinion and by the Government adduced by McDermott, *op. cit.*, pp. 115–19 is convincing.

Arab resistance and ultimately, perhaps, to Germany.[1] But it is indisputable that in attempting to administer so vast an area with inadequate financial resources, and therefore with too few men and too small an armed force, the Company drove the most honourable of its agents into desperate and sometimes dishonest expedients. Passing through the Kenya Highlands in 1893, Sir Gerald Portal discovered that behind the maps and prospectuses published in London there was 'not a single shadow of an attempt at administration or improvement of the country or protection of natives anywhere.'[2] The so-called 'station' at Tsavo was 'a miserable little stockade in charge of a Goanese half-breed boy'. The Nzoi station was a thatched hut ten feet long inhabited by a decrepit ex-porter on a salary of fifteen rupees a month. At Machakos there was one European who tried to trade a little, but who carefully refrained from exercising any jurisdiction over the natives. At Kikuyu, the European in charge 'does not dare venture 200 yards from his stockade without an armed escort . . . and maintains the Company's influence and prestige by sending almost daily looting and raiding parties to burn the surrounding villages and to seize the crops and cattle'.[3]

Such was the nature of Lugard's line of communications when he entered Uganda with an effective force of about 100 men in December 1890, with the task of imposing his authority 'impartially' on the 'religious factions', each of which was capable of putting some 2,500 armed men in the

[1] e.g. Macdonald to Portal from Kampala, 13.xii.92 in F.O. 2. 61. 'The first effects of the anarchy in Uganda . . . would be felt by our German neighbours.'
[2] Portal to Rodd from Nzoi, 22.i.93. F.O. 2. 60.
[3] Portal to Sir H. P. Anderson from Kampala, 22.ii.93. F.O. 2. 60.

field at any moment.[1] In Lugard's defence it must be remembered that the full dangers of the situation were not apparent at the time of his arrival, since the Muhammedan party was once again threatening war, and he was therefore able to rally both the Christian armies to his side to put down the revolt. But, having thus dissolved the last link binding the Catholics and the Protestants, Lugard abandoned Williams, his only English subordinate, with a merely token force at Kampala Fort, and himself departed to make treaties with the surrounding kingdoms of Ankole and Toro and to establish Emin's abandoned Sudanese troops in four forts round the borders of Buganda,[2] with the understanding, since the Company was unable to pay them, that they were to support themselves by raiding into the hostile territory of Bunyoro.[3]

Throughout 1891 the political rivalry between Catholics and Protestants grew steadily. The division of offices made between the parties themselves after the restoration of the king in the spring of 1890 proved the chief ground of contention. The system then instituted had provided, on the one hand that the chiefdoms within each horizontal rank of the hierarchy should be equally divided, and on the other

---

[1] The fact that Lugard was accused of partiality by both Catholics and Protestants is taken by McDermott to prove his impartiality. The term is hardly appropriate, since Lugard had not the force at his command to be truly impartial. 'Independent' would be a better word.

[2] It is in this part of his report that Macdonald casts his most unjustified aspersions on Lugard's conduct. There seems to be no evidence to support his assumption that had Lugard remained at Kampala with the pitiful force at his disposal, he would have been able to maintain the peace. Moreover, it is at least arguable that his primary duty was not to keep the peace in Buganda, but to secure by treaty the much wider area now known as 'Uganda' to British influence.

[3] Portal to Rosebery from Kampala, 27.iii.93. F.O. 2. 60.

hand that alternate ranks in any one vertical section of the hierarchy should be held by members of opposite parties.[1] If therefore a chief of any class changed his religious allegiance, he had also to vacate his office. Since, moreover, much of the land in Buganda, together with the political allegiance of the tenants who tilled it, went with the office and not according to any hereditary principle, it can be readily understood that, apart from the limitation imposed by the agreement, the race for converts between the two denominations was synonymous with a race for political power. The Catholics, having the allegiance of the king, were, by reason of the traditional prestige of his office, in the ascendancy. Some chiefs had become Catholics and submitted to eviction, and it was known that many more would do so if they could keep their lands. The Catholic party, therefore, pressed for 'freedom of conscience' and for revision of the agreement. The Protestant party on the other hand, realising that their opponents held the trump card in their influence over the king, stood fast by the agreement and pressed forward the eviction of converts.[2] In the circumstances of the Company, the policy of Williams at the Fort could only be to favour the most equal balance of power between the two parties, and therefore to support the existing agreement. This was bound to create among the Catholics the belief that the

[1] Thus the ten chieftainships of the first rank were divided five and five; but the five Protestants chiefs had only Catholic chiefs of the second rank under them and these in turn had only Protestant chiefs of the third rank under them, and so on down the hierarchy. See Macdonald's 'Report', loc. cit.

[2] Macdonald clearly thought that the Catholic claim was the juster. But it is arguable from the evidence that Mwanga's allegiance to Catholicism was of a political rather than a religious nature, and that it was due to the superior political ability of the French priests.

Company favoured the Protestants, a belief, said Mac-donald, 'which the weaker party seem to have fostered by every means in their power'.[1]

The situation was still rapidly deteriorating when Lugard returned to Kampala on the 31st December and when, on opening his mail, he found a letter from the Company ordering him to evacuate Uganda immediately. These instructions he decided to ignore pending further reference to England; and on the 2nd January he wrote to the C.M.S. missionaries authorising them to deny any reports that the Company was intending to evacuate which might have reached them either direct or through the French missionaries.

The cause of this incident, which was to exercise such a profound influence upon Lugard's conduct during the impending crisis, was the failure of the Salisbury Government to pass a disguised subsidy for the Company in the Parliamentary session 1890–91. In September 1891 Sir William Mackinnon had informed the C.M.S. that unless £40,000 could be raised by private subscription, Lugard would have to be withdrawn. He had offered to give £10,000 himself and to raise £15,000 among his friends, if the C.M.S. would be responsible for the remaining £15,000. The C.M.S. had replied that their funds could not be so allocated, but that the President and Secretary would as private individuals receive subscriptions for the purpose. For a month no contributions had come in, and the Company had sent the threatened instructions. In October, however, Bishop Tucker had addressed a meeting of the

---

[1] 'Report', *loc. cit.*

C.M.S. Gleaners' Union, as a result of which £16,000 was subscribed in a few days. The countermanding order reached Lugard at Kampala on 7th January, 1892, five days after his public repudiation of the first.

'On Captain Lugard's return from Kavalli', reads the most damaging portion of Macdonald's indictment, 'he does not seem to have realised the changed conditions, and by adopting a high-handed policy, and by injudicious management of the crisis, he precipitated civil war in Uganda.' At what point in the course of events Lugard decided to force an issue is uncertain; but it is clear that he acted under the impression (later proved unfounded) that the French missionaries were in possession of the rumours of the Company's intended evacuation and that they were using them to undermine the prestige of the Fort. It is equally clear that his policy throughout January 1892 was deliberately aggressive. Although the Catholic Party was already aggrieved on the question of land and offices, he reopened the vexed question, which had been shelved at the time of his previous visit, of the king flying the Company's flag. About a week later a Catholic shot a Protestant in circumstances which in Buganda law indisputably constituted self-defence.[1] The king tried and acquitted the offender,

[1] *The incident*: 'Mongolaba [R.C.] had a gun stolen from him by one of the Katikiro's [P.] men. Mongolaba adopted the correct course of laying his claim before the Katikiro [Chief Judge] and the King. The Katikiro [P.] had had a gun stolen from him by the Kauta [R.C.]; and said that if his [the Katikiro's] gun were returned, he would return Mongolaba's. Mongolaba waited a few days; and as his gun was not returned, he made a plot to steal one in exchange. Some of Mongolaba's [R.C.] men pretended to sell native beer by the roadside near Mongolaba's enclosure and waited till a Protestant came to bargain for it. One of the Catholics then slipped behind him and snatched away his gun. The Catholics then ran into Mongolaba's enclosure. The Protestant did not report the matter and claim redress. He summoned some

F

explaining his reasons to Lugard's Somali interpreter who was present. Yet Lugard, acting on a letter from the Protestant mission, ordered that the acquitted man should be handed over to him, as the Catholics understood, for execution. Mwanga refused, whereupon Lugard, noting in his diary that the French Fathers had been telling their adherents 'that we were only a trading company, and that one of them had said that he could drive us out of Kampala with a stick, and not a gun would be fired', drew the conclusion that the Catholics had definitely determined to fight. Instead, however, of making the issue a clear matter of political authority between the Company and the king, by sending an ultimatum, Lugard secretly armed the leaders of the Protestant party with 300 muzzle-loaders and 150 Snider rifles, and waited for events to develop. It is not clear which side fired the first shot; but the result, whether or not it was intended, was that the Catholics, on 24th January attacked the Protestant headquarters at Namirembe and not the Company's fort at Kampala. Lugard did not take

armed friends with guns. . . . The Protestants followed the Catholics and tried to force a way into Mongolaba's enclosure and forced open the gate. Shots were exchanged. Both parties claimed that their opponents fired the first shot, but I am inclined to think that the Catholics fired first. A Protestant was shot, whereupon the other Protestants ran away. The Catholics guarded the dead body and would not allow it to be removed.

If this case is to be judged by Uganda usage, we must note the following points: (a) the Catholic, on having a gun stolen from him adopted the peaceable and legal course of appealing to the Katikiro for restitution. (b) The Protestant on having a gun stolen did not adopt this proper course, but took the law into his own hands. (c) The Protestants were the first to appeal to arms. (d) Shots were fired on both sides. (e) By Uganda custom the Catholic was justified in defending his enclosure against forcible entry, even to the point of killing his opponent. (f) By Uganda custom, when a man is killed in the capital, the corpse must remain until the King has sent to verify the place and cause of death. (g) A man guilty of murder is punishable by fine. . . .' Macdonald, loc. cit.

part in the battle at all until the Protestant commander cunningly placed his forces on the opposite side of Kampala Fort to the Catholics. Upon these, as they streamed up Kampala Hill, Lugard directed a withering fire with his only Maxim gun, and in a few minutes put them to flight.

Lugard at first made no attempt to follow up his victory. He allowed the native Catholics to escape with the king to the island of Bulingugwe; and sending for the French missionaries he offered to reinstate both the king and the Catholic chiefs provided that they would recognise the supremacy of the Company. The White Fathers, however, had lost all trust, both in Lugard's good faith and in his ability to impose these terms on his victorious Protestant allies, and on the last point at least events proved them right.[1] The following day Mgr. Hirth, the French bishop, was permitted to rejoin his flock in order, on his own admission, to persuade the king to return to the capital. Again on his own admission, he did the exact opposite;[2] and after waiting five days Lugard sent a hundred Sudanese troops and a body of Protestants to recapture the king by force. The islands were

---

[1] In this section of his report Macdonald seems to have made the same error of judgment as in the part which deals with Lugard's departure from Kampala in 1891. He does not recognise the essential fact, that it was the Protestant Party and not the Company's troops which won the battle of Mengo, however much they may have been aided by the Company's arms and ammunition. Lugard was not therefore at this stage, any more than later, in a position to propose liberal terms to the Catholics without the consent of the Protestants.

[2] G. Leblond, *Le père Achte*, Paris, 1904, quoting a letter from Hirth dated 11.ii.92: 'Le 26 janvier on nous permit de quitter le Fort pour aller presser le roi à revenir. . . . Mais il ne pouvait songer à rentrer à Mengo, où il eût été l'esclave des protestants. Pour les catholiques il n'y avait plus qu'à choisir entre l'apostate, la mort ou l'exil. . . . Tous ensemble nous primes lentement le chemin de la Kaguera. Nous allons nous créer de ce côté une nouvelle patrie. . . . Le Bouddou va devenir province catholique.'

invaded with some slaughter; but the king and the bishop escaped southwards to Buddu, and what had hitherto been mainly a conflict between the political parties at the capital developed into preparations for a general war throughout the country. There were mass migrations of Catholics into Buddu, and of Protestants out of Buddu, and both sides took prisoners of war whenever possible.

What happened in the next three weeks to soften the pugnacity of the Catholics, or at least of their missionary advisers, is by no means clear.[1] On 18th February, however, Père Achte, of the White Fathers, wrote to Lugard suggesting a partition of the kingdom, with a separate British officer to administer the affairs of each denominational province.[2] Lugard in his reply insisted that the immediate return of the king was the first condition of any settlement and threatened to enthrone a Muhammedan uncle of Mwanga's if there was any further delay.[3] But at about the same time, in a verbal

---

[1] The answer would presumably be found in Hirth's correspondence at the White Fathers' headquarters at Algiers, which is not available. In 1891 Cardinal Lavigerie wrote to Cardinal Manning that the Catholics would not object to a British Protectorate in Uganda provided that an English Catholic be placed at the head of the protectorate. Mgr. Livinhac made the same demand and threatened: 'If this means of pacification were neglected, war would break out and it would perhaps be the German Colony from the West of Nyanza which would profit from the victory.' Baunard, *Le Cardinal Lavigerie*, Paris, 1912, II, p. 435. Quoted Buell, p. 280. P. McDermott, *op. cit.*, p. 167, states that Captain Langheld, the German officer at Bukoba, hinted strongly that Hirth had expected assistance from him. It seems likely that the French missionaries thought that if the British Company was driven out, the Germans would immediately move in and support their cause. In fact some sort of guarded assurance to this effect may have been made by the Germans at the time when the British Company was contemplating withdrawal. Hirth visited Bukoba after his retreat from Uganda and the Germans may then have convinced him that since the British Company now meant business they could not interfere.

[2] Achte to Lugard (in French) from Kasenyi, 18.ii.92. Macdonald, *loc. cit.* Evidence IX.   [3] Lugard to Achte (in Latin) from Kampala, 6.iii.92. *ibid.*

interview with Père Guillemain and Frère Gaudibert, he indicated that if the king returned, he would attempt to negotiate an equal partition of the country between the rival parties.[1] In March the king was spirited away from his Catholic followers and brought by boat to his capital which was now entirely in the hands of the Protestant leaders, under whose forceful influence the fickle Mwanga quickly changed his religious adherence.[2] Since the Protestants now held the trump card which had formerly given the numerical superiority to their opponents, they were even less disposed than before to agree to an equal partition, and Lugard had perforce to agree.[3] At the end of the month a new treaty was signed, which made clear the Company's supremacy, provided for the registration of existing fire-arms, prohibited the importation of more, and assigned only the Buddu chiefdoms to the Catholics, pending a final revision in two years' time.

*　　*　　*　　*

10

Meantime, in March 1892, the Conservative Government had reintroduced the vote for £20,000, which they had unsuccessfully tried to pass through without debate, as a 'non-contentious measure', at the close of the previous session. Though it was described as a grant-in-aid of a

[1] *ibid.*, Père Guillemain's evidence, 16.i.93.
[2] cf., Mwanga to Colville, 24.vii.94. Enclosed in Colville to Hardinge, 19.viii.94. F.O. 2. 72. 'There was none left except myself, and the Protestant chiefs were coming down every day to me and forcing me to be a Protestant.'
[3] Macdonald 'Report', Section 70.

survey for a railway between Mombasa and Lake Victoria, and though this project was in turn presented as an anti-slavery measure by which the Government would be merely fulfilling its obligations under the Brussels Act of 1889, the real question at issue, as everyone knew, was whether public funds should be used to subsidise a Chartered Company which was financially incapable of meeting its political responsibilities. The Under-Secretary for Foreign Affairs made it plain that, without the prospect of a railway, the Company would have to retreat from Uganda and from most of the territory between Lake Victoria and the coast. This region would in that case revert to the slave-traders, and the missionaries settled in Uganda would probably be the first to be sacrificed.[1] The vote was passed; but not before the Liberal leaders, Gladstone, Bryce and Harcourt, had individually dissociated themselves from all responsibility for imperial extension in East Africa, and not before Mr. Labouchere, the Radical editor of *Truth*, had uttered the first of many lurid denunciations of spending money and building railways in order to prevent missionaries from cutting each others' throats.[2] Sir John Kennaway, the President of the C.M.S., and himself a Liberal, though supporting the vote as an anti-slavery measure, stated that his Society, which had spent over £200,000 in forming 'what is admitted to be the only Christian state in Africa', had never asked for protection and did not do so now.[3]

In the summer of 1892 news of the battle of Mengo[4] reached Europe, and provoked a controversy in the highest

---

[1] Hansard, 3.iii.92, col. 1836.
[2] *ibid.*, 4.iii.92, col. 0050.
[3] *ibid.*, 4.iii.92, col. 0059.
[4] *supra*, pp. 146-7.

degree relevant to the establishment of a British protectorate in Uganda. Mgr. Hirth's account arrived a month
before the others, British correspondence having been
delayed in German territory. On 25th May, Ribot, the
French Foreign Minister, sent for the British Ambassador,
Lord Dufferin,[1] and on the same day M. Waddington, his
Ambassador in London, called on Lord Salisbury, demanded
an inquiry into the maltreatment of French subjects by the
officers of the I.B.E.A. Company and presented a list of
material losses suffered by the mission, including one
cathedral, sixty chapels, twelve schools and 50,000 Catholics
said to have been sold as slaves by the Protestants.[2] A translation of Hirth's letter was published in the *Tablet* on
4th June and produced repercussions throughout the English
press. Irish Members diverted the House of Commons by
asking whether care would be taken that any additional
force under Captain Lugard would not be used for con-
fiscating the property of Catholics or of taking their lives.[3]
Cardinal Lavigerie, now on his death-bed, lived long enough
to address an open letter to Lord Granville. Lugard's
reports, when they arrived, together with those of the
C.M.S. missionaries, attracted a corresponding publicity;

[1] Dufferin to Salisbury, 25.v.92, in 'Further papers relating to Uganda', 1893.
Accounts and Papers, LXII, p. 335.

[2] Waddington to Salisbury, *ibid.*, 25.v.92. Inevitably, both sides had the greatest
difficulty in restraining their humbler supporters from enslaving and selling their
prisoners of war. In para. 67 of his report, Captain Macdonald estimated the number
of Catholics enslaved at 5,000 to 6,000, the majority of whom had by then been
returned. Macdonald, *loc. cit.* F.O. 2. 60.

[3] Hansard, 16.vi.92, col. 1278. Question by Colonel Nolan. Others by Mr. O'Brien
and Mr. Healey, 31.v.92, col. 0364; Mr. O'Connor and Mr. O'Kelly, 9.vi.92, col.
0577.

and on 24th June Salisbury telegraphed to the Consul-General at Zanzibar to appoint an independent Commissioner to inquire into the causes of the war. In August, Lord Salisbury's government was replaced by Mr. Gladstone's, Lord Rosebery becoming Foreign Secretary; and to him the French Ambassador repeatedly pressed his demands for reparations. Finally, in November, Rosebery agreed to pay suitable compensation, as and when the Catholic statements were found correct by the Commission.[1] The statement had a wider importance, in that by it the Government admitted a measure of responsibility for the actions of the Chartered Company.

By the side of the diplomatic issue with the French Government there ran the question of what was to happen to Uganda when the funds privately raised by Sir William Mackinnon and the friends of the C.M.S. became exhausted. It was becoming steadily more evident that the railway would not, even if Parliament could be persuaded to vote the money for its construction, be completed in time to save the Company from bankruptcy; and in April the Directors informed both the Foreign Office and the C.M.S. that it would have to withdraw from Uganda at the end of 1892 unless a subsidy for the maintenance of Captain Lugard could be granted.[2] The imminence of a General Election prevented the Conservative Government from acting during the early summer; while the return in August of a Liberal

---

[1] Rosebery to Dufferin, *Accounts and Papers*, LXII, p. 335, 8.xi.92. The Commissioner appointed was Captain Macdonald, whose Report has already been discussed. While refusing to admit any responsibility, the Government in 1898 made an 'ex gratia' payment to the White Fathers of £10,000. H. B. Thomas and R. Scott, *Uganda*, 1935, p. 33.

[2] I.B.E.A. to Lugard, *ibid.*, 16.v.92. Copy to F.O.

Government, whose Home Rule Policy for Ireland was supposed to imply an anti-imperialist policy abroad, threw the whole future of East Africa into the gravest doubt. The hopes of interested parties, however, revived when Lord Rosebery, who was known to hold more favourable views than the majority of his colleagues, took charge of the Foreign Office; and during the autumn the battle for public opinion was fought and won.

As in the case of Nyasaland, there were by 1892 other men and other interests at work than those of the British Mission. There was the Anti-Slavery Society which sent a deputation to Lord Rosebery in October.[1] There were the Directors and shareholders of the Company, whose patriotic opinions were reinforced by the certainty that the redemption of their capital depended upon whether the Government could be persuaded to take over the country and buy them out.[2] There was Lugard, who, returning to England in October, plied the press with long and closely reasoned letters,[3] and by addressing meetings in the industrial towns initiated a steady stream of memorials from Chambers of Commerce on the potentialities of Uganda as a new market for British manufactures.[4] There was the inevitable Mr. Rhodes, who wrote to Lord Rosebery in October, offering to lay at his

---

[1] And received from Lord Rosebery the encouraging reply that it was his belief that 'having put our hand to the plough, we shall not be able, even if we are willing, to look back'.

[2] G. S. Mackenzie to the *Standard*, 28.ix.92; Lord Brassey to *The Times*, 24.x.92; and above all the volume by P. L. McDermott already quoted which was specially prepared at the request of Sir William Mackinnon.

[3] Lugard to *The Times*, 8.x.92 (with Leader) and 17.x.92; Lugard to *Glasgow Herald*, 15.x.92.

[4] Collected in F.O. 84. 2192.

own expense a telegraph from Nyasaland to any point in Uganda which the Government might deem convenient.[1] There was Stanley, and Jephson, his companion on the Emin Relief Expedition, who contributed in speeches and to the press, estimates based on first-hand evidence of Africa of the probable consequences of 'a cowardly and disgraceful scuttle'.[2] Conservative politicians, taunted by wavering Liberals with the quiet acceptance at the end of their term of office of the Company's notice of withdrawal, made public denials that they had ever intended to allow such an evacuation to take place.[3] *The Times*, which alone had sent a special correspondent to Uganda, was in the forefront of the campaign, and, with the variety of evidence contributed to its correspondence columns, drowned the scepticism of the *Manchester Guardian* and the reiterated denunciations of the *Daily News*.[4]

At least as important, however, as any of these interests which were fighting for imperial extension in East Africa, was the missionary interest of the C.M.S., supported by its home 'constituency' as well as by the ecclesiastical hierarchy of the Established Church.

Immediately the Liberal Government came to power,

[1] Rhodes to Rosebery, 30.x.92. *Accounts and Papers*, LXII, p. 335 *sq*. There is in F.O. 2. 61 an unexplained letter from Rhodes to Portal, dated 8.xii.92, which is even more suggestive of his interest in Uganda. 'My idea is that when you reach Mwanga's you should organise a force of 300 or 400 men . . . [who] should be placed with a Commissioner at the king's kraal. . . . Meanwhile we will come up from the south and then jointly deal with the Mahdi on the basis of diplomacy and not of fighting.'

[2] Jephson to *The Times*, 30.ix.92 (with Leader); *Western Mail*, 4.x.92: 'H. M. Stanley at Swansea: Great Speech by the Explorer: British Responsibilities in Africa.'

[3] *e.g.* Lord Salisbury's private secretary to *The Times*, 28.x.92, and Sir Michael Hicks-Beach at Bristol, *The Times*, 12.x.92.

[4] F.O. 2. 61 contains a valuable collection of the relevant press cuttings.

instructions were telegraphed to Sir Gerald Portal, the Consul-General at Zanzibar, to inform Bishop Tucker, then at Mombasa, that if he or any of his missionaries went up to Uganda during the present crisis, they would do so at their own risk.

Fifteen years ago [replied the Bishop] our missionaries entered Uganda, carrying their lives in their hands, never looking for, never expecting, Government protection. In course of time Her Majesty's Government granted a Royal Charter to the Imperial British East Africa Company, in which it delegated to the Company its powers of influence and functions of government within the sphere of British influence. In virtue of the powers entrusted to it under that Charter, the I.B.E.A. Company made its appearance in Uganda some two years ago. Its representative at once entered into a treaty with the king and chiefs. That treaty has now been superseded by another one, signed on March 30th, 1892. In both treaties the Company is pledged in the strongest possible terms to protect the king and people and to maintain its position in Uganda.

Naturally the adherents of the English Mission supported the English Resident in the exercise of those powers entrusted to him by the English Government through the I.B.E.A. Company. The result was that they incurred the hatred and hostility of all other parties in the State.[1]

The position of the mission, it was claimed, had been radically changed by the arrival of the Company, so much so that it could not now resume its former relations with the natives. If the Company tore up its treaties and withdrew from Uganda, not only the lives of the missionaries but also those of their adherents would be endangered.

[1] Bishop Tucker to Sir Gerald Portal in September 1892. Quoted in Stock, *op. cit.*, III, p. 445.

Such was the missionary case, as it was presented to Lord Rosebery by a deputation in September[1] and to the public in an Open Minute of the General Committee dated the 11th October. Mortified by the resignation of one of their members, who refused to be associated with a political agitation, the Committee added that the sole reason for their intervention was that 'at the present grave crisis in the history of Uganda . . . a special responsibility devolved upon them to communicate to the British public their sense of the grave wrong which will be inflicted upon the people of Uganda, if this determination to withdraw the protection in which they have been led to trust be carried out'.[2]

Having thus delivered themselves, the Committee withdrew from the arena; but memorials and resolutions flowed in daily to the Foreign Office, from the Society for the Propagation of the Gospel and the Missionary Committees of the Scottish Churches, from Diocesan Conferences and Ruridecanal Chapters, from branches of the Young Men's Christian Association and the Ladies' Negro Friend Society.[3] At the Church Congress at Folkestone, Archbishop Benson prayed that 'our country's course may be so shaped that the Christian converts of Uganda be not abandoned to imminent destruction'.[4]

The Government conceded the first step in September 1892, when it undertook to pay the Company's expenses

---

[1] The Memorial presented by the deputation on 23rd September is printed in *CMI.*, 92. 516.

[2] Minute of the C.M.S. General Committee, 11.x.92.

[3] All these memorials bear the initials of Lord Rosebery. They are collected in F.O. 84. 2192.

[4] Stock, *op. cit.*, III, p. 444. Benson's prayer is quoted in the minute referred to above.

in Uganda for the three months January to March 1893, in order to give Captain Macdonald time to complete his inquiries.[1] The real decision, however, was taken in November, when Sir Gerald Portal was dispatched to Uganda to report on 'the best means of dealing with the country', armed, as it later transpired, with full powers to establish a provisional regime.[2] The debate on the Queen's Speech in January 1893 provided Liberal ministers with opportunity to assure their Radical supporters that they had not prejudged the issue, that they had merely sent Portal to discover for them how deeply they were committed by the actions of their predecessors in office.[3] Nevertheless, Mr. Labouchere, after impugning the integrity of the Company's Directors and of the Special Commissioner himself, and after describing the missionary agitation as 'the very last outcome of Church and State',[4] in March led 46 Radicals into the opposition lobby against the vote for Portal's expenses, the Conservatives swelling the Government majority to 368.[5] But the Cabinet still needed the Radicals' support for their domestic policy; and it was not until 12th April, 1894 that they dared to ratify the Protectorate over Uganda which Portal had set up more than a year before.[6] In presenting the financial account on 1st June, 1894, Sir Edward Grey still disclaimed any definite views 'with regard to either a forward or a backward policy in Africa'. The Government's action had been determined by circumstances which had occurred before they came to office.

---

[1] ibid., p. 438.
[2] Hansard, 6.ii.93, col. 0586.
[3] ibid., 31st January–6th February, 1893.
[4] ibid., 3.ii.93, col. 0455.
[5] ibid., 20.iii.93, col. 0539.
[6] ibid., 12.iv.94.

It was true that chambers of commerce had been very constant in pressing the Government to retain Uganda. The missionaries, too, had put a case which was not one to be 'answered by generalisations'. But Sir Edward Grey's principal justification of the Government's conduct was a negative one. A magnificent illustration of the manner in which public opinion enters into the calculations of statesmen, it provides perhaps the soundest assessment of the influence of the missionary interest on the British occupation of East Africa. 'If we had abandoned Uganda, we should have had month by month the news of most sinister consequences reaching this country. The Government would have been assailed on all sides as being responsible.' Turning to the Radical members, Grey told them that if they wished for bold and far-reaching measures at home, they could not have got them passed or even proposed by any government which had taken such a 'limited, narrow and ungenerous view' as to have deliberately abandoned Uganda 'to revenge, disaster and ruin'.[1] Sir Charles Dilke fired a parting shot at the missionaries by reminding Members representing the C.M.S., who were about to support the vote, that they would now be pagans if St. Augustine had landed in Kent with Maxim guns.[2] But the shot fell wide. Sir Gerald Portal in his final report had confirmed every warning which Mackay and his colleagues had uttered:

Everything, I fear, seems to point to a desperate and perhaps long-continued struggle in the centre of Africa between the advances of European civilisation from the coasts on the East and West, and the

[1] Hansard, 1.vi.94, col. 0181.   [2] *ibid.*, 1.vi.94, col. 0195.

old class of Arab traders. . . . In determining both the nature and the result of this contest, the position of the Christian country of Uganda is of vital importance. Even now it is known that frequent communications pass from the Arabs of Tanganyika and Tabora to the fanatical Mohammedans at Wadelai and along the White Nile, as well as to the nearest and most dangerous neighbour of Uganda, Kaba-Rega, King of Unyoro. So long as Uganda is under European supervision, there is little or no danger of these probable disturbances spreading from South to North, but I fear that the withdrawal of the present control, and the consequent loss of prestige . . . would shake the position of Europeans throughout East and Central Africa and would react seriously on the neighbouring colonies of Germany, Italy and the Congo State. Any one of these countries, and more especially the first-named, would be fully justified, in their own self-defence, in insisting that, on our withdrawal, our place should at once be taken by some other European power.[1]

Joseph Chamberlain might advocate the ultimate importance to the British economy of new markets, and the strategic value for imperial defence of an East African base. The professional advisers of the Government might stress that the opportunity now presented would not recur. But to any Liberal contemporary however preoccupied he might be with domestic issues, the historical analogy suggested by Portal would have been unmistakeable. The real strength of the missionary interest was in the last analysis the physical presence of the handful of Europeans, French as well as English, living on the shores of the Nyanza Lake. The public meetings and the deputations, the memorials and the statistics of the missionary constituency at home, were chiefly

[1] Portal to Rosebery, 1.xi.93. F.O. 2. 60.

important as a foretaste of the protests and the unpopularity which would follow 'a repetition of Khartoum'.

The declaration of a protectorate over Uganda clearly involved also the territory now known as Kenya. During the debate on the Uganda vote, Sir Edward Grey announced that a Sub-Commissioner would be appointed under the Consul-General at Zanzibar, whose duty it would be 'to establish such friendly relations . . . as shall make it possible for British capital and enterprise to enter the country between Lake Victoria and the coast'.[1] To complete the transaction it was only necessary to find the money with which to buy out the Company's interest. The Foreign Office had long cast covetous eyes on the £200,000 with which the German Government had in 1891 bought those territories of the Sultan of Zanzibar lying within their portion of the mainland; and in 1895 Seyyid Hamed, aptly describing himself as 'only a little bird in the claws of an eagle', agreed to invest this sum at an interest of three per cent in redeeming for his masters the concession which had been granted by his uncle Barghash to Sir William Mackinnon.[2] Simultaneously the Company, which had spent £538,000 on East Africa,[3] agreed to accept £250,000 in compensation for its assets and for the repeal of its Charter. On 13th June, 1895, Parliament voted the balance of £50,000, thus completing the acquisition of the East

[1] Hansard, 1.vi.94, col. 0181.

[2] This sum was originally paid over as the private property of the Sultan; but on Seyyid Ali's death in 1893, the British Government made it a condition of their support of Seyyid Hamed that the £200,000 should be transferred to the Zanzibar Government. F.O. to Rodd, 9.ii.93. F.O. 107. 6, No. 13. For this reference I am indebted to Mr. L. W. Hollingsworth of the School of Oriental and African Studies.

[3] Hansard, 13.vi.95, col. 1134. Mr. Burdett-Coutts.

African Empire at a cost to the British taxpayer of something under £220,000.[1]

It was, of course, inevitable that the mere presence of missionaries of various European nationalities in a territory like East Africa should have become one of the determining factors as soon as that territory became an object for competition among the European powers. In assessing how far missionaries consciously tried to influence the course of that competition, however, one generalisation can be made. No mission ever tried to invoke the aid of the secular power of its own country in order to increase its influence over the African populations which it had come to evangelise. The German inruption, and the Arab resistance which it provoked, taught the missions to regard imperialism as a merciful intervention by Europe, which was necessary to save Central Africa from Islam and all its works. Further, once the necessity for intervention was recognised, missionaries used all their influence to ensure that the intervention should be carried out by their own countrymen, or, failing that, by the power which seemed to offer the best prospects for the work of their own denomination. It was in promoting the British part in the scramble for East Africa that the missionary interest exercised its most decisive influence. Only the most far-sighted of English statesmen could see

[1] Portal's mission to Uganda, 20.iii.93   £5,000
        Supplementary   September '93   £12,000
        Supplementary   15.iii.94   £27,000
        Uganda   1.vi.94   £50,000
        Uganda   22.viii.94   £45,000
        Kenya and Uganda   13.vi.95   £80,000
                                              _____
                                              £219,000

that the British economy was beginning to be threatened by the growth of industrialism in America and in the rest of Europe, and that new markets in Africa were therefore worth the expense of administration and development. In Nyasaland, thanks to Rhodes, the diplomatic action of the State was at first all that was necessary, and a single brief démarche by missionary supporters was considered sufficient to justify its exercise. In Kenya and Uganda, where money had to be spent, and where private economic enterprise had already been forced to retreat, public opinion was of far more vital importance, and every measure of support, economic or religious, idealistic or sentimental, was of consequence. Of the missionary factor in that decision, it is at least symbolic that the flag, so far from following the line of trade from the coast inland, followed the cross from Uganda to the sea.

Chapter Four

THE ZENITH OF THE MISSIONS, 1884–1914

I

THE EUROPEAN OCCUPATION, promising to remove many of the difficulties and dangers of missionary work in East Africa, and attracting the attention of new sections of the supporting public in Europe, provoked a remarkable reinforcement of missionary enterprise, by new societies as well as by those already established in the field.

As early as 1884 the Freiherr von Gravenreuth, a leading member of the German East Africa Company and a devout Roman Catholic, had organised and to a large extent financed the foundation of a missionary congregation of the Benedictine Order, named after St. Ottilien, with its head-quarters at Reichenbach in Bavaria. Three years later the first novices were ready, and the Propaganda divided in two the Apostolic Vicariate of Zanzibar, hitherto worked by the Holy Ghost Fathers, and allotted the southern half to the Benedictines of St. Ottilien.[1] Abbeys were founded at Dar-es-Salaam (1889), at Lukuledi[2] in the south-east of the territory (1895), at Peramiho in the south-west (1898) and at Madibira in the Southern Highlands (1894); and from

---

[1] J. Schmidlin, *Die Katholischen Missionen in den deutschen Schutzgebieten*, 1914, p. 113.

[2] Moved to Ndanda, 1907.

these centres small priories were gradually dispersed into the surrounding districts.[1]

Cardinal Lavigerie's Memorandum on Africa and the Slave Trade,[2] presented to a gathering of German Catholics at Frankfurt-am-Main in July 1888, resulted in the formation of the 'Afrikaverein deutscher Katholiken' which became a powerful propaganda organ for the missionary cause throughout the country. It started a periodical, *Gott es will*; and it assisted in the formation of German Provinces, for recruitment and training, of the White Fathers at Trier, and of the Congregation of the Holy Ghost at Knechtsteden. Abbot Norbert Weber of St. Ottilien and Pater Acker of Knechtsteden were tireless publicists. Lay members of the Verein formed an important group in the Reichstag; and its chairman, Dr. Hespers, was given an official appointment to represent the interests òf Catholic Missions when the Kolonialamt was established in 1907.[3]

The new missionaries recruited by the White Fathers and the Holy Ghost Fathers in Germany formed no distinct divisions in the field, but their presence enabled the former to consolidate their position in the western and north-western part of the colony and the latter to press northwards from their existing sphere of influence between Bagamoyo and Morogoro to the densely populated slopes of Kilimanjaro. In 1886, following the foundation of the Congo Free State, the western side of Lake Tanganyika was divided from the old pro-Vicariate of Tanganyika as the Vicariate of

---

[1] *Catholic Handbook of East Africa*, Mombasa, 1932.
[2] *supra*, p. 118.   [3] Schmidlin, *op. cit.*, p. 2.

the Upper Congo, while in the following year the supporting station of Kipalapala, near Tabora, gained its independence as the Vicariate of Unyanyembe. The missionaries of the new Tanganyika Vicariate, temporarily reduced to the single station of Karema, spread southwards along the lake to Kala (1892) and Kirando (1894) and in 1899 crossed the Fipa plateau to Lake Rukwa and Mkulwe. On the establishment of the Uganda Protectorate in 1894, the old Nyanza Vicariate was divided, and the Anglophobe Bishop Hirth[1] henceforward confined his pastorate to the German shores of Lake Victoria as the Apostolic Vicar of South Nyanza, where the work grew so rapidly in the districts of Ruanda and Urundi, Mwanza and Bukoba, as to necessitate a further sub-division in 1912, when the indomitable Hirth became the first Vicar Apostolic of Kivu. In the north and east of the German colony the Holy Ghost Mission, though growing rapidly, remained under the superintendence of the Vicar Apostolic of Zanzibar until the creation of the Bagamoyo Vicariate in 1906 which was in turn subdivided in 1910, when Kilimanjaro became a separate Vicariate.[2]

During the early nineties, when the German Government had taken over the administration of the colony from the German East Africa Company,[3] when the boundary questions had been solved, and when the imperialist policy had won wider public recognition in Germany, the older established Lutheran societies started to take an interest in the new colony. In 1891 the old Berlin Society (Berlin I)

---

[1] *supra*, pp. 147-8.

[2] *Delegatio Apostolica Africae Orientalis et Occidentalis Britannicae. Status Missionum anni*, 1945–46. Aedibus Delegationis Apostolicae Mombasa.

[3] On 1st January, 1891.

and the Moravians decided in concert to enter the East African field, though it was significant of their abiding distrust of the Kolonialbewegung that they chose to do so at the point which was, and which was likely to remain, the remotest from secular European interest. They agreed upon a boundary following the thirty-fourth degree of longitude from the north end of Lake Nyasa. The first stations were to be planted close enough for mutual assistance; and from them the Moravians were to expand north and west towards Tabora, the Berlin Society north and east towards Dar-es-Salaam.[1] Both missions moved fast. By 1914 the Moravians had established about thirty missionaries in fifteen small stations among the Nkonde, Ndali, Safwa and Nyika tribes and had taken over the old L.M.S. station at Urambo.[2] During the same period the Berlin mission sent out more than sixty missionaries and founded twenty-two stations stretching from the Nkonde and Kinga tribes in the Livingstone mountains, through the Bena and Hehe uplands to Usaramo.[3]

In 1892 the missionaries of the lonely C.M.S. station at Moshi came into conflict with the German administration by defending the behaviour of their local chief, Mareali, in the face of ill-controlled aggression by German soldiery. In deference to the wishes of the British Foreign Office, Bishop Tucker reluctantly decided to withdraw.[4] The Leipzig

[1] *AMZ*. 91. 79.
[2] *ibid.*, 02. 546 and K. S. Latourette, *History of the Expansion of Christianity*, 7 vols., New York and London, 1937–45, v, p. 407.
[3] *AMZ*. 02. 298 and Latourette, *op. cit.*, v, p. 406.
[4] *AMZ*. 08. 409. cf. Bishop Tucker's account in *Eighteen years in Uganda and East Africa*, 2nd edn., London, 1911, pp. 85–6. For the origins of the Moshi mission *vide infra*, p. 169.

Society, which was then prospecting for a field in East Africa immediately entered the Chagga district and by 1914 had thirty-four missionaries spread over the southern slopes of Kilimanjaro and the Pare Hills farther south.[1]

During the nineties, too, the Berlin III Society passed into more effective hands.[2] Pastor von Bodelschwingh was appointed to the committee, and in 1891 he started a seminary at his country house at Bethel-bei-Bielefeld. Here he recruited and trained a generation of missionaries who were fit to take their place beside those of the older societies. He sent them to a new and more promising field in the Usambara Highlands, handing over the older stations in Usaramo to Berlin I.[3] By 1907 the Berlin III mission was strong enough to take on a second sphere of work in Ruanda.

For the Anglican missions working in German East Africa the period from 1884 to 1914 was a time of holding and developing ground previously gained, the fruits of which scarcely became apparent until after the First World War. Relations with the German administration were amicable enough; but both the C.M.S. and the U.M.C.A. had pressing interests in neighbouring British territories, and both were affected by the natural desire of missionary recruits to work under a British rather than a foreign government. The group of C.M.S. stations round Mpwapwa, which had originated as stepping-stones on the old caravan route to Uganda, were held, after much heart-searching by Bishop Peel, as a remote appendage of the Mombasa

[1] Latourette, *op. cit.*, v, p. 407.
[2] *AMZ.* 94. 503 and *Berliner Jahresbericht*, 1904, p. 141.
[3] *supra*, p. 96.

diocese.[1] The lonely station of Nassa on the southern shores of Lake Victoria was fitfully supervised from Uganda until it was handed over to the Africa Inland Mission[2] in 1909. The most spectacular developments of the U.M.C.A. during this period occurred in British Nyasaland and Northern Rhodesia. The Nyasaland diocese, separated from Zanzibar in 1892, spread its work along the German shores of the lake, but did not penetrate on to the high plateaux behind them.[3] The diocese of Zanzibar developed, especially under the dominant hand of Bishop Weston, a healthy life, but remained what it had been under Smythies, a pair of disconnected Archdeaconries. Magila in the Usambara hills, and Masasi, three hundred miles farther south, an enclave between the Muhammedan coastal belt at Lindi and the Muhammedan Yaos of Tunduru, were bound together only by a Bishop and a central theological school on the Muhammedan island of Zanzibar.

The establishment of the British East Africa Protectorate,[4] and even more the building of the 'Uganda Railway', which was begun at Mombasa in 1895 and reached Lake Victoria at Kisumu in 1901, provoked a hurly-burly race among missions new and old into hitherto unoccupied territory. For the railway provided a cheap and safe route

---

[1] cf. Bishop Peel's reports on his visitations of 1901 and 1908 in C.M.S. archives. In the first report he merely defers to the wishes of the local missionaries: in the second he is impressed by the results of the work.

[2] *infra*, p. 171.

[3] The area now known as Nyasaland, inseparable from East Africa during the period before the European occupation, now disappears from the present story. The Anglican diocese of Nyasaland, however, continued to include the north-eastern shores of Lake Nyasa after these had become politically German East Africa.

[4] Since 1919 the Colony and Protectorate of Kenya.

across the blistering desert of thorn-scrub lying behind Mombasa, inhabited by straggling groups of Kamba herds-men and preyed upon by the dreaded Masai, to the healthy highlands occupied by the Kikuyu and the dense populations of Kavirondo.

In 1894 the C.M.S., for all its fifty years of experience at the coast, had only advanced its influence some fifty miles westwards from the freed-slave settlements of Rabai and Freretown, though it had planted in 1885 two isolated missions, among the Teita in the northern foothills of Kilimanjaro, and among the Chagga to the west of the mountain.[1] In 1899, however, the diocese of Equatorial Africa which had sprawled in a great crescent from Mombasa south through the centre of German East Africa and north again to Uganda, was at last divided. The veteran Bishop Tucker retained Uganda, including, as that Protectorate then did, the Nyanza Province to the north-east of Lake Victoria; while W. G. Peel inherited the eastern portion of the old diocese as Bishop of Mombasa.[2] In the following year the C.M.S. began its occupation of the Kikuyu country, founding stations at Kihuruko (1901), Weithaga (1903), Kahuhia (1906), Mahiga (1908) and Embu (1910). In 1905 Archdeacon Willis was posted by Bishop Tucker to the Nyanza Province to open work among the Joluo, which spread to the Bantu Kavirondo, the Nandi and the Lumbwa.

[1] *supra*, p. 166.
[2] Although the Nyanza Province was ceded by Uganda to British East Africa in 1902, the ecclesiastical boundary remained unchanged until 1921. It was as the Bishop in charge of missionary work in the Nyanza Province that Bishop Willis of Uganda played his part in the Kikuyu Conferences.

Roman Catholic interests in British East Africa originated in connection with the Kilimanjaro missions of the Holy Ghost Fathers. Mgr. de Courmont, the Vicar Apostolic of Zanzibar, established a coast agency for this mission at Mombasa in 1890, and a half-way station at Bura, near Voi, in 1891.[1] In 1899, however, his successor, Bishop Allgeyer visited the growing railway town of Nairobi and planted a mission among the Kikuyu eight miles to the west of it. Realising that the new field exceeded the resources of his own Congregation, he accepted offers of help from the Consolata Society of Turin.[2] The first Italian Fathers arrived in June 1902 and were stationed at Kiambu (1902), Limuru (1903) and Mangu, near Thika (1906). The Kenya mission remained a joint concern of the two societies until after the First World War, though it was separated from Zanzibar in 1905. Catholicism, like Anglicanism, entered the Nyanza Province of British East Africa from the west. Mill Hill Fathers from Uganda[3] were posted to Kisumu in 1903, and established their first stations at Mumia's and Kakamega's.

Three directors of the Imperial British East Africa Company, Mackinnon, Bruce and Buxton, had in 1891 established a mission of their own called the East African Scottish Industrial Mission. Its only station, at Kibwezi, some 150 miles inland from Mombasa served some useful purpose as a resting-camp for officials of the Company travelling to and from Uganda until the mysterious disappearance of the Superintendent, David Charters, in 1894, but no impression was made upon the surrounding Akamba.[4]

---

[1] MC. 93. 386.   [2] ibid., 02. 481.   [3] infra, p. 182.
[4] V. T. Coats, David Charters, 1925.

In 1898, however, the Rev. Thomas Watson moved the mission to the celebrated site of 'Kikuyu' high up on the railway escarpment to the west of Nairobi; and in 1900 the venture entered upon a new lease of life when it was transferred to the direction of the Church of Scotland Foreign Missions Committee and when David Clement Scott was moved from Blantyre to take charge of it. A second station was opened at Tumutumu near Mount Kenya in 1908.[1]

In 1895 there was formed the interdenominational Africa Inland Mission, comprising many Baptists, and also some Methodists, Presbyterians and Anglicans. The pioneers, like so many others, frittered away their strength upon the unresponsive Akamba, until in 1901 C. E. Hurlburt moved the mission to Kijabe, 25 miles to the west of the Scottish mission at Kikuyu.[2] In 1902 a Pentecostalist element in this mission constituted itself into the Gospel Missionary Society, but remained in the same district.[3] Finally, in the same year, groups of American Adventists and Quakers moved into the Kavirondo district near the railhead, narrowly forestalling the C.M.S. and the Mill Hill Fathers from Uganda.[4]

[1] Church of Scotland Foreign Missions Committee, 1948, *Kenya 1898–1948*, pp. 18–20.
[2] H. R. A. Philp, *A New Day in Kenya*, 1936, pp. 17–18.
[3] *ibid.*, p. 61.
[4] Latourette, *op. cit.*, v, p. 411.

*   *   *   *

2

The first lesson of the new period of missionary history, which opened with the European occupation, was that the isolationist methods of the pioneers had not been just a product of the difficulties and dangers of missionary work under the old régime. In both German and British East Africa all the stations of the new missions, and most of the new stations of the missions already established, had to pass through a pioneer phase during which their teaching met with complete indifference from the tribal communities, and during which their only adherents were men and women who had to some extent cut themselves off from the tribal life, who had settled on the mission's land and were at least partly dependent on the mission's wages.

To Roman Catholic missions, of course, this phase presented no moral difficulties; and it was taken so much for granted by them that it scarcely provoked any comment. To build around a plantation was both the cheapest and the most effective method of starting a mission. It was a natural development of the older system of freed-slave settlements. The first employees of a new mission station might well be a few families brought from one of these settlements some hundreds of miles away.[1] Local inhabitants who came to work for the mission were expected to receive instruction and in due course to pray at the mission. The fact that many of them might be still, in the Protestant sense of the word,

---

[1] This would seem, for instance, to have been the state of affairs at the new Rukwa station described by Mgr. Lechaptois in *MC*. 02. 289.

unconverted, was immaterial. At a later stage of the work adherents would no longer need the mission's wages and protection. The permanent settlers could be gradually displaced by temporary employees, and a larger number could thus be brought within the mission's influence. At a still later stage the mission plantation would serve mainly for the support of regular catechumens, coming from a distance to receive their final months of pre-baptismal instruction at the station.

The substantial identity between the Catholic and the Presbyterian attitude to this problem has already been noted;[1] and it is not, therefore, surprising that Dr. Henry Scott, who had served his apprenticeship in the 'Industrial Gospel' under Hetherwick at Blantyre, should have planned at Kikuyu a self-supporting mission based upon an agricultural estate of 3,000 acres. The enterprise proved a commercial failure, but the earliest evangelistic progress occurred among the mission's numerous tenantry.[2]

Of the German societies, the Moravians, working to the north of Lake Nyasa, were also traditional believers in economic as well as spiritual rebirth. Their object had never been to convert whole nations, but rather to gather within each nation communities of elect souls, self-supporting and in other ways sufficient unto themselves.[3] Hundreds of Africans were employed in the building of substantial villages and in the laying out of plantations, which 'gave excellent opportunities for language-study, for gaining

[1] *supra*, p. 58.   [2] *Kenya 1898–1948*, p. 18.
[3] See, for example, 'Zinzendorfs Methode' in *Missionsblatt der Brüdergemeinde*, 1900, p. 37.

confidence and also for the first missionary contacts'.[1] Only Christians were allowed to settle permanently at the stations,[2] while all catechumens were obliged to do so at least during the period of instruction.[3] As one village filled up another was founded, a native council of elders being formed in each to supervise the agricultural work, to maintain law and order and to make contact with intending settlers.[4] The Moravians further insisted that commerce was an essential ingredient of all lasting mission work. 'If you seek economic improvements, you must either give or trade.' Rather than allow their converts to make dangerous contacts with Indian and Swahili merchants, they set up a wharf and a warehouse at Kyimbila on Lake Nyasa and appointed two missionaries to conduct the import and export business for the whole area.[5]

The other German missions, though strongly critical of the offering of economic incentives and aware of the dangers of bringing up their converts in isolation from their tribal environment, were nevertheless forced by circumstances to do so. The Leipzig missionaries in the Kilimanjaro area were supplied with youths detailed to serve them as pages by the Chagga chieftains;[6] and in 1904 they were obliged to

---

[1] *Jahresbericht der Brüdergemeine*, 1910, p. 38.

[2] *ibid.*, 1900, p. 31, mentions that Isoko differed from the other stations in that 250 heathen Bandali lived on the mission land. These were the remnants of the original inhabitants, who, when the land was bought, had been given the choice of leaving or else observing some of the rules of Christian morality, including monogamy.

[3] Decision of first conference at Rungwe, 1905, *ibid.*, 1906, p. 29.

[4] *Missionsblatt der Brüdergemeine*, 1903, p. 350, and 1900, p. 238.

[5] *ibid.*, 06. 219: 'Handel in irgend einer Weise wird mit jeder dauernden Missionstätigkeit verbunden sein, wo nicht bereits ein geordnetes, ausgebildetes Geschäftsleben neben der Mission besteht.'   [6] *Jahresbericht*, 1900, p. 98.

confess that in spite of persistent attempts to teach in the villages these 'boarding pupils' were the only successes they had yet achieved.[1] The Berlin I Society likewise admitted that all their early converts had been men who worked for the mission and who had originally been allowed to settle on the stations on the condition of observing a modified form of Christian morality.[2] These men, they added, were disowned by their chiefs as 'Leute der Weissen'.[3] As early as 1895 the Berlin III missionaries reported that at Mlalo in Usambara a Christian village had 'formed itself' on account of the incompatibility of heathen and Christian morality.[4] Summing up the experience of twenty years, Direktor von Schwartz of Leipzig concluded that even if the European missionary was by African standards the greatest known farmer, carpenter, smith, doctor, dentist, linguist and story-teller, he must still fail in his work unless he provided 'an alternative community' to the heathen tribe.[5]

Among the missions of the Anglican communion, the U.M.C.A. were not seeking to add to their already far-flung footholds; but neither did they command the European resources to develop their work sufficiently to produce any striking exception to the general pattern of missionary methods at this period. They were still concentrating upon their four great boarding-school centres, at Zanzibar and Magila, Newala and Likoma, where all day and every day was given up to school work, religious instruction and

[1] *ibid.*, 1904.
[2] *Berliner Jahresbericht*, 1900, p. 52 *sqq.*
[3] *ibid.*, 1912, p. 108.
[4] *Nachrichten aus der ostafrikanischen Mission*, 1895, p. 89.
[5] *Ev.-Luth. Missionsblatt*, 1904, p. 498.

church services;[1] although time had made possible some slight relaxation of the original discipline. 'Till 1898', wrote Father Barnes from Likoma, 'the boarding-school had involved almost total adoption with all expenses paid.' In 1902 the pupils came at sundown, slept the night and went home after morning school.[2] In British and German East Africa the C.M.S. were no less introverted in their methods than their Lutheran and Roman Catholic neighbours. At the Teita station natives were 'consenting, as conditions of residence, to attend the services, to send their children to be taught and to refrain from work on the Sabbath'.[3] The population of Rabai, near Mombasa, had grown by 1897 to some 3,000, of whom only 700 were freed slaves or their descendants. The local administration was in the hands of a body of native elders who were nominally subject to the Mombasa district officials; but as the Commissioner for the territory pointed out, the English clergyman in charge of the mission was the real local authority, was 'doing the work of an assistant district officer and magistrate' and had in that capacity rendered very useful service to the Government.[4]

Uganda excepted, the state of missions in the second pioneer period, which followed the European occupation, differed from the first only in the number of points occupied. The missions remained a thing apart from the local populations; the few natives who came to profess their doctrines were adopted, body as well as soul, into a new way of life and were regarded by their kinsmen as outcasts. Further,

[1] *CA.* 96. 101.   [2] *ibid.*, 02. 62.   [3] *CMI.* 95. 292.
[4] Report by Sir A. Hardinge on the Condition and Progress of the East Africa Protectorate from its Establishment to the 20th July, 1897. *Accounts and Papers*, 1898, LX, p. 199.

the missions of this period did not even have the justification that they were dealing with the unwanted refuse of the slave-trade. At this, more than at any other time, one might expect them to have been accused of undermining the foundations of social order. And yet it is noteworthy that the missions received, not the censure of the early European administrations, but their whole-hearted approval. For the colonial administrations themselves, no less than the missions, were seeking to introduce western concepts, quite as foreign as Christianity, among the communities over which they ruled. Except for the relatively small class of educated Swahilis at the coast, there was no other source than the mission centres to which they could look for their minor officials, clerks, interpreters and policemen, for their semi-skilled builders and joiners, or even for reliable un-skilled labour, messengers, orderlies and domestic servants. At a time when law and order, the introduction of currency, the promotion of local trade and the beginnings of taxation were the main preoccupations of government, mission employees and adherents stood out from the rest as pros-perous and orderly. They paid their taxes and they under-stood the new régime. Until private European settlement became extensive, the mission plantations alone produced the sorely needed cash crops.[1] At a time when the Com-missioner of the East Africa Protectorate was advocating the employment of more District Officers, on the grounds that

[1] The Holy Ghost Fathers introduced coffee into the Nairobi area in 1905 and cotton and rubber near Morogoro. The Uganda Company, founded by Mr. Victor Buxton in 1904 to undertake the industrial work which the C.M.S. felt to be outside the province of its regular missionaries, was very largely responsible for introducing cotton into Uganda as the staple cash crop.

G

they would cost the Government but £500 a year each and would each collect £1,000 in dues and taxes,[1] it can readily be understood that the opening of a new mission station had seemed to him:

> to be generally as efficacious for the extension of European influence as the opening of a government station. . . . There are districts in East Africa such as Teita and the Lower Tana, in which European influence has hitherto been represented almost entirely by missionaries, but which have made as great progress as the regions which have been taken in hand by government officials.[2]

The colonial administrations had come to East Africa expecting to develop national assets for their home countries, expected by their home governments at least to make their remote territories self-supporting; but they encountered tribal solidarity in the economic field as the missions encountered it in the religious field. Europe invested capital in great enterprises like railways only to find that the 'raw' African, so far from being able to make them pay, was unemployable, that he worked under the whip for a fortnight and then slipped silently away to his village. Where the missionary found African customs wicked, the administrator found them a barrier to progress; and in breaking down their solidarity he saw the missionary as an ally.

> It facilitates a better and more civilised life if natives can engage in some form of trade or occupation which causes them more or less to break with their old associations and come under Christian supervision. From this point of view I think it a great mistake to isolate

[1] Sir Charles Eliot, *The East Africa Protectorate*, 1905, p. 189.
[2] *ibid.*, p. 241.

natives and place them in reserves, for such isolation inevitably confirms them in their old bad customs and cuts them off from contact with superior races, which might improve them.[1]

The cynic would, however, be wrong to label the missionary enterprise for the years 1884–1904 as merely an auxiliary arm of the imperialist expansion. There is no evidence from either of the British territories in East Africa to suggest that this early community of interests between missions and governments was regarded by either side as anything more than a happy accident. Neither agency had any idea of deviating from its own natural course in order to form a more powerful combination with the other. In German territory, where Government-sponsored settlement had figured in the earliest plans, and where colonial policy was controlled far more effectively by the commercially interested parties, these parties, united in the Kolonialbund, exerted continuous pressure to influence missionary policy in the direction of European economic aims; but all overtures were indignantly rejected by the Lutheran leaders. If only, said Count Pfeil,[2] the missions would bring themselves to preach a little less the dangerous doctrines of the brotherhood and equality of all men, and give all their instruction in practical tasks, they could become a powerful

[1] *ibid.*, pp. 241–2.
[2] In a speech at the Allgemeiner deutsche Kongress zur Förderung überseeischer Interessen, September 1886. Quoted in *AMZ*. 87. 31. It was entirely typical of the views of the Kolonialbund, which in its newspaper, the *Koloniale Zeitschrift*, frequently expressed them yet more forthrightly: *e.g.* another quotation in *AMZ*. 04. 297 reads: 'Nicht für die Missionierung der Farbigen, nicht für ihr Wohlergehen in erster Linie haben wir die Kolonien erworben, sondern für uns Weisse. Wer uns in dieser Absicht entgegentritt, den müssen wir aus dem Wege räumen.'

factor in the education of the native races. If they would scrap all this reading and writing and praying, and concentrate exclusively on teaching the native to work, they would find that their pupils would acquire in the process as much religious instruction as was suitable for the nigger. The African, replied Direktor Merensky of the Berlin I mission, was not lazy. He was like the rich man in Europe. He did not need to work. The missions were indeed concerned to introduce new arts and methods of agriculture to the extent of making it possible for their converts to lead truly Christian lives. They would encourage conditions in which family life was possible, with sanitary housing and clothing, and in which the husband did his fair share of the work. Missionary influence, he admitted, might even create material demands among the natives which could only be satisfied if they received some wages from Europeans; but the missionary interest was not, and never could be, directly concerned to solve the labour problems created by the entry of European settlers.[1] Husbandry (Ackerbau), declared the Berlin III missionaries, and not daily wage-earning, was the essential basis for Christian family life.[2]

There is, on the other hand, positive evidence that in many respects the missionary's view of the tribal society was a more optimistic one than that of the governments. There is perhaps no more conclusive proof that the missions always intended to work within the framework of the tribal system than the patient, sometimes almost hopeless study which

[1] A. Merensky, 'Welches Interesse und welchen Anteil hat die Mission an der Anziehung der Natürvölker zur Arbeit?' *AMZ.* 87. 148.

[2] *Nachrichten aus der ostafrikanischen Mission*, 1902, p. 166.

they devoted during the first fifteen years of European rule
to languages spoken by as few as ten thousand people each.
At a time when the German administration was pressing for
German to be taught in the schools, the Continental
Missionary Conference at Bremen decided that subsidies, if
offered, should be refused unless the principle could be
preserved that education should be given in the vernacular.[1]
It was a policy which no mission would have adopted whose
permanent objective was to train up Africans in European
ways. In education it was bound sooner or later to defeat its
own ends, since it would clearly be impossible to translate
enough books even for the purposes of primary, much less for
secondary education, into the scores of vernacular languages.
Even for evangelisation, Swahili was already widely understood as a lingua franca, and with a consistent policy it could
easily have become the lingua franca of East African
Christianity, had the Livingstonian principle been less
firmly established in the minds of missionaries that Africa
would only be converted by Africans. However exotic, the
school for native catechists formed the core of every single
missionary community. Catholic missionaries and Protestants alike looked forward to the time when their pupils,
fully instructed in the Word of God, would spread out into
the villages and preach it with the full wealth of African
metaphor and simile, to the millions whom they themselves
could never hope to reach.

[1] Report in *AMZ*. 97. 417.

*   *   *   *

3

In order to understand how the missionaries' hopes of an indigenous propagation of the faith were in due course fulfilled to a degree beyond their expectations, it is necessary to consider first the course of events in Uganda, where alone there was no prolongation of pioneer conditions of missionary work into the period of European government. Until 1891 there had been in the whole of Uganda only one Roman Catholic mission station, at Rubaga, the capital of Buganda. In 1894, when the British half of the old Nyanza Vicariate was divided, the White Fathers retaining the area to the west of Kampala as the Vicariate of North Nyanza and the Society of St. Joseph from Mill Hill taking over the eastern portion as the Vicariate of the Upper Nile, there were still only five stations, all of which were still in Buganda. Twenty years later the White Fathers had 26 stations, occupied by 118 European priests, 14 lay brothers and 34 nuns. The kingdom of Toro had been occupied in 1894, Bunyoro in 1900, Ankole in 1902.[1] By the same date the Mill Hill society had 31 priests and 7 nuns dispersed in 15 stations in Buganda (1895), Busoga (1901), Bugishu (1908) and Teso (1910).[2] During the same period the Church Missionary Society, with a staff of 37 clergy, 11 laymen, 32 wives and 33 single women,[3] had occupied several stations in Buganda, and others in Busoga (1894), Toro (1896), Bugishu (1900), Ankole (1901), Bunyoro (1902), Teso (1905) and Acholi (1913). And yet in nearly all these vast developments the

[1] *MC.*, June 1914.   [2] *ibid.*, June 1915.   [3] cf. Stock, *op. cit.*, IV, p. 102.

foreign missionary expansion, both Catholic and Anglican, had followed and not preceded the expansion of the faith through indigenous channels. In most of these new districts missionaries came at the request of the peoples, and they came to consolidate bands of neophytes already gathered by unordained, very often unbaptised, African enthusiasts who had been in contact with Christian teachings at the older centres.

In Buganda itself, it has been shown that Christianity had been for some time the religion of nationalism and revolution. The first dissemination of Christian teachings occurred when some of the adherents of the missions at Rubaga fled into the country districts from the persecutions of Mwanga in 1886. It occurred again during the Arab *coup d'état* of 1888, when the leading Christians fled to remote parts of the country and organised the armies of resistance. The Christian–Muslim war of 1889 brought the Christian leaders into political power and established the principle of *cujus regio ejus religio*, which furnished the new religion with much of the prestige and many of the economic advantages of an Established Church. It was above all the war between Catholics and Protestants, arising out of the presence of the British Company, which created the social conditions most favourable to the spread of a new religion. The flight of Mwanga with the Roman missionaries in January, and Lugard's temporary settlement of March 1892, set in motion a vast migration of peasants, who had hitherto been little concerned with the religious questions of the capital, into the territories allotted to their chiefs under the religious settlement. The old villages and plantations were laid waste in the war. The communities which had inhabited them were split into fragments and dispersed over long distances. Even the minor chieftaincies were occupied by upstarts of the religious wars.[1] The Baganda retained their strong sense of nationality, but the solidarity of ancient beliefs and customs was utterly destroyed, leaving an appetite for a new synthesis which Christianity was able to appease.

At the end of 1893 the Protestant community at the capital experienced a typical manifestation of evangelical 'revivalism', but associated in this case with one of the most remarkable and spontaneous movements for literacy and new knowledge which the world has ever seen. The movement, in both its facets, owed its origin to George Pilkington, a lay missionary of the C.M.S., who after some three years of Bible translation retired in November 1893 to the island of Kome in Lake Victoria, in order to reconsider his vocation. There he received an experience which he described as his reception of the Holy Spirit.[2] Inspired by this 'lost Truth, the loss of which gives Satan his opportunity of introducing both Muhammedanism and Popery',[3] he returned in haste to Mengo and held a number of mission services, at which he asked people to 'stand up and explain, for the help and encouragement of others, how they came to know the Lord. All of them told us that it was reading the Word of God that had enlightened them to see the way of salvation, and each of them gave us passages, quoting chapter and verse, that had most appealed to them.'[4] Scenes occurred which put one

[1] Walker in *CMI*. 97. 364.
[2] He had already been 'saved' during his undergraduate days at Cambridge.
[3] C. F. Harford-Battersby, *Pilkington of Uganda*, London, 1895, p. 235.
[4] Walker from Mengo in *CMI*. 95. 132.

in mind of Gregory Nazianzen's description of Constantinople on the eve of the Arian controversy.[1] The missionaries were constantly being stopped as they walked about the streets by people racing out of their houses with books in their hands to ask the meaning of obscure passages. What was a winepress? How far was it from Jerusalem to Jericho? In what did the wealth of Capernaum consist? The embarrassed clergymen had to write home to headquarters for reference books and commentaries.[2]

A few months later the revival movement in Mengo was harnessed to the work of spreading the faith in the country districts. In January 1894 Pilkington visited the Rev. A. B. Fisher, who was working in Singo county, and was struck by his colleague's system of 'synagogi', or reading-houses, where 'people could be instructed by native teachers under the direction of more experienced workers, these in turn being supervised by the European in charge of the district'.[3] In March he launched an appeal for African missionaries; and in April eighty native evangelists went out two and two from Mengo, carrying Gospels and reading-sheets, to the principal places in the land.[4] The district (gombolola) chiefs of their own persuasion gave them banana-plantations for their support, and they received in addition minute stipends

---

[1] 'This city is full of mechanics and slaves, who are all of them profound theologians, and preach in the shops and in the streets. If you desire a man to change a piece of silver, he informs you wherein the Son differs from the Father; if you ask the price of a loaf, you are told by way of reply that the Son is inferior to the Father; and if you inquire whether the bath is ready, the answer is that the Son was made out of nothing.' Gibbon, *Decline and Fall*, Chapter XXVII.

[2] Miller from Mengo in *CMI*. 96. 341.

[3] Harford-Battersby, *op. cit.*, p. 231.

[4] Walker from Mengo in *CMI*. 95. 37.

from the Mengo Church Council. In December 1894 Pilkington reported that whereas at the beginning of the year there had been not more than 20 country churches or reading-rooms, there were now 200, attended by perhaps 4,000 people daily and by as many as 20,000 on Sundays. Eighty-five of the churches were in the care of 131 official evangelists paid by the Church Council: the rest were managed by unpaid volunteers. Twenty more evangelists were stationed outside Buganda, in Buvuma and Busoga, as foreign missionaries, and these were paid by the C.M.S.[1] When Bishop Tucker went up to Uganda in 1896 he found that there were 200 of these teachers in regular employment, and 500 others in 'local connection'.[2] When he went again in 1902, there were 2,000 men and 400 women, and they were spreading rapidly into the provinces of Busoga and Toro and even to the pygmy forests of the Congo.[3] Pilkington was dead; but his complete Bible sold 1,100 copies in the year of publication, together with 4,000 New Testaments, 13,500 single Gospels and 40,000 'readers'.[4]

Roman Catholic missionaries used a somewhat different terminology to describe the events of these years; but it is plain that the facts themselves were not dissimilar. Mgr. Hirth announced in 1891 that open-air catechisms held on Rubaga Hill were attended by as many as 3,000 people.[5] Père Guillemain reported that neophytes arrived at the mission, knowing their prayers and the abridged version of the Catechism by heart before they had even set eyes on a

---

[1] Harford-Battersby, *op. cit.*, pp. 236–7, quoting Pilkington's annual letter to the C.M.S.
[2] *CMI.* 97. 183.   [3] *ibid.*, 04. 496.   [4] *ibid.*, 04. 601.
[5] *MC.* 91. 206. Hirth to Lavigerie, dated February, 1891.

European missionary—'car ils s'instruisent entre eux avec un zèle vraiment extraordinaire'.[1] To the French Fathers Pilkington was a 'révérend visionnaire'; nevertheless the missionaries at Bikira in southern Buddu, describing how neophytes of three years' standing duly presented by their chiefs were so numerous that they had to be turned away from the six months' courses for Baptism, passed the comment: 'En vérité le vent violent de la Pentecôte a soufflé sur ce peuple.'[2] Pilkington would doubtless have questioned the statement of Mgr. Streicher that the Baganda felt an irresistible need to love the Blessed Virgin—'le jour ou un paien fait son premier signe de croix il jette ses amulettes et va à la recherche d'une médaille;[3] aussitôt qu'une paienne consente à prier avec nous, elle dédaigne son collier de perles et ses bracelets d'ivoire pour soupirer après une médaille'.[4] But it may be doubted whether this desire was less significant as a sign of grace than the desire to spell out with infinite labour the syllables of a Gospel text.

In the small but densely populated kingdom of Toro the spread of Christianity was almost simultaneous with the mass movement in Buganda. Toro had been until about fifty years before the European occupation a province of the ancient kingdom of Bunyoro. Between about 1830 and 1870, however, a collateral branch of the royal house had been allowed by peaceable kings to develop there an independent status of its own. This independence had been challenged

---

[1] *MC.* 91. 375. Guillemain to Lavigerie, dated, 13.iv.91.
[2] *ibid.*, 93. 170. Moullec to Livinhac, dated 29.x.92.
[3] Refers to the medal of the Virgin Mary, worn round the neck by neophytes. Catechumens were also given a cross.
[4] *Missions d'Afrique*, No. 117, May, 1896.

during the seventies and eighties by the same Omukama Kabarega of Bunyoro, who had allied himself with the Muslim party of Buganda in the war of 1888, and who maintained a vigorous opposition to the British administration until his capture and deportation in 1899. The princes of Toro had been compelled by his frequent invasions of their country to seek refuge and help from the traditional enemies of Bunyoro in Buganda and Ankole. They were rescued by Lugard, who established the Toro confederacy under Daudi Kasagama in 1891. Daudi's cousin, Yafete Byakweyamba, who now became the county chief of Mwenge, had been brought up in Buganda, where he had been baptised by the C.M.S.; and he took Baganda evangelists with him to his new post. Kasagama himself became a 'reader', and was baptised during a visit to Mengo in 1895.[1] Just as Christianity in Buganda had derived much of its momentum from the nationalist uprising against the Arabs, it now became associated through the restoration of Kasagama in Toro with local patriotism against the hated domination of Bunyoro. Toro, like Buganda, hailed the European occupation of 1894 as a deliverance, and like Buganda gained great advantages by its early association with the new invader. These two states alone enjoyed civil administration from the declaration of the Protectorate. They were the first to benefit from the Pax Britannica, from economic reforms such as the introduction of money and the promotion of local trade. By placing their armies at the disposal of the British against Kabarega they gained large territories on the defeat of Bunyoro. To a great extent it

---

[1] Tucker, *op. cit.*, p. 188.

was the confidence given them by European missionaries and the stimulus of Christian teaching which enabled them to take advantage of the new situation. This fact was recognised by Sir Harry Johnston, an avowed agnostic, when, comparing the Buganda of 1900 with the blood-stained and barbarous kingdom of Mutesa, he informed the Foreign Office that the larger share in this improvement was undoubtedly due to the teaching of Anglican and Roman Catholic missionaries:

It must not be imagined, of course, that the Baganda or Batoro have none of the old Adam in their composition since they accepted Christianity; but their intelligence is quickened, their ideas are enlarged—to a very notable extent—and their harmful old superstitions are swept away by their acceptance of the new faith.[1]

As Christianity had helped Buganda (and to a lesser extent Toro) into its position as the nation most favoured by the British administration, so it gained by the prestige which the Baganda soon acquired among their less progressive neighbours. It has already been shown that Busoga became in 1893 the earliest mission field for Baganda evangelists. European missionaries of the C.M.S. occupied two stations in Busoga in the following year, and devoted their first efforts to language work and translation; but, significantly, Bishop Tucker discovered during his visitation of 1899 that the Basoga had no desire to be taught in their own language: they wished to learn Luganda.[2] The spread of Christianity,

[1] Report by Sir H. H Johnston on Uganda for 1900. *Accounts and Papers*, 1900, LVI, p. 865.
[2] Tucker, *op. cit.*, p. 262.

therefore, was associated with a desire to abandon the old particularisms which had served them ill, and with a desire to participate in the successful adaptation of the Baganda. In Bunyoro, Christianity had perforce to await the final defeat of the Omukama Kabarega, who had consistently opposed the new régime. When he was driven out of his kingdom in 1898, Baganda evangelists accompanied his son Kitehimbwa, who was sent by the administration to succeed him.[1] Their presence was symbolic of Bunyoro's reconciliation. In Ankole the old Omugabe, Ntale, had always refused to meet the Europeans. He died in 1898, and two years later Bishop Tucker at last persuaded his son Kahaya to admit Baganda evangelists into the country. He owed his success above all to the influence of Mbaguta, in the Bishop's words 'a progressive', the one great chief among Kahaya's pastoral nobility who affected Kiganda dress and lived in a Kiganda house, away from the filth of the cattle kraal.[2] In both these countries the spread of Christianity was assisted by Johnston's introduction of the Kiganda system of county and district chieftaincies, into a high proportion of which Baganda chiefs were at first imported. These satraps took their followers and relations with them, clad not in skins or bark-cloth but in the graceful cotton kanzu with European coats and hats, and they lived as great lords among the Banyoro and Banyankole peasantry. They organised the compulsory labour for public works. They built roads, rest camps and court-rooms for European officials on tour, fine houses for themselves, and, often enough, churches and schools for the Baganda evangelists of

[1] Tucker, *op. cit.*, p. 240.   [2] *ibid.*, p. 275.

their own persuasion. Their notions of the distinction between Church and State were of the slightest, and frequently, to the dismay of European officials, they refused to issue tax-receipts until a Church contribution had also been paid. For the local populations, to know Luganda was the path to promotion and the way to suffer the smallest inconvenience from these foreign administrators. To learn Luganda one went to the evangelist, and later, perhaps, one appreciated the wider significance of his teaching.[1]

In the densely populated region between Mount Elgon and Lake Kioga it was the Muganda general, Semei Kakunguru[2] who, with the encouragement of Sir Harry Johnston, founded the British administration among the Bagwere, Badama, Kumam and Bagishu; and it was he who by bringing representatives of these peoples on visits to Mengo introduced them to the attention of the C.M.S. A European officer was posted over him in 1902; but Kakunguru, with his large colony of Baganda, stayed on as the county chief of Mbale. When Tucker visited him there in 1903, he commented that he had made 'the wilderness and the solitary place to blossom as the rose'. In the Baganda colony there were broad roads and well-built houses, cultivated gardens and trim fences. There was also a church, in which regular services were being conducted by Anderea Butulabude, a native pastor from Buganda. In considering the silent witness of this community, said the Bishop, 'we could not but

[1] These observations are based upon a preliminary examination of the Secretariat archives at Entebbe, for the years 1900–10.

[2] He was actually born in Koki. For the biography of this remarkable man, see H. B. Thomas, 'Capax Imperii', *Uganda Journal*, January 1939.

speculate as to its possible influence upon the tribes around'.[1] Even in the distant regions to the north of the Somerset Nile, inhabited by the Acholi, the Lango and the Teso, where the British administration for long contented itself with keeping open the Nile waterway and maintaining military patrols, the influence of the Christian Baganda was felt. Lloyd of the C.M.S. found no less than fifty of them in far-away Nimule in 1903 and noted that the Acholi chief Awich, who had heard of the development and prosperity of Buganda from these travellers, was most anxious to receive teachers.[2]

> Wherever [wrote Archdeacon Willis, expounding the strategy of C.M.S. expansion] houses are to be built, caravans organised, Government stations established, roads constructed, there the Baganda will be found. . . . You will see them at every centre of any importance on the Nile, down the railway, far north of Mount Elgon: the whole country for a radius of hundreds of miles is today being travelled by the Baganda.[3]

When the Gordon Memorial Mission started work in the southern Sudan at Lord Cromer's invitation in 1905, twenty Baganda evangelists accompanied the European missionaries under Bishop Gwynne.[4] When Bishop Tucker received a grant of £4,500 from the Pan-Anglican Congress of 1908, his mind turned to Teso, and he calculated that the interest on this sum of money, though scarcely sufficient to maintain

---

[1] Tucker, *op. cit.*, p. 314.
[2] Letter from A. B. Lloyd dated August 1903 in *CMI*. 04. 821.
[3] *ibid.*, 06. 82.
[4] *ibid.*, 05. 81 and H. Gresford Jones, *Uganda in Transformation*, 1926, p. 148.

a single European missionary would provide a hundred
Baganda evangelists. By 1911 he was able to report that
eighty-five out of the hundred had volunteered.[1]

The picture of an ebullient Kiganda nationalism, apparently in full harmony with its European governors and
teachers, flooding its influence over the other tribes of the
Uganda Protectorate, which emerges from the European
records of the period 1894–1914, is so significant that it is
liable to eclipse the many acts of individual heroism and
devotion of which it was composed. Of the many hundreds
of Roman Catholic catechists[2] who worked for the White
Fathers and the Mill Hill Fathers during these years
scarcely a trace survives in the published records. Of the
African Anglican evangelists the most rightly celebrated was
the saintly Apolo Kivebulaya, a Muganda of Muslim
parents, who sought out Mackay during the persecutions of
1886, and who ten years later crossed the Semliki river from
Toro, and, after suffering the bitterest persecution at the
hands of a brutal chief, lived on to found the flourishing
mission of Mboga in the Congo to the west of Lake Albert.[3]
Tomasi Semfuma, who worked in Koki and afterwards alone
in Bunyoro, and the Filipo and Andereya who converted the
king and prime minister of Ankole, appear but briefly in
Tucker's pages; and they must be typical of many more who
have received less than their share of fame.

The census of 1911 showed the population of Buganda
as 660,000, of whom no fewer than 282,000 had declared

[1] Tucker, *op. cit.*, p. 343.
[2] *M C.* of June 1914 speaks of 1,168 African catechists employed in the Vicariate
of North Nyanza alone.
[3] A. B. Lloyd, *Apolo of the Pygmy Forest*, London, 1923.

themselves to be Christians.[1] This proportion, which cannot
have been approached in any other tribe in East Africa, must
be explained by the fact that in Buganda the establishment
of European government marked only the final stage of a
political and social revolution, which had started at least
eight years before Sir Gerald Portal's arrival, and in which
Christianity had played from the first a prominent part.
The British administration crystallised that revolution by
confirming in their positions the natural leaders which it had
thrown up, and by providing them with conditions of peace
and economic progress such as it seldom falls to the lot of
revolutionaries to enjoy. In the remaining districts of the
Protectorate the revolution which gave Christianity its
opportunity was that set in motion by the European government itself, though even here the figure of 140,000 Christians, out of an approximate total of 2,000,000,[2] is high
enough to suggest that the employment of Baganda in
the extension of the administration to other tribes,
though it later came to be resented by the peoples concerned,
did much in the early stages to smooth the progress
of Christianity through Baganda evangelists and to dis-
guise the connection of the movement with its European
originators.

[1] Stock, *op. cit.*, IV, 1897. 155,000 declared themselves as Roman Catholics;
127,000 as Anglicans.

[2] *ibid.* It is to be remembered that the figure of 2,000,000 included large tribes
such as the Lango, the Acholi and the Karamojong, still almost untouched by any
form of western influence.

*   *   *   *

4

As in the outlying districts of Uganda, so in other parts
of East Africa the evidence would seem to show that it was
the spirit of inquiry and the desire for cultural renaissance
set in motion by the European governments, as their
occupation became effective, which enabled the missions to
expand beyond their closed communities, until each station
occupied by European missionaries became the centre of a
network of out-stations from which African teachers and
evangelists could carry their influence into the villages
around. In the north-east of the German colony, close to
the seat of government and to the earliest European plantations, the U.M.C.A. had rejoiced as early as 1891 over the
growing interest of the Wabondei and Wazigua in the
education provided by the mission.[1] Near by, among the
progressive Wachagga, the Holy Ghost Fathers achieved
during the first ten years of German rule one of their swiftest
victories. Thirteen years after the foundation of the first
station at Kilema it was reported that the neighbourhood
was 'virtually Christian'.[2] Just before its division in 1907
the Vicariate of North Zanzibar counted 14,000 Christians,
and its European staff of 165 had been supplemented by 130
African catechists.[3]

After the destruction of the Arab strongholds to the south

[1] Bishop Smythies in *C.A.* 91. 46: 'The effect of German rule is salutary. . . . We
are now able to take the line that we will send teachers when the people themselves
build the school.'

[2] *MC.* 04. 462.

[3] *ibid.*, 06. 566.

of Lake Victoria and around Lake Tanganyika,[1] the old-established missions of the White Fathers began to report considerable expansions. In the South Nyanza Vicariate, the Wasumbwa provided the first of many examples of mass movements following upon the conversion of the para-mount chief.[2] The kingdom of Ukerewe followed next, and lastly the seven sultanates of Bukoba district. In the Vicariate of Unyanyembe, with more than 7,000 adherents, there were in 1905 sixty-one African catechists as against forty-three European missionaries.[3] The Vicar Apostolic of Tanganyika, Mgr. Lechaptois, reported in 1902 that a European staff of thirty-five and forty-three African cate-chists were instructing 9,300 catechumens and 2,400 neophytes. In addition to the seven European stations, there were thirty more in charge of Africans; while at Karema there was a regular training school for catechists, who were emerging at the rate of ten a year.[4]

In the isolated and unexploited areas of the centre and the south, however, it was not until the suppression of the Maji-Maji rebellion that the missionaries noticed any significant change from the pre-European conditions. In 1905 throughout the southern half of German East Africa, the forces of tribal paganism made their last fling and were defeated. During the rising, faith in magic achieved an unprecedented intensity. Thousands of tribesmen believed

[1] *MC.* 91. 130 reports the destruction by Emin Pasha of the Arab centre of Masansa to the south of Lake Victoria, and there are numerous references to the fall of the Tanganyika Arabs in reports from that Vicariate. An examination of the German archives at Dar-es-Salaam is, however, an urgent necessity for the events of this obscure period.

[2] Père Dessoignies to Livinhac from Ushirombo. *ibid.*, 94. 245.

[3] *ibid.*, 06. 124.   [4] *ibid.*, 02. 289.

steadfastly that baptism with water from the hot springs at Kibambare would deflect the bullets of the Europeans; and even when the event proved it otherwise, they believed just as firmly that the dead would rise again in three weeks. Tribe fought alongside tribe in defiance of all the established particularist traditions, and, most amazing of all, the secret of the preparations was perfectly kept.[1] According to the considered opinion of the Governor, Count von Götzen, the explosion was not to be attributed merely to the hatred of foreign overlordship by the chiefs and witch-doctors whose vested interests had been affected, but rather to the deep reaching changes which the European occupation was bringing into the rhythm of daily life, with the inevitable but unwanted obligations that it laid upon individuals.[2] When such an effort as this proved to be in vain, it was natural that the reaction should be swift and widespread. The central stations of the Lutherans were just beginning to put forth their first generation of pupils when the demand for teachers arose. Two years after the rising the Berlin I missionaries reported that their work had completely changed in character. Beside the four European stations among the Nkonde, there had grown up twenty-one out-stations and eighty-eight preaching-points (Predigtplätze). Contact with

[1] *Berliner Jahresbericht*, 1905, p. 96.
[2] 'Nicht dass Weisse über sie herrschten und durch Araber, Sudanesen und andere Landfremde dies Regiment ausübten, ist den Häuptlingen, Zauberern und anderen Grossen, von denen der Aufstand ausging, unerträglich gewesen, sondern die tiefgreifende Veränderung, welche diese Fremdherrschaft für ihre alte Lebensweise brachte . . . eine Reaktion heidnischer Barbarei gegen dei übermächtig, einbrechende Kultur, und die mit ihr notwendig verbundene, ungewohnte Lebenszucht.' Quotation from 'Deutschostafrika im Aufstand.' *ibid.*, 1911, p. 3.

the heathen was now almost entirely in the hands of native Christians, the task of the European missionary being to train and supervise African teachers and catechists, and to examine and receive into the Church the catechumens trained at the out-stations.[1] Even more significant was the case of the three or four C.M.S. stations grouped around Mpwapwa. In 1899 there were only 200 baptised Christians after twenty-two years of work.[2] In 1902 Bishop Peel had reported 'indifference, disrespect and contempt of the Gospel' among the Usagara and Ugogo chiefs.[3] But in 1908 the missionaries announced that 'a great wave of interest and inquiry' was passing over their district: new villages were asking for schools, while those already served were pleading for more frequent instruction.[4] By 1914 the mission had more than 5,000 adherents, while reading and writing were being taught at 370 different centres in the district.[5] Even the Moravians, receiving spontaneous requests for education from the Basafwa round Rungwe, were starting to expand beyond their close-knit communities.[6] In 1910, of 1,087 baptised Christians only 714 lived on the central stations, and the native evangelist was becoming the chief instrument of progress.[7]

British East Africa seems to provide no exception to the rule that it was the pressure of a new social order which

[1] *Berliner Jahresbericht*, 1907, p. 119.

[2] Stock, *op. cit.*, IV, p. 78.

[3] Bishop Peel to C.M.S. from Mpwapwa, 29.xii.02. C.M.S. papers.

[4] J. H. Briggs to C.M.S. from Mvumi, near Mpwapwa, 17.iii.08.

[5] Stock, *op. cit.*, IV, p. 78.

[6] *Jahresbericht der Brüdergemeine*, 1906, p. 95. Rungwe had been built and settled by imported Nkonde workmen, who were also the first converts. *AMZ.* 07. 31.

[7] *Jahresbericht der Brüdergemeine*, 1910, p. 38.

provided the conditions under which Christianity could expand, although, the coastal area apart, the missionary occupation was itself so late that no very marked expansion occurred until the First World War. It is significant, however, that the first expression of interest by the Kikuyu in the activities of the C.M.S. occurred in 1909 in the shape of a desire for the knowledge of reading and writing as accomplishments connected with the most highly paid employment on the newly established European farms.[1] It is significant, also, if only of the experience which David and Henry Scott had brought to Kikuyu from Nyasaland, that in 1911, when the Church of Scotland Mission numbered but twenty-three baptised Christians and forty-two catechumens there were already eleven out-stations under African teachers and twenty-two pupils in the 'teachers' class'.[2] Describing the agricultural activities of his mission, the Superior of the Consolata Fathers in 1908 made the following luminous comment:

Si la religion est, par sa nature même, la mère de la civilisation, bien souvent, pour arriver à la religion, il faut passer par la civilisation. La connaissance de Dieu est pour l'homme (pour le sauvage en particulier) proportionnée à la connaissance qu'il a des choses qui l'entourent.[3]

Faced by new problems for which tribal precedent offered no solution, it was to the Christian mission that the bemused

[1] For this information I am indebted to a manuscript 'History of the C.M.S. in the Highlands' by Mr. C. Granston Richards of Nairobi.
[2] *Kenya 1898–1948*, p. 21.
[3] Article by Phillippo Perlo in *MC*. 08, 211.

African often turned for help. If he lived within a few days'
journey of a mission station, the pagan African knew well of
the existence of white men who were teaching black men
the new wisdom. Before the European occupation had
become a real factor in his life, he had not troubled himself
very much about them. Once or twice, perhaps, they had
come to his village, and told a tale, badly mangled by an
interpreter, of one Jesus, who had fertilised the earth with
His blood, and who had left His words in a book which the
preacher had held in his hands while he talked. In those days
the African's world had been stable enough. He had felt no
need to place himself in the hands of a stranger who would
probably bewitch him. Now, however, when the sands were
shifting under his feet, when, perhaps, his chief had been
imprisoned by the Europeans, when their soldiery patrolled
the land, collecting taxes and conscripting him to work on
the roads, he recalled the tale of the new and powerful
medicine, and in consultation with the headman or the
village elders he agreed that it would be wise to send a
deputation to the mission to ask for a teacher of the new
ways. At the station, the missionary told him that if the
chief or the headman would build a large hut, a teacher
would be sent as soon as possible. He also explained to him
something of the significance of the great white chieftaincy
which had in many fields of life displaced his own, and
advised him to meet its demands for taxes and labour. In
cases of special hardship, if there had been a famine or an
epidemic, the missionary might even write a letter to his
European brother at the government station, asking for a
temporary exemption from the imposition; and this would

be construed by the village as a foretaste of the magic which would follow with the teacher.

Imagine [wrote Bishop Kitching] a rough shed, built of mud and wattle . . . and thatched with grass. . . . Very likely, it is leaning sideways and is propped up with extra poles at varied angles. A few gaps left in the mud serve for windows and doorways. At one end the floor is raised a few inches by way of a chancel, and a pole or bamboo runs across as a Communion rail. At each side a mud-walled enclosure does duty as reading-desk and pulpit. On the inside of the roof hang innumerable hornets' nests, and possibly a few bats. On the walls, suspended from little pegs, are sheets displaying the alphabet, or rows of syllables, some of them nibbled by intrusive goats or fretted by the ubiquitous termites. Look in at about 8.30 in the morning and you will see groups of readers, of mixed ages and sexes, seated on the floor in front of the sheets, saying over the letters or syllables in a singsong voice. . . . Somehow they get the syllables memorised and eventually are promoted to reading consecutive print. . . .[1]

Such was the out-station. It was the least spectacular branch of the missionary enterprise, but also the most important; for it was in this form that Christianity reached the big battalions. The native catechist, of slender intellectual attainments, presiding over the syllabic chorus and interspersing it with crude denunciations of drunkenness and dancing, of polygamy and witchcraft, from beneath the shelter of a wretched hut, has seemed to many European observers a pitiable reflection of western bigotry. To the

[1] A. L. Kitching, *From Darkness to Light*, 1935, p. 31. The date is immaterial. What was true of the remote diocese of the Upper Nile in the twenties was certainly true of less remote places in the 1900's; and is true of minor villages all over East Africa today.

African villager he was the apostle of the new learning, preaching emancipation from the old law, and opening vistas of a more ideal life which was attainable at least by the young and enterprising. No other interpretation can account for the phenomenal expansion of these out-stations, both Catholic and Protestant, during the early years of European rule. The entry to the one lay through symbol and ceremony, to the other through literacy and the Book: the strength of both was their conquest of the newly realised limitations of the tribal life.

*   *   *   *

5

The final illustration of the motives which brought the pagan African to seek out the teaching of the missions is to be found in the closely corresponding expansion of Islam in certain parts of East Africa. Though its adoption had been a natural consequence of the intermarriage of Arab and Persian settlers with the coastal populations since the tenth century, it seems that the penetration of Islam into the interior started only shortly before the arrival of the Christian missionaries, and that its wholesale diffusion was, like that of Christianity, an indirect result of the European occupation. The Arab slave-trader had not in general been a missionary: to have proselytised his victims would indeed have precluded him from enslaving them. But among the tribes who were allied to the Arabs, there had certainly been some religious assimilation to Islam before the arrival of Europeans. The Baganda remember the name of one Ahmed bin Ibrahim who had expounded the principles of Islam to Suna, the father of Mutesa; and the Arab or Swahili scribe had long been a familiar figure at the courts of the Yao chiefs living round the headwaters of the Rovuma. It was difficult even for eye-witnesses to assess the religious influence of these travelling Muslims, since, unlike Christian missionaries, they demanded no baptismal renunciation of ancient beliefs, and their followers could express their adherence by an infinite number of gradations, from simple imitation of dress and demeanour to the stringent obser-vance of circumcision, fasting and prayer. It is significant that, away from the coast, no missionary of the pioneer period had seen the Arabs as anything more than political rivals. W. P. Johnson, who had been travelling the Rovuma and Nyasa regions since 1875, first commented on the appearance of Islamic proselytism in 1892, a few months after the last slave-dhow on the lake had been sunk by the British gun-boats,[1] and the Uganda missionaries, for all their knowledge of the Arab 'faction', seem scarcely to have con-sidered the religious impact of Islam until Lugard's intro-duction of Sudanese troops.

The European occupation, however, gave to the superior Swahili population something of the same prestige as it gave to the Baganda, and thus carried a militant host of Muslims from the coast into the interior. In Buganda itself, the first domestic servants of the European officials were Swahilis

[1] W. P. Johnson, *My African Reminiscences*, p. 202: 'It seemed as if the slavers, checked by the Government, were determined to extend their *moral* force.'

from the coast.[1] Throughout East Africa the first military
garrisons were manned with Sudanese or Swahili troops.
Most of the skilled craftsmen, many of the earliest traders, a
high proportion of the government interpreters and the
foremen on the European farms were Swahili Muslims. In
the German colony, the administration for many years
developed and extended the system by which the Sultans of
Zanzibar had governed their possessions on the mainland.
The District Officers ruled directly through Swahili akidas
and jumbes, who were recruited in the coastal towns and
trained in government schools at Dar-es-Salaam and Tanga.[2]
To the African villager, especially if he lived far from a
missionary centre, these black invaders must have appeared,
both by weight of numbers and by racial propinquity, the
most significant element of the new régime. They were
often the visible instruments of the new authority which
was shaking the foundations of his world. Frequently, it
was they who brought for sale the wonderful wares of the
West. If he sought employment on a European farm, or if
he was conscripted for work on a road or a railway, it was
they who stood in comfort and watched over his toil. They
knew something of the wider world at the coast and beyond,
which worshipped the One God and followed the precepts of
the Prophet. Their understanding of the Koran might be
imperfect, their observance of religious practices might be
meaningless; but to the pagan African it would at once be
apparent that membership of the great brotherhood of the
faithful would confer at least that sense of sophistication,
which, in his tribal parochialism, he so signally lacked.

[1] Stock, *op. cit.*, IV, p. 96.   [2] Hailey, *An African Survey*, p. 435.

Significantly, it was during the same three or four years in which the German missions were experiencing a spontaneous demand for their ministrations that they noticed that Islam was moving as fast or even faster than Christianity. Nyamwezi porters were found to be observing the fast of Ramadhan in 1904. In 1907 Islamic proselytism was noticed by Berlin I and by the Moravians, and was even reported by the Berlin III missionaries in far-off Ruanda.[1] In the same year the German officer at Mpwapwa advised the C.M.S. to spread northwards into the Kondoa district, where Muslim teachers were said to be at work.[2] By 1908–9 the progress of Islam was high on the agenda of every missionary conference in East Africa and was filling the pages of the missionary magazines at home. At the World Missionary Conference at Edinburgh in 1910 a letter was read from the venerable Professor Gustav Warneck, who had ruled the policy of the Lutheran societies for thirty years, in which he said that priority over every other missionary problem of the day should be given to the race against Islam for the animist peoples of the world.[3]

The rivalry of Islam first brought the German missions into politics. Its prestige, they soon realised, arose largely from the fact that there was a Muslim in nearly every subordinate post in the Government.[4] In 1906 the Moravians reported that pagan Africans, who had formerly identified the Government and the missions, were now beginning to distinguish between them on precisely this

[1] Klamroth, 'Islam in Deutschostafrika', *AMZ.* 10. 481.
[2] Minutes of C.M.S. Executive Committee, Usagara section, 30.i.07. C.M.S. papers.
[3] *Berliner Jahresbericht*, 1910, p. 80.   [4] *ibid.*, 1909, p. 84.

matter.[1] They now knew that they could have civilisation without Christianity, for they saw educated yet polygamous Muslims at every government station.[2] In 1907 the Konde Synod of Berlin I, which ten years earlier had so flatly opposed the movement for 'Erziehung zur Arbeit', decided upon a policy of education for government posts.[3] At the Kolonialkongress at Berlin in 1910 it was argued by missionary supporters that a Muslim East Africa would be an anti-European East Africa;[4] but it was not until 1913 that the German Government agreed to subsidise missions to train subordinate officials for the pagan districts of the interior.[5]

In the British territories, strangely, it was the governments rather than the missions which saw the dangers of the Islamic expansion, and which took what steps they could to forestall it. Sir Arthur Hardinge, in his first report on the East Africa Protectorate, did indeed remark that the Arabs and higher Swahilis were 'the only element with any comprehension of politics, justice or government', and outlined a scheme by which an administrative class could be trained up in special schools, where, side by side with instruction in the Koran, the pupils could receive a practical education in English and mathematics, 'besides being taught athletics, riding and out-door games and thus weaned from those habits of indolence and vice which are so rapidly corrupting the race'.[6] But Hardinge's school, and indeed the just interests of the Arabs, faded from the picture when Nairobi

[1] *Missionsblatt der Brüdergemeine*, 1906, p. 165.   [2] *Berliner Jahresbericht*, 1908.
[3] *ibid.*, 1907, p. 119.   [4] *ibid.*, 1910, p. 80.   [5] *ibid.*, 1913, p. 94.
[6] Report by Sir A. Hardinge on the East Africa Protectorate from its establishment to the 20th July, 1897. *Accounts and Papers*, 1898, LX, p. 199.

replaced Mombasa as the seat of government; and Sir Harry Johnston, who ruled Uganda from 1899–1901, held very different views on the Muslim question. The Government, he said, could not afford to ignore the political issues involved in the religious conflict. Since paganism must eventually yield all along the line either to Christianity or Islam, it was 'in every sense to be desired' that it should be to the former. 'To those who fear the possibility of a Muhammedan revival the importance of Uganda as a strong bulwark in Equatorial Africa gradually spreading Christianity to its surroundings must be at once apparent.'[1] Wherever Islam had not obtained complete control of the people, therefore, the administration, 'without anything like compulsion or undue pressure', was advising the native chiefs to encourage Christian schools and mission stations.[2]

*   *   *   *

6

The fact that Islam was able, without the assistance of professional missionaries, to expand, if not at the expense of Christianity, at least side by side with it, is in itself a reason for qualifying the assertions of a later generation of missionaries that Christianity was 'the natural sublimation of African animism'.[3] It may perhaps be argued that both

[1] Uganda Report for 1903–04. *ibid.*, 1905, LVI, p. 275.

[2] Uganda Report for 1901. The implementation of this policy is evident from a preliminary examination of the Secretariat records at Entebbe, especially from the documents relating to Busoga.

[3] The phrase is that of Bishop Gresford Jones, *op. cit.*, but it could be paralleled many times over from the pages of the *International Review of Missions*.

Christianity and Islam found a *point d'appui* in the notion of a Supreme Being, which lay in the dim background of most of the tribal religions of East Africa.[1] But it is more probable that, had the element of monotheism been in fact a considerable one, African beliefs would have offered a stouter resistance than they did. Evidence concerning the nature of the Christian expansion shows rather that it was the parochialism of tribal religions which proved their undoing—the fact that the basic monotheism had been so overlaid by the cult of tribal ancestors and the sanctification of tribal customs, that belief was shattered by the first impact of wider-than-tribal government.

Moreover, if missionaries found that belief in Christian doctrines came easily to Africans, they soon discovered also how difficult and foreign was the practice of Christian morality. 'When the white man brings him so much knowledge that is obviously superior to anything he has so far met with, he is ready to believe that most of what is taught is true. . . . But the holiness of God is a strange novelty.'[2] This was a fact which had scarcely come to light in the days when handfuls of Christians lived in isolated communities round the mission-stations, or under the conditions of persecution endured by the infant churches of Mackay and Lourdel. The period of deployment through African catechists into villages far from the mission centres, however, brought a flood of disciplinary issues among baptised Christians, which well illustrated the difficulties of transition from a communal to an individual code of morality. It

---

[1] cf. J. J. Willis, 'Presentation of Christianity to Primitive Peoples'. *IRM.*, July 1914.   [2] A. L. Kitching, *op. cit.*, p. 16.

is recorded that Bishop Weston heard 500 cases of marriage offences during a single visit to Masasi,[1] and again that in 1911 he interviewed more than 1,000 people who had been disciplined for moral offences, only about half of whom could be received back into communion.[2] In 1910 no less than 73 out of 1,087 Moravian Christians had been placed under the lesser excommunication;[3] and two years later the figure stood at 166 out of 1,557.[4] Subtracting the numbers resident in the mission villages, the casualty rate at the out-stations must have been something like one in four.[5] No other society was courageous enough to publish the statistics. The Leipzig missionaries, however, reported in 1910 that a majority among them had become convinced that 'an African who had passed the age of puberty and who was left in his accustomed environment could never become more than a nominal Christian (Scheinchrist).[6] Anglican missionaries in Uganda also complained of nominal Christianity during the early years of the century.[7] Bishop Tucker was no disciplinarian, but in 1906 he judged the situation serious enough to hold a 'Mission' similar to that inaugurated by Pilkington in 1893.[8] Bishop Willis found it necessary on his accession to institute a searching inquiry into the state of Christian morals and to introduce the threat of excommunication at the Synod of 1913.[9] There is little evidence about Roman Catholic experience during the same

[1] H. Maynard Smith, *Frank, Bishop of Zanzibar*, 1926, p. 87.
[2] *ibid.*, p. 94.
[3] *Jahresbericht der Brüdergemeine*, 1910, p. 38.
[4] *ibid.*, 1912, p. 45.
[5] 713 in 1910. *ibid.*, p. 38.
[6] *Leipzig Jahresbericht*, 1910, p. 90.
[7] cf. *CMI*. 04. 502 and Stock, *op. cit.*, IV, p. 95.
[8] Tucker, *op. cit.*, p. 329.
[9] Stock, *op. cit.*, IV, p. 96.

H

period. The White Fathers always maintained strict rules of probation and pre-baptismal training; and as early as 1893 Bishop Hirth found it necessary to limit still further the number of baptisms at certain stations in order that the missionaries might have time to hear confessions properly.[1] At a conference of Roman Catholic bishops at Dar-es-Salaam in 1912 it was decided that candidates for Baptism must spend one year in the 'Hearers' Class', followed by at least two more in the formal catechumenate, during which their observance of the externals of Christian morality would be carefully watched.[2]

The problems of discipline raised by the rapid diffusion of Christianity called the attention of most missions to the social and economic facts of African life, and set them to probe solutions preventive rather than punitive. In particular, both medical and educational work came to be viewed, no longer as rather dubious auxiliaries of evangelism, but as means of consolidating the Christian life among those who had already been baptised. There had of course been missionary doctors in East Africa since the days of Livingstone. The most prominent of the Presbyterian pioneers, both in Nyasaland and in British East Africa, had been ordained doctors. The C.M.S. had employed doctors in East Africa since 1875. Hine, Bishop of Nyasaland from 1896 till 1901 and of Zanzibar from 1901 till 1908, was a doctor. But the idea of a medical mission as something existing in its own right developed only with the growth of a Christian community, to which the work of a doctor could

---

[1] Hirth to Livinhac, 3.iii.93, in *MC*. 93. 398.
[2] Schmidlin, *op. cit.*, p. iii.

be related.[1] It was not until 1885 that the C.M.S. appointed a sub-committee to consider the place of medical missions; and even then this body reported that they were useful 'where the Gospel could not easily be preached by ordinary evangelists, or among aboriginal and uncivilised people likely to be impressed by the kindly influence of medical work'.[2] The old idea of the missionary doctor was symbolised by Bishop Tucker taking Dr. Albert Cook on his pioneer journeys in Ankole and Acholiland, in order that the preaching of the Word might be reinforced by signs and wonders. But as the Churches grew, and as increasing numbers of baptised Christians had to be disciplined on charges of witchcraft and polygamy, it came to be realised that the medical mission was necessary as a social institution of the Christian community. If the witch-doctor was to be eliminated, with all that he symbolised of sub-Christian fears and hatreds,[3] the missionary doctor must abandon his evangelistic itinerations, stay in his hospital and train African nurses and medical assistants to replace the diviner in village life. And equally, if the children of monogamous marriages were to survive in sufficient numbers to compensate for the renunciation of polygamy, then maternity work, child welfare and infant dietetics must all come within the missionary's sphere.[4]

[1] cf. E. M. Anderson, *Healing Hands*, 1950, p. 11 *sq.*
[2] *ibid.*, p. 18.
[3] See, for instance, Bruno Gutmann's early work on the Chagga in the *Ev.-Luth. Missionsblatt*, 1907, p. 15, or Rösler of Berlin III in *Nachrichten aus der ostafrikanischen Mission*, 1906, p. 192.
[4] cf. Direktor von Trittlevitz of Berlin III on 'Soziale und kulturelle Aufgaben', *Nachrichten*, 1905, p. 150; and S. W. W. Witty, *Medical Missions in Africa and the East*, 1922, pp. 7–18.

Again, as the Christian community increased, education began to outgrow its avowedly evangelistic beginnings. The first schools at the central stations of both Catholic and Protestant missions had been designed to train catechists. When Protestant missions later made literacy the normal test for Baptism, it was intended as a test of sincerity rather than of education.[1] In essence there was little difference between their out-stations and those of the Roman Catholics, where teaching was usually oral. These out-stations or 'bush schools' survived for many years—indeed they still survive—as the normal instrument of Christian expansion. Above them, however, there gradually developed a hierarchy of more regular schools, often self-supporting through fees, and concerned not primarily with religious instruction but with the consolidation of the Christian community. In Uganda both Catholic and Anglican missions were aware of the advantages they had reaped from the stratification of African society: Buganda was perhaps the classic example of conversion from the top. It was natural therefore that both missions should have sought to maintain their initiative with the upper classes by establishing 'schools for the sons of chiefs'. The most exclusive of these institutions, the Eton and Downside of Buganda, were the King's School at Budo[2]

[1] 'Large numbers were coming forward and asking for Baptism. Of their life we knew nothing. 'Very well,' was our answer, 'We don't know you. We must test you We must see that you have an intelligent knowledge of the way of salvation. Here are the Gospels. We will teach you to read them, and when you have read them we shall expect you to give an intelligent answer to the questions which we shall then ask you.' Tucker, *op. cit.*, p. 234.

[2] Budo, founded in 1906 by H. W. Weatherhead, later joined by his brother H. C. T. Weatherhead, was attended by the young Kabaka Daudi Chwa, and in 1908 charged the considerable fee of £7 a year. For a summary of educational developments in Uganda to 1914, see J. J. Willis in *C.M.R.* 15. 654 *sqq.*

and St. Joseph's College at Kisubi; but the idea of the chiefly boarding school spread far and wide, to Ngora in Teso, to Maseno in Kavirondo, to Ushirombo in the Vicariate of Tabora, to both Catholic and Lutheran missions among the Chagga of Mount Kilimanjaro.

Another idea, which was possibly more prominent in theory than in practice, was that of Industrial Education. Whereas literary education developed out of the school for catechists, industrial education sprang from the mission buildings, the mission church, the mission press and the mission estate. As such, it was more characteristically a feature of Catholic missions, who aimed to be nearly self-supporting and who recruited and trained regular orders of lay-brothers to undertake these secular tasks, than of Protestant missions, who relied almost entirely on the salaries they received from the home constituency and who always found the greatest difficulty in recruiting European artisans. Nevertheless, as the expanding Churches suffered increasing disappointments from within their ranks, the minds of Protestant missionaries turned partly to economic remedies. 'I do not see', Archdeacon Farler had written, 'how you can raise man's spiritual life unless you raise his bodily life to correspond.'[1] This was possibly a counsel of despair from a man who was shortly to retire from missionary work on grounds of ill-health; but it reflected a growing opinion that successful adherence to a new faith might involve the adoption of certain new economic and social standards. If the African Christian was to abandon his place on the old ladders of economic prosperity and social prestige

[1] *CA.* 96. 101.

by practising monogamy, he must be compensated by learning a trade or new methods of agriculture which would open the way to new ambitions. If his children were to sleep at home and live a Christian family life, he must have a house with two rooms instead of one. If he was to read his Bible, his house must have windows to admit the light, and therefore its shape must be square and not conical; nor could he afford to rebuild it every five years to meet the needs of shifting cultivation. If his children were to be educated, he must learn to do without their services on the farm and yet earn enough to pay their school fees. Again, to pay the government tax and his Church tithe he must have ready money; and, if he was not to leave his family to work on a railway or a plantation, he must produce not only for himself but for the market.[1]

And so, during the period of consolidation after the first great deployment, the 'pious industrial superintendents', so contemptuously dismissed by Dr. Cust,[2] so strongly advocated by Sir Bartle Frere, began to figure in the plans of the most evangelical missions. Berlin I engaged an agriculturalist to try to solve the economic problems of their converts.[3] Berlin III reported experiments in new crops which their adherents could grow and sell for cash.[4] The Church of Scotland Mission and the C.M.S. taught printing, smithing, carpentry and brick-making. In 1904 Mr. Victor Buxton, a member of the C.M.S. Committee, founded the Uganda Company and East African Industries Ltd. in order to

---

[1] cf. *AMZ.* 09. 134, and *Berliner Jahresbericht,* 1913, 107.

[2] *supra,* p. 25.

[3] *Berliner Jahresbericht,* 1912, p. 108 *sqq.*

[4] *Nachrichten aus der ostafrikanischen Mission,* 1905, p. 150.

provide employment for the mission's industrial trainees.[1]
It is difficult to assess just how far missionary initiative at this
period was responsible for economic developments in East
African society, how far, as distinct from other factors, it
influenced peasant agriculture or helped to produce a class
of artisans. What little evidence there is suggests that industrial education too often lifted Africans out of their own
society only to enmesh them in the web of European economic enterprise. Certainly technical education did not,
like literary education, develop into a mass movement, in
which the pupils of the European missionary themselves
became teachers, supporting themselves directly or indirectly on indigenous contributions. Indeed it is probable
that the greatest service of the industrial movement to the
Christian community lay less in the material enrichment of
its individual members than in the churches and cathedrals
with which it began to adorn a landscape too little tamed by
human arts.

*   *   *   *

7

The most important, the most difficult and the most con-
troversial of all the works of consolidation, however, was the
introduction of order and government into the nascent
African Churches, as distinct from the missionary organisations which had brought them into being. The most striking
feature of the early expansion of Christianity had been its

[1] *CMI.* 04. p. 65 and *CMR.* 09. pp. 9–18.

informality. The pupils of a few years' standing, able perhaps to read a gospel or recite a catechism, had become, almost insensibly, the teachers of a wider circle. But these scarcely commissioned catechists, though they might win adherents from a paganism which was visibly failing to meet the demands of new and outside pressures, were helpless to build up the life of the Church on the traditional basis of the Word and the Sacraments. Until Africans could be set apart as priests and ministers, the growing body of believers would remain dependent, for Baptism and Communion, for Confession and Unction, upon a necessarily limited number of ordained European missionaries. The preparation of Africans for ordination was, naturally, one of the most conscious aims of every mission working in East Africa; but the very idea of holy orders implied a stability, at least in the externals of Christian morality, not impossible for the first generation of converts to achieve, but impossible to count upon in advance in any individual of the age of an ordinand in Europe. Roman Catholic missions, stiffened by injunctions from the Propaganda, aspired from the first to nothing less than a celibate African clergy, versed in Latin, and armed with a theological learning comparable to that which was imparted in the seminaries of Europe. Such requirements could only be fulfilled by the total adoption and prolonged education of young boys. Bishop Hirth opened a junior seminary in the North Nyanza Vicariate in 1893; but it was not until 1914 that two out of more than 400 aspirants were raised to the priesthood.[1] Protestant policy, by contrast, was to ordain only married men of mature age, who

[1] J. Bouniol, *The White Fathers and their Missions*, 1929, p. 117n.

had proved themselves by long service as catechists and lay-readers. Bishop Tucker early decided to regard only that which was possible as essential:

There were those moving in and out daily amongst us whose faith in Christ had been tested and tried in times of fierce persecution, and whose lives for years past had been given up to the service of their Master.

In 1893 he chose seven such men and ordained them deacons after five months of preparation;[1] and in 1896 three of them were promoted to be priests.[2] But even by the less exacting standards of Protestantism the growth of an ordained clergy was slow. By 1914 the Uganda diocese, with more than 100,000 Church members, had only 33 native priests.[3] The Universities Mission, which had ordained Africans to the diaconate in 1879 and to the priesthood in 1890,[4] had by 1914 less than 20 African clergy; and Bishop Weston had written that 'the increase of the native ministry must for years involve us in the increase of our European staff'.[5] The Church of Scotland Mission in British East Africa had ordained no Africans by 1914, but a standard of comparison may be taken from the Livingstonia mission of Nyasaland, founded in 1875, where Dr. Laws in 1907 licensed for probationary service three young men who had made some progress in theological studies,[6] and ordained two of them in 1914.[7]

[1] Tucker, op. cit., pp. 109–10. Bishop Hannington had in 1885 ordained two African catechists who had come from the freed-slave station at Nasik to work in the Mombasa district.   [2] ibid., p. 192.   [3] Stock, op. cit., IV, p. 94.
[4] Wilson, op. cit., pp. viii–ix.   [5] H. Maynard Smith, op. cit., p. 88.
[6] W. P. Livingstone, Laws, p. 309.   [7] ibid., p. 347.

Closely allied to the problem of an African ministry was that of Church government. To Roman Catholics, indeed, it was identical. Catholic missionaries came to East Africa to found, not new Churches, but new provinces of the Roman Church. Christ was the Head of the Church; but the Pope was His Vicar and Head of the one true Church Visible here below. There was therefore no question of preparing bodies of African Christians for sovereignty or independence. The Church must necessarily be planted in East Africa by Bishops and Priests who were not nationals of the country. As nationals became available, they would, wherever it was expedient, replace the missionaries, but still as Priests and Bishops of the Roman Church, recognising the spiritual authority of the Pope, and themselves eligible for service in any part of the world, for promotion to the College of Cardinals and even to the throne of St. Peter. Further, since both legislative power and financial responsibility were matters for the clergy alone, and predominantly for the hierarchy, Catholic missions knew nothing of the problems of educating the African laity into government by Council and Synod which figured so largely in Protestant systems.

In contrast to Roman Catholics, Protestants of all shades of belief from Anglo-Catholic to Free Church, came to Africa to found new Churches which would one day hold the faith in independence, though not necessarily in schism. Apart from the inevitable bias of their teaching, missionaries usually took what constitutional steps were possible to ensure that these Churches would hold the same doctrine, practise the same forms of government and remain in ecclesiastical communion with the Churches from which they had sprung.

But the religious traditions of all the Protestant Churches prevented their missionaries from being in the ecclesiastical sense imperialists. The official regulations of the C.M.S. argued that

> If Christianity is for all races, all races should eventually have their place within the organisation of the Visible Catholic or Universal Church; but it is agreed on all hands that Asiatic or African Christians ought not to be permanently subject to European Churches; that having regard to both the varied character and the varied circumstances of different nations, independent Churches or Branches of the Church are indispensable; and that these Churches or Branches, in order to be independent, must have their own constitutions, and become self-contained and self-governing, able to perpetuate their own ecclesiastical life.[1]

Self-perpetuation depended according to Anglican practice upon the right of four or more dioceses, grouped together as an ecclesiastical Province under an Archbishop, to elect and consecrate its own Bishops; and this stage of development in East Africa was still far off. Even constitutional self-government by smaller units was in general a development of the post-war period. There was, however, by 1914 one Anglican diocese, that of Uganda, which had progressed far along the paths of self-government and self-support. This was due, not only to the exceptional rapidity of Christian evangelism, but even more to the organising genius of Bishop Alfred Tucker. The traditional practice of C.M.S. missions had been to set up congregational or 'pastorate' councils as soon as a community of indigenous Christians had been formed in any place. These councils had the

[1] Stock, *op. cit.*, IV, pp. 393–4.

duty of approving candidates for Baptism and Church employment, and the financial responsibility for maintaining church buildings and paying native clergy and evangelists who worked within the pastorate. The mission, meanwhile, maintained its own organisation, appointing and paying its own native agents, and keeping the work of evangelistic extension, educational, medical and literary work, and the training of native agents, entirely within its own jurisdiction.[1] Tucker resolutely refused to recognise this arbitrary dichotomy between the Church and the mission, which kept the central government almost exclusively in missionary hands. He refused to commission lay-readers or clergy who were not supported by the Church, and he thereby deprived the mission of the financial grounds for its supremacy. The C.M.S. was left responsible only for the salaries of the European missionaries and their equipment. He next prepared a

---

[1] Stock, *op. cit.*, IV, pp. 398–9, expounded in detail in a Memorandum of the General Committee of the C.M.S. dated 13th April, 1909, and printed in the *Reports of the Edinburgh Conference*, II, Appendix K. The basis of C.M.S. policy on the Edification of the native Church was the famous minute of 1851 by Henry Venn, Secretary of the C.M.S. from 1841–72: 'Regarding the ultimate object of a mission, viewed in its ecclesiastical aspect, to be the settlement of a native Church under native pastors upon a self-supporting system, it should be borne in mind that the progress of a mission mainly depends upon the training up and location of native pastors, and that, as it has happily been expressed, the euthanasia of a mission takes place when a missionary surrounded by well-trained native congregations under native pastors, is able gradually to relax all pastoral work into their hands, and gradually to relax his superintendence over the pastors themselves till it insensibly ceases, and the mission passes into a settled Christian community. Then the missionary should be transferred to the regions beyond.' This position was modified in the memorandum of a special sub-committee presented in 1901 (see *CMI.* of April, 1901) which recommended the early promotion of indigenous episcopates ('although the Episcopate of the Future Churches should be characterised by the simplicity of the Primitive Church') in order that constitutional independence might be expedited and that possible subsequent negotiations with non-episcopal Churches might be upon the basis of the Lambeth Quadrilateral.

Diocesan Constitution which provided, not only for parish or pastorate councils, but also for district councils and a Diocesan Synod, on which African laity and clergy would sit alongside members of the mission, and control the central affairs of the Church through Boards of Education, Missions, Theology and Church Estates.[1] The European missionaries opposed Tucker's constitution for more than eight years; but in 1909 it was unanimously accepted by a conference at Mengo, which was attended by 40 clergy, both European and African, and by 250 lay delegates, of whom an overwhelming majority were Africans. The constitution ensured an African majority in the House of Laity from the start and an African majority in the House of Clergy from the first moment at which the African clergy outnumbered the ordained missionaries working in the diocese.[2] The sole safeguards, therefore, were the Bishop's veto, and the first and fundamental article of the constitution that:

> The Church of Uganda doth hold and maintain the doctrine and Sacraments of Christ as the Lord hath commanded in His Holy Word, and as the Church of England hath received and explained the same in the Book of Common Prayer, in the form of making, ordaining and consecrating of Bishops, Priests and Deacons, and in the Thirtynine Articles of Religion, and further it disclaims for itself the right of altering any of the aforesaid standards of faith and doctrine.[3]

When his constitution had been approved by the Archbishop of Canterbury, as the Quasi-Metropolitan, Bishop Tucker at last felt free to retire, rejoicing in the knowledge that the

[1] Stock, *op. cit.*, IV, pp. 98–9 expanded in *CMR*. 13. 431: 'The Native Anglican Church of Uganda.'
[2] Quoted in *CMR*. 13. 437.   [3] *ibid.*

Church of Uganda, which he had ruled for eighteen years, was now self-governing, 'with power to make its own laws and canons, and to administer its own discipline and funds.'[1] It is strange to reflect that Tucker, who walked 22,000 miles in the service of the African Church, never mastered an African language.[2] Perhaps it was his intuition as an artist which enabled him as an administrator to guide so success-fully the religious stirrings of a people among whom he can have formed fewer individual friendships than any other missionary of his time.

*   *   *   *

8

Another and less orthodox experiment in Church order and government, though it had by 1914 been carried no farther than the conference table, had attracted the atten-tion of the whole Christian world. This was the movement, associated with the name of the Church of Scotland mission station at Kikuyu, for a federation of the Protestant missions of the British East Africa Protectorate,[3] conceived as the first step towards a United African Church. The Kikuyu Con-ference of 1913 has been widely acclaimed as a landmark in the ecumenical movement among the Protestant Churches of the world, which has been perhaps the most persistent feature of the ecclesiastical history of the twentieth century. Certainly Kikuyu raised issues which were of world-wide

---

[1] Tucker, *op. cit.*, p. 344.   [2] Gresford Jones, *op. cit.*, p. 40.
[3] Later the Colony and Protectorate of Kenya.

importance and which have profoundly affected all later schemes for union between episcopal and non-episcopal Churches. It is the more interesting, therefore, to notice the almost parochial problems out of which the movement arose. Significantly, the territory concerned in the Kikuyu proposals was from the point of view of Christian evangelism the least advanced of the mission-fields of East Africa. The number of African Christians affected in 1913 was probably less than 5,000; and not one of them had any voice in its proceedings.[1] The need for the movement arose solely from the uncomfortable proximity of European missions of different denominations in the delectable highland region between Nairobi and Kisumu. During the early years of the century these missions had marked out, usually quite informally,[2] spheres of interest within which they agreed to confine their evangelistic work. With the development of European farms, however, and with the growth of the transport industry, African Christians began to travel from one sphere to another in search of employment. The C.M.S. was the first to establish effective missions in the towns,

[1] For this account of the Kikuyu movement, which, for the sake of proportion, is necessarily much condensed, I have used (i) the official reports of the Conferences of 1909 and 1913; (ii) the excellent retrospective summaries of the movement by J. J. Willis and J. W. Arthur, published in *Towards a United Church*, London, Edinburgh House, 1947; (iii) the relevant chapters of Maynard Smith's *Frank, Bishop of Zanzibar*, and G. K. A. Bell's *Randall Davidson*; (iv) a manuscript, 'History of Christian Co-operation in Kenya', by Archdeacon M. G. Capon, a copy of which is in the keeping of the Kenya Christian Council in Nairobi; (v) a considerable body of unpublished correspondence of Dr. H. E. Scott and Dr. J. W. Arthur, now in the keeping of the Rev. R. G. M. Calderwood, Head of the Church of Scotland Mission, Kikuyu.

[2] Capon, *op. cit.*, quotes a case in which Scott of the C.S.M. and Leakey of the C.M.S. climbed a hill near Kikuyu, and agreed upon a boundary running between two clumps of trees, which were subsequently unidentifiable.

especially in Mombasa, Nairobi and Kisumu, which were excluded from the system of spheres, and thus frequently instructed and baptised the former adherents of other missions, many of whom later returned to live in non-Anglican spheres. As time went on other pastoral problems arose which called for co-operation between different missions. Catechists dismissed by one mission for misbehaviour would be engaged by another a few miles away, often at a higher salary than that which they had lost. Christians under discipline from one denomination would transfer their allegiance to another. Adherents of the American 'Gospel' missions would ask to be received by Anglicans or Presbyterians who offered superior facilities for education.[1]

It was pre-eminently J. J. Willis, later Bishop of Uganda, who raised a situation containing all the possibilities of unseemly competition between rival European missions to a higher level. Willis had already given much thought to the strategic disposition of Christian forces against those of Islam in East Africa;[2] and he was genuinely more concerned at the prospect of a Kenya divided in its religious allegiance between eight little Protestant Churches than with the questions at issue between the different missions. As an Anglican, however, he was perhaps better aware than the leaders of other denominations of the limits of immediate compromise; and as a priest of the highly developed diocese of Uganda, of which his own Archdeaconry of Kavirondo was a mission field, he maintained from the first that an ecclesiastical union which involved separation from the outside affinities of the various missions concerned, would be one

---

[1] Capon, *op. cit.*   [2] *CMI.* o6. p. 82.

bought at too high a price.[1] The primary idea which Willis sought to promote was that, while the nascent African Churches of Kenya were still in a passive and plastic state, no unnecessary differences should be allowed to become habitual among African Christians; that, on the contrary, the edification of these Churches should proceed 'upon converging lines', through the recognition by all missions of a single standard for Church membership, a single code of discipline, a common attitude towards certain native customs, a common form of simple worship which could be used with sufficient frequency for it to become familiar to all African Christians, and similar courses of training for African ministers based upon a common recognition of the Scriptures and the Creeds. It was this idea which Willis with the sympathetic assistance of Dr. Henry Scott, the Head of the Church of Scotland Mission presented to a series of preliminary conferences in 1908 and 1909[2] and which resulted in the formulation by the four largest missions working in the territory[3] of the Proposals for a Federation of Missions,

[1] *Report of the United Missionary Conference held at Nairobi, June 7th–11th*, 1909. (Advertiser Coy., Nairobi, 1909). Copy in C.M.S. papers, B.E.A., 1909, No. 126.

[2] Willis had his first conversations with Dr. Scott in 1907. In 1908 a Conference of missionaries working in the Kavirondo district was held at the C.M.S. headquarters at Maseno and was attended by members of the A.I.M. (interdenominational), Seventh Day Adventists, and American Friends. In 1909 a conference for the Kikuyu area was held at the A.I.M. headquarters at Kijabe and was attended by Willis (C.M.S.) and Dr. Scott (C.S.M.). The Nairobi Conference in 1909 was attended by delegates from all the above missions, plus the United Methodist Mission at Mombasa and the English Friends Mission on Pemba. Representatives of all these missions were appointed to the standing committee which drafted the Kikuyu proposals; but the two Quaker missions, and also apparently the Seventh Day Adventist Mission, withdrew their full support during the interval between 1909 and 1913: their representatives attended the Kikuyu Conference but did not sign the proposals.

[3] The C.M.S., the C.S.M., the A.I.M. and the United Methodists.

which were accepted for reference to the home authorities of the various denominations at the Kikuyu Conference of 1913.[1]

The fact that the proposals went beyond what the Anglican Communion as a whole could sanction arose, it would seem, out of the retention of the system of spheres which might logically have been abolished when federation was adopted. For the strict observance of spheres made it certain that large numbers of Christian travellers would remain without access to the ministrations of their own Churches, and therefore made it very hard to refuse the principle that these Christians might seek Communion from ministers of other denominations. And yet, to Anglicans, to admit this principle was to call in question the whole basis of an episcopally ordained ministry. Such an admission, though not explicitly stated, seemed to be clearly implied in the Kikuyu proposals;[2] and the impression of irregularity was reinforced by the Bishop of Mombasa's administration of the Holy Communion to the delegates of all denominations except the Quakers at the close of the 1913 Conference. Much of the celebrity of the proceedings derived from the

---

[1] *Proposed Scheme of Federation of Missionary Societies working in British East Africa* (Leader, Nairobi), 1913.

[2] *ibid.*, p. 6. Rules are laid down for the reception at the Sacrament of the Lord's Supper in any mission of visiting communicants from other missions. The Anglican Church is clearly bound to administer the Sacrament to visiting communicants from other missions, and this practice was upheld by the Central Consultative Body of Lambeth against Bishop Weston's contention that the Sacrament could only be administered to such as were 'ready and desirous to be confirmed'. Equally, other missions are bound to administer the Sacrament to visiting Anglican communicants, if these should apply for it. 'The Kikuyu proposals', says Bishop Willis in *Towards a United Church*, p. 42, 'do not go so far as to bid or advise such intercommunion; but they do not forbid it.'

dramatic and over-hasty action of Bishop Weston of Zanzibar, 'the Zanzibarbarian', in formally indicting his brother Bishops of Mombasa and Uganda before the Archbishop of Canterbury for 'the grievous faults of propagating heresy and committing schism'.[1] While controversy raged in pamphlets and newspapers, the Central Consultative Body of the Lambeth Conference, to whom Archbishop Davidson had referred the issue, expressed every sympathy with the Bishops of Mombasa and Uganda, but upheld the Bishop of Zanzibar in three important points: they deprecated the word Federation; they declared that the united Communion service should not be treated as a precedent; and they ruled that, while Bishops might in certain circumstances admit Christians of other denominations to Anglican altars, 'Anglican Churchmen must contend for a valid ministry as they understand it, and regard themselves as absolutely bound to stipulate for this for themselves'.[2]

Weston's intervention and the judgment of the central Anglican authorities need not have been decisive. Had the early initiative behind the movement been less predominantly Anglican, the other three missions might have proceeded with the federation, with limited Anglican participation. As it was, the standing committee of the Kikuyu Conference in December 1915 put forward an only slightly modified set of proposals—this time for an Alliance of missions—which still professed reunion as their ultimate gaol, and which were accepted by the four societies at the

[1] The formal charge was not admitted by the Archbishop, because Weston had formulated it under a misapprehension that the proposed Federation had actually taken place. See Maynard Smith, *op. cit.*, p. 149 *sqq.*
[2] J. J. Willis in *Towards a United Church*, p. 47.

Second Kikuyu Conference in 1918.[1] Inevitably, however, the Anglican démarche had stiffened the opposite wing of the movement.[2] And Africa Inland Missionaries now realised, as perhaps they had not done before, that communion with the C.M.S. would necessarily involve also communion with the U.M.C.A.; and they persisted in an irrational belief that High Churchmen were modernists.[3] Bishop Weston attended the 1918 Conference and presented a list of startlingly simple proposals for a United Church, which might conceivably have been acceptable to the delegates of 1913;[4] but discussion of them was silenced by C. E. Hurlburt of the A.I.M., who roundly declared that 'no basis was possible which placed the church above the Word of God, no ritual which would take the place of personal communion, and no ecclesiastical control which limited personal liberty in vital things'.[5] Other factors had developed since 1913 which helped to make a United Church in Kenya a remote aspiration. The nascent Churches themselves were no longer so passive and plastic as they had once been; and the entry after the war of large numbers of new European settlers served on the one hand to explode the idea of a purely 'native' Church, and on the other to create problems of race relations calling

---

[1] J. W. Arthur, in *Towards a United Church*, pp. 58–62.

[2] *e.g.* C. E. Hurlburt, Director of the A.I.M. to Bishop Willis of 22.iv.16, requires two concessions from the C.M.S.: (i) Liberty for Anglicans attending Baptist churches to be immersed (*i.e.* re-baptised) if they so desire; (ii) exclusion of non-teetotallers from full membership. C.S.M. papers, Kikuyu.

[3] They had evidently not studied *Ecclesia Anglicana—for what does she stand? An open letter to Edgar, Bishop of St. Albans by Frank, Bishop of Zanzibar*, Longmans, London, 1914.

[4] Arthur, *op. cit.*, p. 56.

[5] *ibid.*, pp. 57–8.

for a more practical kind of Christian co-operation, for which the organisation of the Alliance was peculiarly well suited.[1]

In one respect the course of the Kikuyu movement was symbolic of the course of the missionary movement throughout East Africa. In a real sense, the decade before the First World War may be said to mark the zenith of the missionary influence. The young Churches were still far from having reached their greatest numbers or the height of their power; but they had reached the farthest point of their development at which the influence of the European missionary was still supreme in all departments of their life. The Edwardian missionary governed unaided at the centre of the Church. He legislated about native customs and Church discipline. He controlled the finances. And he still entered at some point into the life of every Christian convert. Already it was the African catechist who made contact with the heathen and who taught to neophytes the elementary doctrines of the faith; but it was, with rare exceptions, the ordained missionary who presided over the final instruction and examination. It was a time when European priests and ministers trudged incessantly over vast parishes, encouraging evangelists, baptising catechumens and dispensing the Sacraments to Church members, when Bishops tramped a thousand miles a year to supervise, ordain and confirm. During the post-war period the systems of theological training established by the Edwardian missionaries bore their fruit. With the steady flow of Africans into the clerical ranks, African Christianity began to acquire a momentum of its own; and

[1] *infra*, Chapter V.

the missionary factor began to recede from its dominant position in the outward life of the African Church and to concentrate upon those still central but more specialised functions, of which theological training was the first and most important example.

Chapter Five

MISSION, CHURCH AND STATE, 1914-49

I

IT IS CURIOUS for a European to reflect upon the conclusion, reached by Professor Latourette after surveying the world-wide development of the faith, that not only was Christianity stronger in 1944 than it had been in 1914 but also that these thirty years had constituted one of the greatest periods in its long history.[1] For in Europe, and especially in the Protestant North of Europe, the Christian outlook had scarcely established its position against the determinist philosophies of natural science and against the first application of scientific method to Biblical studies, when it suffered the much wider impact of the First World War. This catastrophe shattered the faith of Europe in the moral values which it had inherited from the nineteenth century, and gravely injured the Churches which had seemed to be so closely connected with those values. Imperialism in general and missions in particular fell sharply in the esteem of a public opinion which no longer felt that western civilisation had incalculable benefits to confer upon inferior races, and which was even being stimulated by the discoveries of social scientists to a revival of the romantic cult of the noble savage. This unpopularity was inevitably reflected in the financial support of missions

---

[1] Latourette, *op. cit.*, VII, p. 3 *sq.*

in the sending countries and also in the recruitment of new workers. The number of Protestant missionaries working all over the world increased by 43 per cent between 1911 and 1925, but slightly declined between 1925 and 1938.[1] The Roman Catholic Church maintained the momentum of its missionary recruitment but suffered severely in financial support.[2]

It was partly for these negative reasons that missions of the most modern period were so successful in establishing the Oriental and African Churches upon an indigenous basis. Had the supply of missionaries from the sending countries been greater, there might have been a tendency to consolidate western control and to have formed merely a collection of ecclesiastical colonies in eastern lands. Moreover, the prevailing distrust of western civilisation was shared by post-war missionaries themselves. It was less and less assumed that Christianity must be presented to non-Europeans in the political, social and economic context of European culture. Papal pronouncements, Lambeth Encyclicals and the resolutions of missionary conferences stressed the importance of preserving so far as possible the fabric of indigenous societies and of encouraging appropriate varieties in liturgy and devotions.[3] In other ways, too, the faithful core of western

[1] M. Searle Bates, *Data on the Distribution of the Missionary Enterprise*, International Missionary Council, London, 1943.

[2] *Africanae Fraternae Ephemerides Romanae*, the periodical of the Conference of Catholic missionary societies working in Africa, April 1936, p. 81, shows that according to statistics supplied by Cardinal Salotti, Secretary-General of the Propaganda, the central missionary funds of the Catholic Church declined by 50 per cent in the five years, 1931–5.

[3] *e.g.* the 'Summi Pontificatus' of Pius XII, 28.x.39; the Lambeth Conference of 1920, reported by Edwyn Bevan in *IRM.*, July 1921; and E. W. Smith, *The Christian Mission in Africa*, London, 1926, being an account of the Le Zoute Conference.

Christianity responded both to the intellectual attack and to the challenge of world events. The ecumenical movement, drawing its main inspiration from the missionary elements in the Protestant Churches, did much to supplant the older notions of the Christian civilisation of Europe waging war upon the pagan barbarism of the East by the new conception of a world-wide Christianity arrayed against a secularism which was at least as dangerous in Europe as anywhere else. John Mott, the greatest of the ecumenical leaders, was tireless in prophesying that the rising nationalisms of Asia and Africa would destroy Christianity along with western imperialism unless the faith could be early established under indigenous leadership.[1] At the World Missionary Conference at Edinburgh in 1910 the representation of non-European Christianity had been minute; at Jerusalem in 1928 it was substantial; at Madras in 1938 it was preponderant.

The Roman Church under a succession of outstanding Popes achieved a similar revolution in its missionary outlook. Pius X carried out an important reform in 1908, by removing the older mission fields of northern Europe and America from the jurisdiction of the Propaganda, and by empowering the more specialised Congregations, the Consistorialis, the Consilii, the Studiorum and the Sacramentorum, to exercise their appropriate functions even within Propaganda territory.[2] The Cardinals and the regular staff of the Propaganda

[1] John R. Mott, *The Decisive Hour of Christian Missions*, New York, 1912, pp. 29–31.

[2] By the Constitution 'Sapienti Consilio' of 29.vii.08. Hilling: 'Die rechtliche Stellung der Propagandakongregation nach der neuer Kurialreform Pius X' in *ZMW*. 11. 147.

were thus freed from a mass of multifarious and unrelated business and enabled to exercise an effective control over missionary policy and development.[1] Backed by a series of important Encyclicals of Benedict XV and Pius XI, the modern Propaganda became a potent factor in promoting the training of indigenous clergy and in hastening indigenous episcopates in the mission lands.[2] Viewing as it did the Oriental and African situation as a whole, it pressed for development at a pace which incurred among missionaries in the field something of the same suspicion which colonial officials have sometimes felt towards the forward policies of Whitehall.

In East Africa the numerical growth of Christianity between 1914 and 1944 was phenomenal. By 1938 Christians were about 8 per cent of the population in Kenya, 10 per cent in Tanganyika and 25 per cent in Uganda.[3] Roman

[1] The internal organisation of the Propaganda during the modern period is described by Anton Freitag S.V.D. in *ZMW*. 22. 51. The full congregation of about twenty-five Cardinals meets monthly to review important business such as senior appointments and the creation of new dioceses. A more specialised body of seventeen Cardinals meets weekly and is assisted in its deliberations by a panel of about thirty 'Consultants', who are the representatives in Rome of the missionary Orders of the Church. The day-to-day business is conducted by the Cardinal Prefect, assisted by a Secretary-General, an Assistant Secretary for oriental rites, four Secretaries for geographical regions and a staff of 'Minutants' and Clerks. The Pope has regular appointments with the Cardinal Prefect on the first and third Thursday in each month and with the Secretary-General on the second and fourth Monday.

[2] Especially the Encyclicals 'Maximum Illud' of Benedict XV of 30.xi.19, and 'Rerum Ecclesiae Gestarum' of Pius XI of 28.ii.26. Both stress the importance of an indigenous clergy and emphasise that according to experience there is no inherent difference in capacity between Europeans and non-Europeans.

[3] Latourette, *op. cit.*, VII, pp. 234–8, and J. I. Parker, *Interpretative Statistical Survey of the World Mission of the Christian Church*, International Missionary Council, London, 1938.

ROMAN CATHOLIC VICARIATES APOSTOLIC
WITH CHRISTIAN POPULATION 1946

EQUATORIAL NILE
120,000
(VF)

NYERI
25,000
(CF)

UPPER
NILE
UGANDA 247,000
190,000 (MH)
(WF)

MERU
7,500
(CF)

RUWENZORI
185,000
(WF)

MASAKA
121,000
(AS)

KISUMU
175,000
(MH)

BUKOBA
95,000
(WF)

MUSOMA
MASWA
11,000

ZANZIBAR
40,000
(IIG)

MWANZA
24,000
(WF)

(WF)

Mombasa
Apostolic
Delegacy

(HG)

KIGOMA
9,000

(WF)

TABORA
19,000
(WF)

MBULU
7,000
(Pal.)

KILIMANJARO
63,000

DODOMA
23,000
(Pas)

BAGAMOYO
67,000
(HG)

KAREMA
77,000
(WF)

(WF)
TUKUYU
14,000

IRINGA
21,000
(CF)

DAR-ES-SALAAM
32,000
(OMCap)

African Secular Priests   AS
White Fathers   WF
Holy Ghost Fathers   HG
Mill Hill Fathers   MH
Benedictines   OSB
Consolata Fathers   CF
Verona Fathers   VF
Passionist Fathers   Pas.
Pallotine Fathers   Pal.
Capuchins   OMCap

PERAMIHO
110,000
(OSB)

(OSB)
NDANDA
26,000

40°E

Catholics increased from about 300,000 in 1914,[1] to just over 1,000,000 in 1938,[2] and to 1,700,000 in 1946.[3] Three-quarters of the first total and slightly less than half of the second and third were from Uganda.[4] The Anglican Church, despite the fact that it respected the territorial spheres of other missions in Kenya and Tanganyika for the greater part of the period, grew from about 225,000 in 1914 to 400,000 in 1938 and to about 750,000 in 1946;[5] but Uganda was responsible for no less than nine-tenths of the 1914 total and for about three-quarters of the other two. In Tanganyika the Lutheran Churches of the German societies increased, in spite of two serious interruptions in European missionary work from about 20,000 in 1914 to 92,000 in 1938 and to 150,000 in 1949.[6] In Kenya the Presbyterian Church founded by the Scottish Mission, which had numbered less than 1,000 in 1914,[7] grew to 10,000 in 1938[8] and to 15,000 in 1947.

These gains bore but small relation to changes in the strength of the European missionaries working in the territories. In the absence of complete and appropriate statistics it may be estimated that Protestant missionaries remained

[1] cf. Latourette, *op. cit.*, v.

[2] Parker, *op. cit.*

[3] *Delegatio Apostolica Africae Orientalis et Occidentalis Britannicae. Status Missionum*, Mombasa, 1946.

[4] 225,000, 477,000 and 861,000 respectively.

[5] This figure is my own estimate, but based upon information personally communicated by the Anglican Bishops.

[6] 'Reports of the Augustana Lutheran Mission and the former German Missions in Tanganyika, 1949.'

[7] Baptised Christians numbered 1,333 in 1922. *Kenya 1898–1948*, p. 48.

[8] Parker, *op. cit.*, also gives the following statistics for 1938: Africa Inland Mission (undenominational), 13,951 Christians; Seventh Day Adventists, 13,707; Methodist Missionary Society, 1,611.

constant at about 1,000 throughout the period,[1] and that Catholics approximately doubled their numbers, reaching a total strength of 2,300 in 1946.[2] A large proportion of the missionary forces, however, was even in this period engaged in the opening of new work in hitherto untouched areas, where the number of adherents gained was but a small fraction of the total Christian increase. During and after the First World War for instance, the Nilotic-speaking area of northern Uganda was entered in force by the Catholic Verona Fathers from the Sudan[3] and also by the C.M.S. from the south.[4] Again, in the early twenties the Benedictines of St. Ottilien concentrated in the south of their former sphere,[5] leaving Swiss Capuchins from the Seychelles and the Italian Consolata Fathers from Kenya to open what was virtually new work in the area to the south-west of Dar-es-Salaam[6] and in the southern Highlands.[7] In 1925 the C.M.S. began to associate its former German East Africa

[1] M. Searle Bates, *op. cit.*, p. 5, gives a total of 1,181 for 1925, which is probably correct. His figure of 1,858 for 1938 is certainly in error, since in the analysis by territories in Parker, *op. cit.*, p. 21, the total is 958, and this figure is confirmed in the analysis by societies on p. 111.

[2] The last figure is from *Delegatio Apostolica Africae, op. cit.* The first overall statistics are to be found in the *Catholic Directory of East Africa*, Mombasa, 1932, and even here the returns from several vicariates are omitted, so that only a general estimate is possible.

[3] This region was divided from the Bahr-Ghazal Vicariate as 'Equatorial Nile' in 1932.

[4] The Upper Nile Diocese was divided from Uganda in 1926. From 1926 till 1936 this diocese included also the Southern Sudan, which was temporarily divided from the Diocese of Egypt.

[5] The Prefecture Apostolic of Lindi became an Abbacy Nullius in 1927, which was divided into the two Abbacies of Ndanda and Peramiho in 1931.

[6] The Capuchin Vicariate of Dar-es-Salaam dates from 1922.

[7] The Prefecture Apostolic of Iringa, created in 1922, headquarters of the Consolata mission being at Tosamaganga.

Mission[1] with the C.M.S. of Australia, and with this fresh access of strength was able to open up a new field in the remote region bordering on the Belgian mandate of Urundi. In the late twenties White Fathers from the Tanganyika Vicariate started work in the same area[2] and also extended their southern limits beyond Lake Rukwa to the Northern Rhodesia frontier.[3] In 1926 the Augustana Synod, American Lutherans of Scandinavian origin, entered the virgin field to the north of the Tanganyika Central Railway and started work among the Iramba and Turu tribes.[4] During the thirties Roman Catholics filled the gap between the effective spheres of the White Fathers and the Holy Ghost Fathers, Pallotine Fathers staffing a new Vicariate of Dodoma,[5] with Passionists to the north of them in the Mbulu district.[6]

These new fields, absorbing most of the increase in missionary personnel, yielded for the most part only the meagre fruits of pioneer work.[7] The grand numerical progression was registered in the older fields, with southern Uganda still well in the lead; and was due less to the momentum supplied by foreign missionaries than to that of the developing organisations to which they had given rise. In all six of the

---

[1] Erected into a separate diocese (from Mombasa) of Central Tanganyika in 1925.

[2] The Tanganyika Vicariate was divided into Karema and Kigoma in 1946.

[3] Forming an Independent Mission in Tukuyu in 1932 and a Prefecture Apostolic in 1938.

[4] This mission became of great importance during and after the Second World War, since it took over the supervision of the German Lutheran fields on the expulsion of the German missionaries.

[5] Prefecture Apostolic, 1935.   [6] Prefecture Apostolic, 1943.

[7] Two representative example are (i) the Augustana mission, which after twelve years had sixteen missionaries and 3,800 Christians; (ii) the Tukuyu mission of the White Fathers, which after sixteen years had twenty-four missionaries and 14,500 Christians.

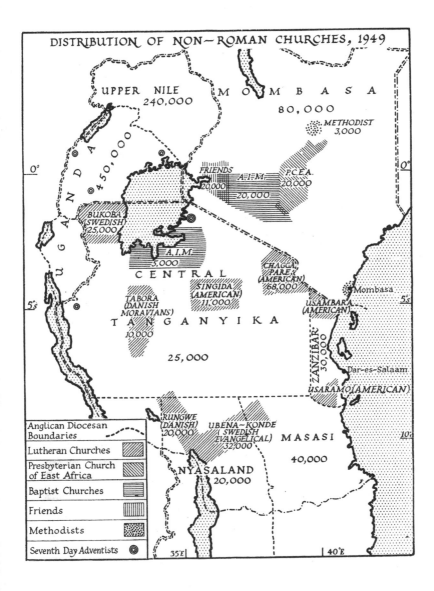

DISTRIBUTION OF NON—ROMAN CHURCHES, 1949

UPPER NILE
240,000

M O M B A S A
80,000

METHODIST
3,000

450,000

FRIENDS
20,000

A.I.M.
20,000

P.C.E.A.
20,000

BUKOBA
(SWEDISH)
25,000

A.I.M.
3,000

C E N T R A L

CHAGGA,
PARE,
(AMERICAN)
68,000

SINGIDA
(AMERICAN)
11,000

USAMBARA
(AMERICAN)

Mombasa

TABORA
(DANISH
MORAVIANS)
10,000

T A N G A N Y I K A

ZANZIBAR
30,000

Dar-es-Salaam

25,000

USARAMO (AMERICAN)

RUNGWE
(DANISH)
20,000

UBENA—KONDE
(SWEDISH
EVANGELICAL)
32,000

M A S A S I
40,000

NYASALAND
20,000

Anglican Diocesan Boundaries	
Lutheran Churches	
Presbyterian Church of East Africa	
Baptist Churches	
Friends	
Methodists	
Seventh Day Adventists	◎

35°E

40°E

Anglican dioceses African clergy by 1938 outnumbered the ordained European missionaries;[1] by 1950 they were about four to one. In the Lutheran Churches ordained Africans were drawing level with the Europeans in 1938; in 1949 they outnumbered them by three to one. In 1947 there were 11 African Presbyterian ministers in Kenya as against three Europeans. African priests in Roman Catholic orders, who were required to undergo about eighteen years of education and to take the usual vows of celibacy, were even at the end of the period in a minority of one to five to the ordained European missionaries. Nevertheless their numbers grew from 2 in 1914 to 80 in 1938 and to 208 in 1946, when there were also 385 aspirants in the last stage of their training.[2] When in 1939 the southern portion of Uganda was divided off as the Apostolic Vicariate of Masaka and entrusted to the care of an African Bishop and fifty-six African secular priests, Catholic missionaries might justifiably have complimented themselves upon their observance of the adage: 'C'est le premier pas qui coûte.'[3]

Beside and under the ordained ministry, moreover, the semi-literate catechists of the pre-war age had developed into an organised body of professionals, closely integrated with the emerging parochial system. The base of the ecclesiastical organisation was still the village evangelist, who was by now a scholar of some four years' standing, who taught literacy and the catechism on weekdays and conducted simple worship on Sunday. Above him, and supervising the

---

[1] In Protestant missions ordained missionaries were about one-fifth of the total in 1938. In Catholic missions they were slightly less than half in 1946.

[2] *i.e.* in the 'Senior Seminary' or last seven years of the course.

[3] Authorities as for pp. 234-6 above.

work of three or four evangelists in other villages, was a superior kind of lay-reader, who had received a year or two of special training over and above his regular schooling, and who in Protestant Churches would often be an aspirant for the ministry. A half-dozen or so of these groups of villages, each under a lay-reader, would form in the Protestant Churches the parish of an ordained minister, a parish rather larger in size than an English Rural Deanery, with a central church, probably by now of brick, at the minister's place of residence. At this centre the parson would preside over the monthly meetings of his Church Council, which dealt with local questions of discipline and finance; and from it he would go out, on foot or by bicycle, to visit his numerous flock, to examine and baptise catechumens and to supervise the work of subordinate Church teachers. The Roman Catholic parish was an even more extensive unit, which might have as many as 150 village evangelists working within its boundaries. This was necessary, since the European missionary priests were regulars and even the African clergy, though secular, were a diocesan clergy of the Augustinian type, living in communities of at least three and usually of six or more. The Catholic 'mission', whether it was staffed by Europeans or Africans, was by this period something of a landmark in the countryside. It was built almost invariably upon a hill, and round the considerable church of sun-dried brick there was usually grouped a clergy-house, a house for lay-brethren, a nunnery, a workshop, a medical dispensary and schools for boys and girls, all solidly built, and set in the middle of gardens and plantations which made it as nearly as possible self-supporting.

I

If these parochial centres of the Roman Church were still for the most part in European hands, the Catholic missionary at least lived close to the native Africans. He seldom returned to Europe more than once in his career, and in the poverty and simplicity of his food and furniture there was little to which an African priest might not aspire.[1] Outside the Roman Church only the Anglo-Catholic missionaries of the U.M.C.A. practised the same simplicity. They too lived unencumbered by the family ties which so complicate the life of the European in the tropics. They too planned their parish centres in such a way that they could be handed over to Africans without any material alterations. The European parish priest of the Universities Mission, living beside his church in a house of mud and thatch without wood in the doorways or glass in the windows, often quite alone and without speaking English for weeks on end, represented indeed the very extreme of missionary assimilation to the environment. At other Protestant stations missionaries lived in comfortable bungalows set in spacious gardens and furnished, though modestly, in unmistakably European fashion. They travelled in motor-cars, albeit old ones. Their wives and families necessitated large domestic staffs and regular visits to Europe. They presented an example of Christian family life, but in an economic setting which was far beyond anything to which an African minister could aspire and in a family and racial privacy which only their domestic servants could penetrate. Still, except in the pioneer areas, the

---

[1] African priests always serve a period of probation at a European mission station, and, so far as it is possible for a visitor to observe, share entirely in the life of the European clergy.

'District' or 'Rural Deanery' tended by the modern period to be the smallest pastoral unit under the care of a Protestant missionary. The Archdeaconry, or its equivalent, was a more usual unit for a European; and the African clergyman was beginning to appear by the end of the period even at this exalted level. The diocesan or other administrative centre still wore a European air, as did the theological college, the hospital and the secondary boarding schools which were usually concentrated within a few miles of it; but elsewhere the European-occupied mission stations of any one denomination tended to be of the order of fifty or even a hundred miles apart.

During the modern period, therefore, ordained pastoral missionaries were rapidly becoming only the apex of the pyramid of Church organisation; and the financial contribution of the missionary societies and Churches which sent them was almost as closely limited. The six Anglican dioceses in East Africa, which were representative of other Protestant Churches in this respect, each received an average sum of about £17,000 from their supporting societies in 1938,[1] and these sums covered little more than the salaries and allowances of European missionaries directly engaged in pastoral and evangelistic work.[2] The contributions of African Church members, though amounting to only a third or a

[1] Parker, *op. cit.*, p. 150 *sq.* According to such figures as were personally communicated to me by the ecclesiastical authorities in 1949, it would appear (i) that European contributions have decreased by about 30 per cent since 1938, although these losses have been partly offset by increases in Government grants, for which see note 2 below; (ii) that African contributions have increased by approximately 40 per cent.

[2] Educational and medical missionaries were by this time very largely supported out of government grants, as will be explained later in this chapter.

half of these sums, in fact covered by far the greater part of the pastoral and evangelistic work carried out by the much more numerous African staff. The salaries of lay evangelists before the Second World War were as low as £5 a year; while the stipend of an African clergyman ranged from £10 to £25, as against the £650,[1] which was the estimated cost of a married European missionary. The distribution of the financial burden between Europe and Africa in the Roman Catholic Church is harder to assess; but in spite of the vastly greater amount of pastoral work performed by Europeans, it would seem that the financial contribution of the European constituency was actually smaller, and proportionately very much smaller, than that of the aggregate of the Protestant constituencies. Apostolic Vicariates and Prefectures[2] received annual subventions of about £2,500 from the central funds of the Society for the Propagation of the Faith, which was the equivalent of about £35 per head of European staff. These sums were augmented by undisclosed amounts from the Congregations to which the missionaries belonged, and individuals were also encouraged to receive assistance from relations and friends up to a certain standard.[3] Even bearing in mind the exiguous material standards maintained by Catholic missionaries and the extent to which they lived off the produce of mission estates, it seems scarcely credible that these European funds sufficed for the needs of the European

[1] This figure was quoted by the General Secretary of the C.M.S. to the C.M.S., Australia, in 1930.

[2] Numbering 24 in 1946.

[3] For this information I am indebted to personal communications by Catholic missionaries, and especially by Mgr. F. X. Lacoursière, the Vicar Apostolic of Ruwenzori, and Mgr. A. Holmes-Siedel, the Vicar Apostolic of Karema.

staff, much less for the subsidisation of pastoral activities by Africans. A tithe of 1*s.* a year was collected from African Church members, and if, as missionaries claimed, the proceeds were insufficient to pay the African clergy and catechists, the 'Mission Funds' used to supplement it must almost certainly have been funds locally raised or earned.[1]

*   *   *   *

2

It is therefore against the background of ecclesiastical organisations already largely African in personnel and increasingly self-supporting in finance that the specific contribution of the European missionary factor during the modern period has to be examined and assessed. It must not be forgotten that at least half of the foreign missionaries and almost the whole of the financial resources which the missions received from Europe were still devoted to the support of these pastoral organisations. Nevertheless, this part of the missionary contribution was steadily diminishing in significance. As the indigenous institutions took shape, the pastoral missionary became less an initiator than a caretaker, holding an already well-defined position until a native of the country should be ready to occupy it. There remained, however, one field in which the action of the foreign missionary was both creative and unique. The young Church had been planted

---

[1] Tithe collected in the Ruwenzori Vicariate amounted to close on £4,000 in 1949. The African staff of the Vicariate in 1946 consisted of 18 priests, 15 brothers, 138 sisters and 1,137 catechists.

in lands which were still governed by a European power, and which became during the modern period increasingly subject to secular European influences, both official and unofficial. As these influences grew in strength, the position of the European missionary as the intermediary between the African Church and the European State became ever more responsible.

During the interval between the European occupation of East Africa and the First World War, missionaries had scarcely needed to consider their relations with the State. The first stages of colonialism had been in nearly every respect favourable to the spread of Christianity. For England the acquisition of Uganda and Kenya had been mainly a grudging concession to philanthropy and national pride. Even Lugard and his small following, who had looked forward to a time when these territories would be valuable as a market for British manufactures, had seen that time as lying in the far future. The East African territories were regarded as being in cold storage against a time of need. The sole requirement of the metropolitan country, therefore, had been that they should become financially self-supporting at the earliest possible moment. Edwardian administrators, with this limited objective before them and unruffled by any local agitation for better living conditions, had not been under any pressure to force the pace of development. Their modest innovations in the fields of law and order, taxation and public works had been sufficient to stir the local populations into a desire for some wider than tribal knowledge, a desire which Christianity had often been able to satisfy. But they had not been so far-reaching as to be an embarrassment to the missions in their work. They had made no breach in the old social order which seemed too wide for Christianity to fill. They had undermined the foundations of tribal paganism, but not so fast as to leave a void exposed to western materialism. Even the beginnings of European settlement in Kenya and German East Africa do not seem to have been regarded by pre-war missionaries as prejudicial to the interests of their adherents. During the modern period, by contrast, the missionary world was conscious of being engaged, with only stationary or diminishing forces, against a steadily growing body of western influences, whose operation was by no means necessarily favourable to the growth of African Christianity. And in these circumstances the struggle with tribal paganism began to assume an air of only transitory importance by comparison with the position of Christianity relatively to the other outside forces which were engaged upon the transformation of the African scene. As at the time when their position had appeared to be threatened by the violent inroads of the Arabs, so now, missionaries felt compelled to enter the political arena and to protect by wider than spiritual methods what they believed to be the interests of the African Church. In these efforts they exercised an influence upon the development of a new phase of colonial policy which no historian of East Africa can afford to ignore.

The first stage of the missionary intervention was occasioned by the decision of General Northey, the first post-war Governor of Kenya, to encourage the settlement of ex-servicemen in the Colony. The African population of Kenya had already suffered severely during the war. Casualties in the army and in the 'carrier corps' had been disastrous, less through enemy action than through a disgraceful lack of quarter-mastering and medical services. Famine and disease had been the inevitable consequence of war. The supply of voluntary labour had already proved too small for the existing body of European settlers; and the Government had been compelled by the war emergency to put political pressure on native chiefs to send their people out to work on the farms. It was clear both to missionaries and to many officials that a further influx of European employers could be supported only by the continuance and intensification of a policy which came perilously close to compulsory labour by Africans for the private gain of individual Europeans. These fears were confirmed when in October 1919 Northey issued the severest of a series of labour circulars, instructing government officials to 'exercise every possible lawful influence to induce able-bodied male natives to go into the labour field'.[1]

Missionary opposition to Northey's policy found an effective channel for expression in the Alliance of Protestant Missions set up at the Kikuyu Conference of 1918.[2] It may perhaps seem a sad anticlimax to the original high objects of the Kikuyu movement that it should have found its greatest importance as a political pressure group asserting the right of Africans to grow eventually to a status of equality with members of other races. But it is arguable that the very existence of racial problems in Kenya exploded the value of the Kikuyu concept of a United Native Church, and made it more urgent for denominational Christianity to transcend

[1] Conveniently summarised in Buell, *op. cit.*, I, p. 332 *sqq.*
[2] *supra*, p. 228.

the barriers of race than for a racial Church to transcend the barriers of denomination. And so, shortly after the publication of the labour circulars, the Bishops of Mombasa and Uganda joined with Dr. Arthur of the Church of Scotland Mission in a Memorandum to the Secretary of State, pointing out that the authorisation of government officers to act as recruiting agents for the European farmers opened wide the door to almost any abuse. To the native chief, who was dependent for his position on the goodwill of the District Officer, there could be no practical difference between 'lawful influence' and a direct command. The Memorandum challenged the justification which was commonly argued by the settlers that by such labour the native was brought into edifying contact with a superior civilisation and taught the dignity of manual work. Compulsory recruiting, it asserted, meant that the African tribesman had to 'leave his house unthatched, his crops unreaped, his wife unguarded, perhaps for months at a time, in return for cash which he does not want'.[1] In May 1920 the Alliance made a further protest to the Secretary of State against the decision of the Legislative Council to raise the native poll-tax from five rupees to eight. They affirmed that in spite of all assurances natives, including women, were already being forced into the labour market by the policy of 'encouragement'; and they now felt that increased taxation was primarily another step in the same direction. No improvement in medical, educational, agricultural or veterinary services had resulted from previous

---

[1] The so-called 'Bishops' Memorandum' reprinted in Milner's *Despatch on Native Labour*, 1920, Cmd. 873. See also *The Serfs of Great Britain*, a pamphlet by the Rt. Rev. Frank Weston, D.D., London, 1920.

increases in taxation; and in the present instance the Legislative Council had refused to accept any proviso that the increase in the revenue should be earmarked for the benefit of the natives from whom it was to be raised. In these circumstances, the letter concluded, missions were finding it increasingly difficult to teach their adherents to be loyal to the Government.[1]

These protests by themselves evoked only a tardy and unsatisfactory reply from the Imperial Government.[2] Their historical importance was due to the presence in London, and at the head of an organisation which could speak collectively for all the British missionary societies, of a man of outstanding vision, ability and tact, who was to figure for many years as one of the most deeply thinking and creative personalities who collaborated in the evolution of modern imperial policy in East Africa. The Conference of Missionary Societies in Great Britain and Northern Ireland had been one of the earliest products of the ecumenical movement, and its first secretary, Dr. J. H. Oldham, had been John Mott's right-hand man since the World Missionary

[1] Alliance to Secretary of State, 20.v.20. In archives of the Christian Council of Kenya, Nairobi: Secretariat File. Accompanying correspondence of Dr. Arthur shows clearly that the real initiator of this protest was a senior government officer who in a letter to Arthur of 17.xii.19, expressed his anxiety at the Government's native policy and suggested that missions might combine in protest.

[2] In two dispatches to Governor Northey (printed in Cmd. 873) Milner instructed the administration to prevent the chiefs from abusing their authority, reasserted the very distinction between advice and commands which the critics had declared invalid and concluded that since there was 'no question of force or compulsion . . . the Protectorate Government would be failing in its duty if it did not use all lawful and reasonable means to encourage the supply of labour for the settlers, who have embarked on enterprises calculated to assist not only the Protectorate itself, but also this country and other parts of the Empire by the production of raw materials which are in urgent demand.'

Conference in 1910. He had been organising secretary of the Edinburgh Conference itself and secretary of its Continuation Committee, which became permanent as the International Missionary Council in 1921. Oldham was young enough to appreciate the new powers of centralised control which governments had taken to themselves during the war, and which they would not easily relinquish. He saw the danger that in such conditions the so-called neutrality of the State in religious matters could in fact mean the elbowing of the religious factor from one department of public life after another.[1] But he was also wise enough to see the openings for expert knowledge in fields where the State was beginning to 'plan'. And he was able and industrious enough to keep abreast of the officials, to counter policy with policy, and often to arrive first with a solution. As early as 1917 he had made his mark with the civil authorities over the difficult question of alien missionaries working in India and Africa;[2] and when, according to the terms of the Versailles Treaty, the property of German missionary societies was transferred to trustees of the same faith as the missions involved, it was once again Oldham's specialist knowledge which was needed at every turn.[3]

And now, during 1919 and 1920, amid the pressure of other business ranging to the ends of the earth, Oldham was patiently making himself an expert on questions of land and labour in Kenya, and in East Africa generally. Great files of correspondence from Kenya missionaries, dealing province

[1] J. H. Oldham in *IRM.*, April 1919.
[2] G. K. A. Bell, *Randall Davidson*, II, pp. 931-4.
[3] *ibid.*, p. 933, Government Memorandum on Alien Missionaries reported in *IRM.* 19. 334.

by province with the application and effect of the labour laws, were received at Edinburgh House.[1] Several government officers home on leave had called and privately expressed their doubts about the policy.[2] Missionary reports had been submitted in strict confidence to senior officials for comment and advice. The views of the Labour Party and of other possible supporters[3] had been ascertained. The Bishops of Uganda, Mombasa and Zanzibar had been consulted during their return for the fifth Lambeth Conference.

In July and August a draft memorandum was circulated to the thirty-one members of the Conference of British Missionary Societies for their approval. In October a slightly amended version started the round of the Heads of Churches. The name of Cardinal Bourne, who was to have been approached by Bishop Weston, was alone missing from the list of signatories.[4] In an almost daily correspondence with Randall Davidson at Lambeth, Oldham unfolded his plans 'to unite the religious and moral forces of the country in a strong approach to the Government'.[5] The Archbishop placed at Oldham's disposal his unrivalled knowledge of public men and their 'weight'; and the final list of signatories

[1] London headquarters of the International Missionary Council and of the Conference of British Missionary Societies.

[2] One of them made the interesting suggestion that either Bernard Shaw or G. K. Chesterton should be invited to visit East Africa.

[3] Notably Lionel Curtis and the Round Table group.

[4] The above statements are drawn from Mr. Oldham's correspondence in two large files marked East Africa: Native Labour.

[5] J. H. O. to A. of C., 6.x.20. Mr. Oldham's correspondence with the Archbishop is collected in a single folder in the files mentioned above, and forms a particularly valuable historical source, in that the two men were working hand in hand over the question and therefore kept each other fully informed of all new developments as they occurred.

included Lords Balfour, Bryce, Cave, Haldane and Salis-
bury; J. R. Clynes, W. E. Elliot, Arthur Henderson, Samuel
Hoare, E. Hilton Young, J. H. Thomas and E. F. L. Wood
from the Commons; Ernest Barker, Louise Creighton,
Margaret Bondfield, Ramsay Muir, Gilbert Murray,
Michael Sadler, R. H. Tawney, J. J. Thomson, Beatrice
Webb, C. K. Webster and Alfred Zimmern. On 27th
November Milner dined at the Old Palace, Canterbury,
and consented to receive the completed memorandum from
a small deputation at the Colonial Office on 14th December.[1]

Under the title 'Labour in Africa and the Principles of
Trusteeship',[2] this document raised issues much wider than
the original protests. Quoting the Covenant of the League
of Nations and Milner's own acceptance of the Trusteeship
doctrine in the House of Lords in May 1920, it pointed out
that behind the question of the Labour Ordinances there lay
the grave situation arising from 'the existence in Kenya and
elsewhere in Africa of two civilisations at very different
stages of development'. Members of one civilisation were
politically conscious and had already acquired a powerful
voice in the Government: members of the other were not
even represented. While the difficulties of the settlers were
recognised as real and deserving of sympathy, attempts to
overcome them must not be allowed to sacrifice irrevocably
the interests of the native population and its chances to
develop.

[1] A. of C. to J. H. O., 29.xi.20.
[2] Three slightly different drafts as well as the final printed version are preserved
at Edinburgh House, representing the different stages of its composition (i) to Dr.
Arthur and the three Anglican bishops; (ii) Heads of Churches; (iii) Public men.
The present summary is taken from the final version.

Without a clear, resolute and continuous policy on the part of Government, directed to the fostering of native life and institutions, there is grave danger that the pressing needs of European farms and plantations, together with the requirements of Government, may make such demands on native labour as may lead to the destruction of village life.

About the desirability of preventing idleness there was no difference of opinion; but it was just as possible to inculcate habits of industry by a policy of education within the Reserves, by the demonstration of improved methods of agriculture, as by forcing the natives to seek work on European plantations. Such methods, combined with the attraction of voluntary labour to European farms by proper inducements and good conditions, and the gradual stimulation of needs through contact with a more advanced civilisation, would in time achieve the desired end 'without the unfortunate results which beset any attempt unduly to force the pace'.

Finally and emphatically, the Memorandum asked for the appointment of a Royal Commission to inquire into the guiding principles of imperial policy in the East African Crown Colonies and Protectorates, with special reference to:

(i) The adequacy of the Reserves and the security of land tenure by natives.

(ii) The amount of land alienated to Europeans and the estimated supply of labour necessary to cultivate it; the capacity of the native population to provide such labour without injury to the healthy development of native life.

(iv) The effect of contact with western civilisation upon the tribal system, the position and authority of chiefs and headmen, native law, custom, habits and family life; the best means of dealing with these changes to ensure a sound and orderly development of native society.

(v) The economic and moral advancement of the native population, by the teaching of improved methods of cultivation, the development of native industries, the dissemination of a knowledge of health and sanitation and education generally.

(vii) The best means of obtaining expression of native opinion in matters affecting their interests and adequate representation of these interests in the government of the country, and in training the natives in responsibility and the management of their own affairs.

The fact that a Royal Commission was for the present refused by the Government is less significant than that the outline of a constructive policy, commanding the approval of an influential group of public men, and suggesting most of the important issues which were to be investigated by the Ormsby-Gore Commission of 1924 and the Hilton Young Commission of 1928, had originated in a missionary agitation, and had been distilled from criticism into counsel by the pen of a missionary leader.

During the spring of 1921 Oldham was away in India; but when he returned he found that Milner had been succeeded at the Colonial Office by Churchill, with Edward Wood[1] as Under-Secretary. Another reason for renewing the attack was that Governor Northey in a new circular had instructed District Officers to discourage natives from growing 'cash crops' in the Reserves; but, in his opening letter to the Archbishop of Canterbury, Oldham discouraged any public

---

[1] Now Lord Halifax.

denunciation of this circular, because it would divert attention from principles to Northey as an individual.[1] Instead, he wrote a confidential 'Memorandum on Native Affairs in East Africa', which was privately transmitted to Wood by the Archbishop.[2] In this document Oldham summed up the evidence from the African field that compulsion was having harmful results, and quoted extensively from the recent Belgian Report,[3] on the dangers of overworking the native labour supply. An honest interpretation of trusteeship required, first, the reservation of sufficient land for the natives to ensure that, if they left the Reserves to work for Europeans, they did so of their own free will and sold their labour on fair commercial terms, and, secondly, a comprehensive and progressive policy of native education.

A policy which leaves the native population no future except as workers on European estates cannot be reconciled with Trusteeship. Nor can it, in the long run, conduce to the economic prosperity of the East African Protectorates. The chief wealth of these territories is the people, and, on a long view, the cardinal aim of policy must be to maintain tribal life, to encourage the growth of population by combating disease and promoting sanitation and hygiene, and to develop by education the industry and intelligence of the population.

If the Government remained inactive, Oldham concluded, the material was at hand for a large-scale agitation; 'but it seems better to lift the whole matter out of the region of controversy and make it the subject of a thorough impartial

[1] J. H. O. to A. of C., 15.v.21 and 17.v.21.
[2] J. H. O. to Hon. E. F. L. Wood, 17.v.21.
[3] *Rapport au Roi de la Commission instituée pour la Protection des Indigènes*, 1920.

inquiry . . .'. On 12th July the Archbishop wrote that he had seen Churchill, who had accepted the memorandum in principle, but had expressed his confidence that he would be able to deal with the matter himself in consultation with the Governors of Kenya and Uganda who had already been summoned to London.[1] Oldham knew very well what this portended, and on 15th August he wrote a last appeal to Wood. The real question was, not the labour ordinance, but in whose interests were the territories primarily to be developed. It would be small use to amend the regulations: unless the natives were actively assisted to grow their own crops 'no alternative means will be provided for their acquiring habits of industry and becoming useful and productive members of society'.[2] But it was too late. On 5th September Churchill addressed a dispatch to the Principal Administrative Officer in Kenya which formally precluded officials and chiefs from recruiting labour for Europeans. And that was all.[3]

Two years later, in 1923, Bonar Law's Government, with the Duke of Devonshire at the Colonial Office and Ormsby-Gore as Under-Secretary, answered the 'real question'; and the missionary interest, operating both in East Africa and in London, exercised a decisive influence in the decision.[4]

As early as 1914 the Government of India had drawn the attention of the Colonial Office to the fact that the Kenya

[1] A. of C. to J. H. O., 12.vii.21.
[2] J. H. O. to Hon. E. F. L. Wood, 19.viii.21.
[3] Dispatch relating to Native Labour, 1921. Cmd. 1504.
[4] The Edinburgh House correspondence referred to below is in two files, marked 'East Africa—Indians', one of which is almost entirely filled with cuttings from the East African Press.

Government was in certain matters discriminating, administratively if not by legislation, between Europeans and Indians in the Protectorate. Feeling in India had risen higher still when the Legislative Council Ordinance of 1919 had provided for eleven members to represent the European community and only two nominated members to represent the Indians, who outnumbered the Europeans in the Protectorate by three to one. Reacting to Indian pressure, the Joint Standing Committee of Parliament on Indian Affairs had in 1921 accepted the principle that Indians should not have a status inferior to other British subjects in Kenya, a decision which had been endorsed by the 1921 Imperial Conference, South Africa alone dissenting. Accordingly in 1922 the Colonial Secretary had amended the Kenya constitution by raising the Indian representation to four nominated members as against eleven elected Europeans; and later in the same year the Wood-Winterton Committee had recommended that Indians and Europeans should have a common electoral roll with a non-discriminating property and education test.[1]

The publication of these proposals raised a storm of protest in Kenya. In February 1923 the settlers formed a Vigilance Committee, and even hatched plans to kidnap the Governor and to set up a republic. The Kenya Indians in their turn held mass meetings; and their supporters in India made it clear that they claimed not only political parity with Europeans in Kenya, but the right of unrestricted immigration into East Africa.[2] The settlers' standpoint, once heads

---

[1] Buell, *op. cit.*, I, pp. 290–4.
[2] Rt. Hon. Srinivasi Sastri to Reuter, *The Times*, 30.iv.23.

had cooled, was straightforward. They stood for European paramountcy and to them, therefore, the question of the franchise was crucial. They wanted a European unofficial majority on the Legislative Council; and they were much less concerned to restrict Indian immigration.[1] The missionary attitude was more complex. Many of them favoured a common electoral roll.[2] On the other hand they feared unrestricted immigration from a vast, over-populated and non-Christian country;[3] and they regarded Indians already in East Africa, with their monopoly of commerce and the skilled trades, as a more immediate threat to African development than the European farmers.[4] But equally, with the labour question fresh in their experience, they did not wish the European unofficial community to achieve complete success by obtaining a commanding vote in the local legislature. One group, represented by Archdeacon Owen of Kavirondo, refused to distinguish between Indian and European settlers, regarding them as alike to blame for the fact that Kikuyu and Kavirondo were not developing as

[1] In the manse at Kikuyu there is preserved an interesting letter from J. W. Arthur dated 2.vi.23, showing that in Delamere's view restrictions on Indian immigration need not be strictly enforced, if a European unofficial majority could be obtained in the Legislative Council.

[2] This and the following statements are based upon correspondence of J. W. Arthur with other members of the Protestant Missionary Alliance relating to his delegation to England described below. The correspondence is preserved at the Church of Scotland Mission, Kikuyu.

[3] cf. Bishop Willis of Uganda to *The Times*, 25.iv.23, quoting a statement by Mr. Jeevanjee in the Leg. Co. in 1912, which advocated the annexation of Kenya to the Indian Empire with provincial government under the Indian Viceroy.

[4] *e.g.* J. W. Arthur in an interview with the *Morning Post*, 28.iv.23. The Indian is a retarding factor. But the Indian problem is only one aspect of the failure of the British Government to develop the native races. . . . Out of £450,000 taken in native taxation only £25,000 spent on native education.

native states on the Uganda pattern. They favoured the restriction of all further immigration and the immediate representation of Africans on the Legislature on the principle of no taxation without representation.[1]

Oldham was in India during the February crisis and there learned to understand not only the strength of Indian feelings but also the hatred of all racial discrimination evinced by leading missionaries in India and Ceylon such as C. F. Andrews of the Cambridge Mission to Delhi and A. G. Fraser, the Principal of Trinity College, Kandy. Thus when he returned to England in April and read his East African correspondence he realised that he would have to resolve by action in the political field an important conflict between missionaries in India and missionaries in Africa. Further, the more closely he studied the evidence, the more firmly he became convinced that here was the instrument which he needed to reinforce his statements of two years ago. The settlers, he saw from his meticulously filed press-cuttings, were basing their opposition, not only on the issue of responsible government, but also on the welfare of the natives, who should be protected, they argued, from the vices of Oriental civilisation. Might not the Indian pressure be used as a lever to secure a declaration from the Imperial Government, and its acceptance by the settlers, that the East African territories from Northern Rhodesia to Kenya were to be developed primarily in the interests of the native populations and that the grant of responsible government to any immigrant community was therefore out of the question? And might not such a declaration, if backed by

[1] Owen to Arthur (undated) received March 1923. Kikuyu papers.

non-discriminating legislation to regulate further immigration, be equally sure to allay Indian suspicions?[1]

Meantime, two delegations had been summoned to England by the Colonial Secretary: one consisting of settlers and Indians from Kenya, with Dr. Arthur to represent the interests of the Africans; the other from India, led by the Rt. Hon. Srinivasi Sastri, and including C. F. Andrews. During the month of May, Andrews, Sastri and Arthur were received in turn, for long conferences at Edinburgh House, were converted with much difficulty to Oldham's policy, were carefully briefed by him for their negotiations with the Government and finally dispatched to Lambeth for interviews with the Archbishop, who was to act as Oldham's liaison with the Duke of Devonshire.[2] On 25th May, the Government having come to no decision, Oldham wrote to Davidson, that Andrews and Sastri were threatening to break off negotiations.[3] On the 29th the Archbishop saw the Duke and left with him a brief summary of Oldham's proposals: (i) a declaration that native interests were to be paramount; (ii) a Royal Commission to examine the application of paramountcy to Kenya.[4] On 12th June Oldham reported a long conference with the Duke, Masterton-Smith and Ormsby-Gore.[5] Andrews by this time had returned to India, ready, if need be, to face accusations of

[1] J. H. O. to A. of C., 11.v.23, expanded on 14.v.23, after spending a week-end with Lugard.

[2] J. H. O. to A. of C., 11.v.23, and 14.v.23.

[3] J. H. O. to A. of C., 25.v.23.

[4] G. K. A. Bell to J. H. O., 29.v.23, enclosing copy of A. of C. to Duke of Devonshire, 29.v.23.

[5] J. H. O. to A. of C., 12.vi.23. Masterton-Smith was Permanent Under-Secretary at the C.O.

treachery, and to convert his supporters to the new policy.[1] Judging by a letter from Oldham to Arthur on the 18th the remaining difficulties came from one quarter only:

> I have never on any occasion made any public use of the wild statements by Kenya settlers. My desire is entirely for co-operation. I have, however, told government people in conversation that, supposing I wanted to take a dead line and go in for agitation, I had all the material at hand required to rouse an ordinary British audience to great excitement in the utterances of the settlers themselves.[2]

Finally the Government overcame its scruples, and in July the Duke of Devonshire issued a White Paper in which it was stated that:

> Primarily Kenya is an African territory, and His Majesty's Government think it necessary definitely to record their considered opinion that the interests of the African natives must be paramount, and that if, and when, those interests and the interests of the immigrant races should conflict, the former should prevail. . . . His Majesty's Government cannot but regard the grant of responsible self-government as out of the question within any period of time which need now be taken into consideration. . . . As in the Uganda Protectorate, so in the Kenya Colony the principle of Trusteeship for the Natives no less than in the Mandated Territory of Tanganyika is unassailable.[3]

---

[1] J. H. O. to A. of C., 1.vi.23.
[2] J. H. O. to Dr. Arthur, 18.vi.23.
[3] White Paper entitled *Indians in Kenya*, 1923, Cmd. 1922.

*　　*　　*　　*

3

The Kenya White Paper of 1923 has been severely criticised even by those who have stood outside the conflicting
racial and political interests of East Africa.[1] Considered
apart from the Indian question in which it originated, it was
no doubt an unstatesmanlike document. The doctrine of
African paramountcy wherever racial interests conflicted was
probably never intended as a thoroughgoing statement of
internal policy as distinct from the wider issues of immigration and immigrant franchise; and certainly, if it was, it
went far beyond the consensus of expert opinion as expressed
in the Royal Commissions of 1924 and 1928 and in the Report of the Joint Select Committee of 1931. Nevertheless,
the declaration has been consistently upheld in maintaining
that responsible self-government could not be granted to
members of one minority race; and it is significant that even
before the final decision on the Indian question had been
reached, the Conservative Government had given proof of
its support of at least one aspect of a constructive native
policy, designed to raise the African section of the population
to a position in which it could eventually play its part in a
self-governing community.

The promptness with which Ormsby-Gore applied himself to the problem of native education took even Oldham by

[1] 'It was no doubt a genuine attempt to indicate a liberal policy; but the subsequent
attempts to elucidate the meaning of this declaration led to a controversy which was
as barren in result, and often as bitter in character, as any of the great theological
disputes of the past.' Hailey, *An African Survey*, p. 142.

surprise. The latter, when he had addressed his important paper on Native Affairs to Wood in May 1921, had confessed that the type of education best suited to give African society its chance of developing was a matter which required further study.[1] But, even as he wrote, he had known that the most impressive contribution yet made to the subject was about to be presented, and'presented from a missionary source. At the instance of American missionary societies working in Africa, the Phelps-Stokes Fund had in 1920 agreed to finance a commission of missionaries and educationists to survey the existing systems of native education in West and South Africa, and in particular, to try and apply to the African scene the results of experience in negro education in the United States. The Commission, headed by Dr. Jesse Jones and including an African member, Dr. Aggrey of the Gold Coast, made detailed suggestions as to how education could be adapted to the needs of African society, so as to promote its development without causing its disruption. In recognising that the education of the masses must be related both to the physical environment in which they lived and to the social groupings into which they were organised, it forestalled by several years the random criticisms of anthropological scientists and those of the officially promoted inquiry undertaken by Professor Julian Huxley in 1930.[2] Moreover, the members of the Commission were, as believing Christians, at a certain advantage over Huxley and others who, while recommending some sort of ethical religion

[1] J. H. O. to Hon. E. F. L. Wood, quoted above.
[2] Julian Huxley: (i) *Biology and its Place in Native Education*, Colonial Office, Africa (East), No. 1134; (ii) *Africa View*, London, 1930.

to remedy the defects of tribal beliefs, were nevertheless unable to suggest an object for that religion to worship.[1]

The Report of the Phelps–Stokes Commission was published in 1922,[2] and found immediate favour with the colonial governments, who were becoming increasingly aware of the futility and even the positive dangers of a literary education of the Western type in societies which were economically more primitive than those of Europe in the Dark Ages.[3] When, therefore, missions, which as monopolists in the educational field had been responsible for most of the mistakes committed in the past, had shown such signs of enterprise and sanity as regarded their intentions for the future, it was doubly natural that the Under-Secretary of State, wishing to institute a Government policy of native education as recommended by Oldham in 1921, and yet uncertain where to look for his resources both in

[1] See an account of a discussion at the Royal Anthropological Institute in *A*. 38. 228, 'Major Hanns Vischer spoke on the difficulty of inculcating a moral code as part of a system of education. . . . In the subsequent discussion it was suggested by one of those present that the assumption that the Christian code of ethics provides the answer is open to the criticism that this code is at variance with the reality of the social system which European administrations have introduced into Africa, and is apt to be rejected by Africans when they become aware of that fact. It was suggested that a task which awaits the anthropologist is the construction of a code based on sociological realities, but that he has not at present the data to equip him for such work' (*sic*).

[2] *Education in Africa*. A Study of West, South and Equatorial Africa by the African Education Commission, under the Auspices of the Phelps-Stokes Fund and Foreign Missionary Societies of North America and Europe, New York, 1922.

[3] cf. Lugard, who, in the *Dual Mandate*, 1922, p. 426 *sqq*., questioned whether missions had used the weapon of education with a due regard to the stability of the social order. 'After more than a millennium of political development, the western democracies have in the last century tried to increase the elasticity of the social order by introducing equality of opportunity in education, and even now it is highly questionable whether they have not proceeded faster than the fragile conditions of human association seem to justify.'

money and in European staff, should turn once again to
Edinburgh House. Accordingly, in March 1923, Ormsby-
Gore invited Oldham to submit suggestions for a *modus
vivendi* between missions and Government under the new
scheme.[1]

Reporting the Government's intentions to Garfield
Williams, the Educational Secretary of the C.M.S., Oldham
confessed that he was somewhat taken aback: he had hoped
to work out a policy of co-operation with the Government
in East Africa slowly, over the course of two or three years.[2]
His hesitation certainly did not arise from any lack of
testimony from missionaries in the field as to the importance
of education as a medium for evangelism. The C.M.S.
missionaries in Tanganyika had as early as 1921 importuned
the Governor, Sir Horace Byatt, to introduce a system of
grants-in-aid to mission schools, in exchange for which they
had promised to augment the number of schools, to raise
their educational standards and to introduce a larger measure
of industrial training, for which qualified instructors would
be obtained from England.[3] The situation was shortly to be
summed up with great frankness by the Bishop of Mombasa
in a private memorandum to his Society. Rapidly increasing
numbers of Africans were realising the possibilities before
them; most of whom felt that the missions offered them
their best chance of 'rising', and they connected Christianity
with this opportunity. Doubtless, their motives were
seldom 'high or spiritual'; but, whereas in India boys would

[1] J. H. O. to Garfield Williams, Educational Secretary of the C.M.S., 28.iii.23.
[2] *ibid.*
[3] Executive Committee of the C.M.S. Tanganyika Mission to Sir H. Byatt,
16.ix.21, C.M.S. Papers.

troop to mission schools without any intention of accepting Christianity, in Africa it was the case that nearly all were anxious to be prepared for Baptism.[1] The demand for education and the demand for Christianity were, as the General Secretary of the C.M.S. expressed it,[2] 'so inextricably interwoven', that if the first was driven, through the failure of missions, to seek satisfaction in a secular system run by the State, the second might vanish away. But Oldham, it appears, would have preferred to wait until a second commission under missionary auspices had surveyed the East African scene, and until the Societies had reorganised their forces in the light of its recommendations, before defining their relations with the Government. The initiative would then have remained with the missions. If Government concessions and increased subsidies preceded the missionary reorganisation, there would be a danger that the societies would regard them as a reward for past services and not as a contribution towards fresh advance, and that missionary education, instead of setting the pace, would trail hopelessly behind the ever-rising demands of the government inspector.[3]

[1] Bishop of Mombasa to C.M.S., undated, received 1925.

[2] W. W. Cash to Secretary of C.M.S., Australia, 26.v.26.

[3] e.g. (i) J. H. O. to Manley (Africa Secretary of the C.M.S.), 15.xii.24. 'If and when grants are given it is desirable that the whole of the amount received should be spent on increasing the efficiency of the schools and not simply accepted as relieving the present strain on missionary resources.'

(ii) 'Missions cannot properly undertake the task, unless they are prepared in this generation to more than double the number of efficient educational missionaries. No sane government could hand over to the force that is at present in occupation. Methods will also have to improve. Mass education is proceeding with incredible rapidity: school education is not keeping pace with it. From the point of view of secular education, hundreds of our schools are practically useless.' Garfield Williams in *IRM.*, January 1925.

Ormsby-Gore's offer, once made, however, could not be refused; and accordingly in May 1923 a confidential memorandum was submitted by Oldham to the Colonial Office, setting forth the missionary claim. 'In some of the British Colonies and Protectorates in Africa', it opened, 'the whole, and in most of the others at least nine-tenths, of the native education is being given in mission schools.' The task of education was so vast in proportion to the resources available that it would be sheer folly if the agencies concerned were not to work in co-operation. It was a simple matter of fact that, apart from their own financial contributions, missions were able to attract the services of qualified men and women at a lower wage than any government. Statistics were quoted from Lord Meston's 'Aspects of Indian Education', showing that the cost to the Government of a pupil in an aided mission school could be as little as one-fifth of his cost in an identical government school. The Indian Education Despatch of 1854 had encouraged a policy of partnership with private agencies as a safeguard against the rigidity and uniformity of a bureaucratically managed system: in Africa this argument had additional cogency, in that there was 'an overwhelming weight of competent testimony' that if education was not to be destructive of morality and the social order, it must have a religious basis.[1]

Mere recognition of the principle of co-operation, wrote Oldham in a covering letter to the Archbishop of Canterbury,

[1] 'Educational Policy in Africa—A memorandum submitted on behalf of the Education Committee of the Conference of Missionary Societies in Great Britain and Ireland.' Copies at Edinburgh House in file marked 'Advisory Committee on Native Education'.

was not sufficient. The opportunity must be used to secure permanent and effective machinery for consultation, both locally and at the Colonial Office. Could the Archbishop see the Duke of Devonshire, and possibly also the President of the Board of Education?[1] Oldham himself had long talks with Lugard and Guggisberg, who were advising the Government,[2] and on the 25th had an interview with Ormsby-Gore.[3] On 6th June the Memorandum was considered and approved by a conference, chaired by Ormsby-Gore and attended by the Archbishop of Canterbury, Oldham, Jesse Jones and Garfield Williams on the one hand, and by Lugard, the Governors of Nigeria, the Gold Coast, Sierra Leone, Kenya and Nyasaland, and the Colonial Secretary of Tanganyika on the other.[4] The formation of Advisory Boards of Education, to include missionaries and other non-officials, in the several territories was left to the returning Governors; while in London it was determined to form a permanent Advisory Committee on Native Education in Tropical Africa, in which the Parliamentary Under-Secretary of State and the Head of the Africa Department at the Colonial Office were to meet in consultation with high representatives of missions, both Protestant and Roman Catholic, and with distinguished educationists and other experts, to study the wider questions of policy.[5]

[1] J. H. O. to A. of C., 3.v.23 and 11.v.23.

[2] J. H. O. to A. of C., 14.v.23.   [3] J. H. O. to A. of C., 25.v.23.

[4] J. H. Oldham, 'The Educational Policy of the British Government in Africa'. *IRM.*, August, 1925.

[5] G. K. A. Bell, *Randall Davidson*, II, p. 1,234. The first members of the Committee were: Ormsby-Gore (Under-Secretary); Sir Herbert Reid (Colonial Office); Bishop Bidwell (nominated by Cardinal Bourne); J. H. Oldham; the Bishop of Liverpool (A. A. David, previously Headmaster of Rugby); Sir Frederick Lugard; Sir Michael Sadler; Sir James Currie; and Major Hanns Vischer, Secretary.

The 'Derby Day Meeting', as it was always called,[1] was a turning point in the history of African education. Once the principle of co-operation had been agreed, the practice followed quickly. A second Phelps-Stokes Commission departed to East Africa early in 1924, accompanied by a Colonial Office representative, Major Hanns Vischer, who was to become the first Secretary of the Advisory Committee. The lessons of its report were plain for all to read. On the one hand the colonial governments of Kenya, Uganda and Tanganyika, the last a Mandated Territory, were spending respectively, the grotesque proportions of 4 per cent, 2 per cent and 1 per cent of their revenue on education. Uganda, though subsidising mission schools to the extent of £10,000 a year, had no Education Department at all. In Tanganyika, the Director of Education was the only man in a European staff of five who was not actively engaged in teaching; and no grants-in-aid had been paid to missions since the establishment of the British administration. On the other hand the vast, amateur education systems of the missions, supported necessarily out of the infinitesimal fees chargeable to the local populations, were crying out for expert advice and co-ordination by a professional inspectorate, as well as for the finance to train and employ higher grades of African teachers.[2] The Commission was, however, able to report that far-reaching reforms were already being planned by all three governments;

---

[1] It was indeed a high testimony of the importance of the event that so many distinguished people were able to be convened on Derby Day.

[2] *Education in East Africa.* A study of East, Central and South Africa by the second African Education Commission under the auspices of the Phelps-Stokes Fund (New York and London, 1924).

and a fresh stimulus was added to official efforts by the report of the East Africa Commission under the chairmanship of Ormsby-Gore, appointed by the first Labour Government in 1924, which concluded in one section after another, that the successful application of a 'Dual Mandate' policy depended upon ensuring that the native peoples received a fair chance of 'economic and moral development' through a constructive programme of 'education, in the widest sense of the word'.[1]

It remained only to ensure that the rank and file of the missionary organisations understood that the new policy of co-operation involved, not merely the subsidisation of existing systems, but their rapid development to professional standards of efficiency. At Le Zoute in 1926 Oldham told representatives of every Protestant mission working in Africa that missionaries would, despite their physical presence in Africa, drift outside the real life of the Continent, unless they bore their witness among the new forces which were reshaping the lives of the African peoples.[2] This Conference itself contributed little that was new to missionary thinking. It approved the policy of co-operation with the new education policy of the British Government. It accepted the recommendations of the Phelps-Stokes Commissions. It endorsed Oldham's action in relation to land and labour problems. It studied the part that missions could play in solving problems of health and population. And it set up a Standing Committee to hasten the production of Christian

---

[1] *Report of the East Africa Commission,* 1925, Cmd. 2387. Sections on Education, Labour, Native Production, Medical Services.
[2] Introductory address by J. H. Oldham, printed in *IRM.* 27. 24.

literature in the African vernaculars. Under the heading of
Evangelism it passed a resolution recognising the essentially
social character of African life, and countenancing the adoption and purification of customs which were 'valuable in
substance', even though their 'accidents' might be evil.[1] All
these matters had been publicised by individual missionaries
during the years since 1918, and had attracted the attention
of the experts at the headquarters of the missionary societies
and at Edinburgh House: what was significant was that they
should now receive the most formal degree of support that an
inter-denominational and unofficial gathering could confer.

The entry of the Roman Church into full co-operation
with the new native policy came about in a more circuitous
manner. Cardinal Bourne had indeed nominated a representative to the Advisory Committee at the Colonial Office;
but the relationship of the Archbishop of Westminster to the
missionary congregations working in British Tropical Africa
was obscure, and Rome at first did nothing to clarify them.
It so happened, however, that one of the first questions
examined by the Advisory Committee was that of the place
of vernacular languages in African education; and it was in
connection with the highly technical problems of classifica-
tion and orthography which were seen to be involved that
the idea was conceived of an International Institute of
African Languages and Cultures, which should act as a
clearing-house between governments, missions and academic
centres in these matters. Thanks largely to the enthusiasm
of Vischer, this organisation came into being in June 1926,
with an already world-wide membership and with Lugard

[1] E. W. Smith, *The Christian Mission in Africa*, p. 108.

at its head.[1] Four Roman Catholic missionaries were delegated by the Propaganda to attend the inaugural meeting;
and one of them, Father Dubois, S.J., was provisionally
elected to the Executive Council. It was apparently Dubois
who on his return to Rome awakened the Vatican to the
significance of the new developments in British colonial
policy, for early in 1927 Cardinal Van Rossum, the Prefect
of Propaganda, called a meeting of the Procurators of all
the missionary orders working in Africa and instructed them
to form a Standing Committee which could be officially
represented on the Governing Body of the Institute in the
same way as the Protestant International Missionary
Council.[2] In its external relations the first duty of the
resultant 'Conférence des missions catholiques d'Afrique'
was to ensure that the contributions of missionaries to
ethnology and the related sciences found their way into the
secular journals and in particular into that of the International Institute:

Nous pouvons travailler ainsi l'opinion publique [wrote its
Secretary, Fr. Dubois]. Il nous faut des Savants qui s'imposent et qui,
par le chemin de la science, puisque ce n'est guère que par là qu'ils
peuvent y pénétrer, se fassent une place dans les Conseils Supérieurs
et auprès des suprêmes autorités. . . . Mais prenons-nous y garde! On
nous appelle, on nous consulte actuellement à cause de notre avance

[1] The idea was first conceived at a conference of Protestant missionaries which met
at High Leigh in 1924 to consider the report of the Phelps–Stokes Commission on
Education in East Africa. The draft constitution was prepared by Mr. E. W. Smith
of the British and Foreign Bible Society, Dr. Warnshuis of the International
Missionary Council, and Major, later Sir Hanns Vischer, Secretary of the Colonial
Office Advisory Committee. *Africa* 1934, p. 1.
[2] Anonymous article in *A.* 31. 235 and H. Dubois, *Le Répertoire Africain: Traité
de Missiologie pratique*, Rome, 1932, p. 185 *sq.*

K

dans la connaissance de l'Afrique, mais de toutes parts se lève une armée de chercheurs. Avant vingt ans, si nous n'avons pas des hommes de valeur reconnue, on nous laissera parfaitement de coté.[1]

Though it is hard from the published evidence to assess the internal authority of the Conference, it is clear that it was far more than a piece of machinery for collaboration with a learned society. The scope and thoroughness of its own researches into all aspects of missionary education from the 'bush school' to the higher seminary,[2] together with the fact that its reports and publications were sent with the official imprimatur of the Propaganda to all Apostolic Vicars and Prefects in charge of African dioceses,[3] suggests that it was the first of a series of moves by the Propaganda to co-ordinate the activities of its dependent missions in relation to the native policy of the colonial powers, and to pursue what Pope Pius XI is said to have described as a 'politique de présence'.[4]

An even more significant move in the same direction was the appointment later in the same year of Mgr. Arthur Hinsley, Rector of the English College in Rome, to the special post of Visitor Apostolic to the Catholic Missions in the British Colonies in Africa. After consultations with the Colonial Office in December 1927, Hinsley spent two years touring the length and breadth of British Africa, preaching co-operation with the education policies of the several colonial governments to an extent which involved a

---

[1] *AFER.*, *June* 1932, p. 7 *sqq.*   [2] Results published in *AFER.*, 1932–9.
[3] *ibid.*, *June* 1932, p. 34.
[4] 'Les absents ont toujours tort et, comme on l'a dit la politique de présence doit être partout la nôtre.' *ibid.*, *June* 1932, p. 14. cf. Dubois, *op. cit.*, p. 157.

regrouping of the existing dispositions of Catholic missionary forces. Hitherto 'extensive' methods had been the rule in Catholic missions in Central Africa. The networks of 'bush schools' remotely controlled from the European stations had been larger in number and even more rudimentary in character than those of the Protestant missions.[1] And, in terms of quantity rather than quality, the dividend had been high. Mgr. Lechaptois, the Apostolic Vicar of Tanganyika, had held them responsible for nine-tenths of all his converts.[2] But the Departments of Education were not interested in 'education' of this standard; and even from the religious standpoint Hinsley judged them to be insufficient 'now that civilisation is advancing with giant strides'.[3] At a conference of Bishops and leading missionaries at Dar-es-Salaam in August 1928 the Apostolic Visitor gave his orders: 'Collaborate with all your power; and where it is impossible for you to carry on both the immediate task of evangelisation and your educational work, neglect your churches in order to perfect your schools.'[4] At least one Normal School was to be started in every diocese; missionaries were to study to attain a perfect command of English; women missionaries were for

[1] I am here quoting Hinsley's own opinion in what appears to be a personal communication to Dubois, *op. cit.*, p. 135.

[2] J. Becker, *Die Katholische Kirche im neuen Afrika*, Geneva, 1947, p. 180. According to another estimate, from the Vicariate of Dar-es-Salaam, 70–80 per cent of bush-school pupils were heathen, and of these some 60 per cent became Christians. Date uncertain, but certainly post-1918.

[3] Dubois, *op. cit.*, p. 136.

[4] J. Mazé, *La Collaboration Scolaire des Missions et des Gouvernements*, Algiers, 1933, p. 14. who also quotes a directive from the Superior-General of the White Fathers: 'Il ne faut pas hésiter . . . à supprimer une station entière, sans vous laisser arrêter par les protestations des catechumènes, à qui vous aurez le crêve-coeur d'enlever leurs prêtres.'

the future to receive some medical training, if possible at the London School of Tropical Medicine.[1]

Thus, if the Roman Catholic Church had left it to others to advocate a forward native policy which would keep open the road to racial equality in the future, Hinsley's visitation of 1928–9 made it clear that there could be no question of its standing aside once that policy had been adopted. Indeed, entering the political arena when it did, after the fighting was over, it was able to see the problem more clearly and simply than the Protestant missions, which had argued their case so frequently in social and economic terms for propaganda purposes, that its religious object had sometimes seemed obscure.[2] Who owned the schools, wrote Father Dubois in his handbook for Catholic missionaries, would own Africa. 'La question des écoles est pour toutes les causes qui veulent durer une question de vie ou de mort.'[3] In the absence of competition, bush schools had sufficed for the conversion of agrarian animists into a Catholic peasantry. Now that the colonial governments were forcing up the standard both by direct competition and by subsidy, Catholic missions must either follow suit or else lose not only the subsidy but also the cream of the younger generation.

[1] *ZMW*. 30. 142. Also refers to Dar-es-Salaam conference.

[2] C. C. Martindale, S.J., in his *African Angelus*, London, 1932, p. 338 *sqq.*, makes some justifiable comments to this effect about the literature relating to the Le Zoute Conference. 'The [Protestant] missionary now tries to create an environment rather than to save individual souls. World evangelism requires a change of sanitation quite as much as a change of heart. . . . Concomitantly, governments see that government is based on consent; they therefore desire no less a change of heart.'

[3] Dubois, *op. cit.*, p. 133.

*　　*　　*　　*

4

The alliance between the imperial and the missionary factors in education amounted to much more than an alignment of theoretical policies. In terms of finance, the annual contribution of the Government to mission schools rose during the generation between 1923 and 1949, from nothing to £285,000 in Tanganyika, from £10,000 to about £400,000 in Uganda, and from £14,000 to about £300,000 in Kenya.[1] By the end of the period grants to missions were absorbing between a half and two-thirds of the educational budgets of the territories, and the individual missions were receiving more money from Governments in respect of their educational work than their combined receipts from their home societies and from their local church members.[2] In some denominations more than a third of the European missionaries came to be mainly supported out of government grants, while an even higher proportion received some official allowances in respect of part-time educational

[1] The 1923 figures are taken from the Phelps–Stokes report, pp. 118, 155. The 1949 figures are calculated from evidence supplied by the Education Departments concerned. In Kenya grants to mission primary schools are made by the African District Councils which do not distinguish in their returns between mission schools and others. The figure quoted is therefore approximate. In the Uganda figure, allowance has been made for the contributions of the Buganda Lukiko and also for the mission element in the so-called 'Independent Schools'.

[2] Various factors, including the difference between civil and ecclesiastical units, decentralisation in the administration of grants, undisclosed items in the 'home contributions' of Roman Catholic Missions, etc., make it impossible to quote exact statistics; but the piecemeal evidence available suggests that in some cases the Government educational contribution may be as much as double the income of the mission from all other sources.

work.[1] Mainly, however, the vast sums allocated to missions by governments represented the salaries of African schoolmasters and school-mistresses, trained, employed and organised by the missions, who had become by the end of the period even more numerous and much more highly paid than the pastoral workers of the Churches.[2]

The most immediate practical result of the alliance was to turn a number of the former missionary 'out-stations'—aptly described by the Phelps-Stokes Commission as the 'frontier of civilisation'—into regular elementary schools, providing three or four years of simple education in the vernacular language. Schools selected for financial support were at first staffed by the better educated of the old class of mission teachers and evangelists, and were brought under closer supervision, both by the European missionaries and by the government inspectorate. Gradually higher qualifications were demanded of the teachers themselves, until by the end of the period only men and women who had passed through a recognised Teachers' Training Centre were eligible for grants-in-aid. At first large numbers of scholastically unqualified 'Church' teachers and catechists continued to operate in unaided 'bush schools', but as grant-aided schools multiplied, Church teachers declined in number

---

[1] Although Protestant missionaries were less than half as numerous as Roman Catholics, the Protestant educational effort, measured in terms of grants earned, was almost equal to that of Catholics. In general, therefore, a higher proportion of Protestant missionaries were engaged in educational work, although there were some exceptions to this rule, notably among the Fundamentalist element in the Africa Inland Mission.

[2] Figures supplied by the Education Department in Dar-es-Salaam show that about 15 per cent of the grants were in respect of European missionaries and 85 per cent in respect of African staff.

and became more distinctively pastoral in character.[1] The older type of evangelist was employed only in primitive and still pagan districts. But where missions were well established and Christians predominated, the religious instruction of children was increasingly left to the grant-aided mission schools.

The next transformation was that of the former schools for catechists and Church teachers, usually situated at the European mission stations, into regular training centres for primary teachers. In the course of a decade a few of these were so far developed as to be producing English-speaking teachers who were capable of carrying primary education into the fifth and sixth years. At a higher level still, the former mission boarding schools and 'schools for the sons of chiefs' were integrated with the new system as the first secondary schools, where a handful of the best pupils were able to continue their education, at first to the ninth, and eventually to the twelfth year, English being used as the vehicular language. Whereas at the lower levels of education the contribution of the European missionary lay in administration and supervision, in the field of secondary education the missionary schoolmaster was himself a pioneer; and the great headmasters of the period, Grace of Budo,

---

[1] This important tendency was more marked in Protestant Church organisations than in the Roman Catholic system. The following examples are representative of the present-day situation:

	Native Clergy	Catechists	Grant-aided teachers
(1) Upper Nile Diocese (Anglican) 1950	44	225	695
(2) Vic. Ap. Equatorial Nile (R.C.) 1946	7	425	488
(3) Masasi Diocese (Anglican) 1950	35	100	233
(4) Abbacy Nullius Ndanda (R.C.) 1946	3	350	140

Francis of the Alliance High School and Gibbons of Minaki, were perhaps the most outstanding figures in the modern missionary enterprise.

It was certainly at the level of secondary education that the alliance between missions and governments produced its most decisive results. Thanks to the progress achieved by the mission secondary schools during the first fifteen years of the alliance, the East African governments were able in 1938 to take the first steps in promoting the vocational school of the Uganda Government at Makerere to be the University College of East Africa. The emergence from the secondary schools, and later from Makerere, of an African professional class contributed powerfully to the programme of native development, by providing recruits for the medical, agricultural and veterinary services, for the developing native administrations, and, of course, for education itself. The appointment of Africans, even though in small numbers, to positions of responsibility outside their own tribal organisations provided an important vindication of the Christian doctrine of man over against racialist heresies, and lessened year by year the danger of the emergence of the economic and political colour-bars which have darkened the history of Africa south of the Zambezi. The fact that the majority of the Africans who reached the new professional status owed their rise to mission schools gave to Christianity an influence which far surpassed the numbers of its adherents, while the continued identification of the missions through their schools with that which was in African eyes most progressive and most liberating must be accounted a powerful reason for the remarkable extent to which African Christians remained loyal to the traditional forms of the religion even under the pressure of rising nationalism.[1]

Nevertheless, the passage of a generation made it at least questionable whether the policy of co-operation was of more than temporary significance. Progress at the higher levels of education, while narrowing the cultural and economic gap between the immigrant races and the African élite, created an only slightly less dangerous hiatus between the educated and the uneducated within African society itself,[2] and called for a vast expansion at the base of the educational system which the missions were ill able to meet and yet unwilling to refuse. The employment by a missionary society of a devoted Christian teacher in a secondary school or a training college, especially when nine-tenths of the financial cost was

[1] East Africa has not indeed been free from African splinter sects. In 1913 an ex-teacher of the Anglican Church in Uganda, named Malaki, who quoted Old Testament texts in support of polygamy and who opposed all forms of medicine, started to baptise independently of the Church. He gained the support of the influential ex-chief Kakunguru (vide supra, p. 191), and in 1921 his followers were estimated at 91,000. But his success was ephemeral and most of the Malakites have long since rejoined the Church. In more recent times the African Orthodox Church of 'Bishop' Sparta has attracted some political notice in connection with the Bataka agitations in Buganda; and more recently still, another sect known as the 'Dina ya Msambwa' has been responsible for violent agitations among the Suk tribe of western Kenya. In neither case has it been possible to obtain reliable information regarding doctrines or numbers. It is much to be hoped that someone with local knowledge and the necessary sympathy will attempt a study on the lines of Dr. B. G. M. Sundkler's Bantu Prophets in South Africa, London, 1948.

[2] The growing awareness of the Advisory Committee on Native Education in the Colonies to this trend is well illustrated in the succession of its statements of policy: 'The Education of the Community in African Society' (1930), 'The Education of Women' (1935), and 'Mass Education in African Society '(1944). Trenchant criticisms to the effect that grants-in-aid were being applied too exclusively for the training of a déclassée élite were made as early as 1930 by Mgr. Hinsley, in his report to the Propaganda of his Visitation of 1927–29, cf. Dubois, op. cit., p. 137.

borne by the government, called for no more justification than the employment of a missionary doctor. But the increasing diversion of ordained missionaries from pastoral work to the administration of great networks of elementary schools, involving the selection and supervision of teachers, the mastery of government syllabuses and all the routine work of official consultation and statistical returns, in theory a part-time occupation, tended in practice to become an all-absorbing burden, justifiable only if the objective recognised by both parties to the alliance had been the establishment of a permanent system of denominational education to be confided to the African Churches at the earliest practicable moment. The very fact, however, that the direction of policy lay with the European officials of the government departments made it difficult for missions to transfer responsibility to Africans as fast as they had done in the pastoral organisations. Government grants were made to the missions and not to the Churches, and it was therefore inevitable that European missionaries should have to bear a detailed responsibility for their administration.

It is significant that co-operation with the governments made it necessary for the missions to reconstitute themselves as employers of African workers in competition with the native Church organisations, and so to defy the very principle which Bishop Tucker and other pre-war missionaries had fought to establish. The former system of bush-schools, which for all its professional limitations had been a spontaneous movement of mass education by the people themselves, had been brought under European control, and its spontaneity had withered. In the Protestant Churches, whose ministries were recruited from the bush-school teachers, the status of the clerical profession declined relatively to the new secular professions which were opening to the educated élite. A qualified teacher in a government-aided mission school, who was earning perhaps four or five times the salary of an African clergyman, no longer regarded the ministry as the summit of his profession. The native clergy continued to be drawn from the dwindling body of unqualified and unaided Church teachers and evangelists, who were now merely the lowest grade of the educational hierarchy. Thus, though the clerical ranks might be full and still increasing, though the masses of the people were still served, though pagans were still joining the Churches and though their children were still being educated in Christian schools, the men who would have been capable of real leadership within the ecclesiastical organisations were being drawn off by economic inducements, into the service of the missions as schoolmasters, as well as into the growing departments of government.[1] The Roman Catholic Church was less obviously affected, since in that Church vocations to the priesthood were detected among primary-school pupils, who then received the whole of their further education in seminaries which were quite independent of the State-aided system. Those who finished the course were still among the best educated Africans in the territories, and, being committed to celibacy, were less subject to economic distractions than their Protestant counterparts. But, though positive

[1] The position has been well summarised by Bishop Stephen Neill in a private memorandum to the International Missionary Council on 'The Training of the Ministry in Africa', London, 1950.

evidence is lacking, it would be difficult to assert that progress towards an African hierarchy was unhampered by the educational commitments of the European missionary orders. Though Catholic missionaries were in one sense more disinterested than Protestants in that they broke with all European ties and identified themselves body and soul with the country of their adoption, this very fact was apt in another sense to give them something of the spirit of the colonist. Formal education was a new field to conquer, and one which much enhanced both the prestige and the resources of the mission. It is difficult to resist the conclusion that it was sometimes welcomed as an excuse for meagre progress in the training of an African clergy who would one day inherit the land.[1]

Finally, the close association of missions and governments, which was most obvious to Africans in the intensified control exercised by European missionaries over the lower levels of education, was itself becoming by the end of the period a positive danger to the Church. For during the very years in which the alliance was taking shape, nationalism was making its appearance in East Africa. The generation which remembered the chaos and the tyranny of pre-European times, and which had usually appreciated the benefits of the Pax Britannica, had died. The natural leaders of the

[1] This is not intended as an unqualified generalisation. From the statistics issued by the Apostolic Delegacy in 1946 it would appear that the White Fathers' mission has in all its districts made creditable progress in training an African ministry. The opposite tendency is, however, apparent in the Benedictine sphere in southern Tanganyika, where a substantial mission with ninety-five ordained missionaries has only produced eight African priests. True, the area is backward. But the very much smaller mission of the U.M.C.A. in Masasi diocese, with sixteen ordained missionaries, has a staff of thirty-five African clergy.

people who had so often been successfully confirmed in positions of authority by the early European administrations were irreplaceable in the second and third generations. No amount of attention to heredity and native custom could prevent the ossification of indigenous political institutions which had been subjected to fifty years of authoritarian control by an outside power. The very acceleration of development had necessitated the multiplication of European officials, had widened the impact of the foreigner upon African life, and had emphasised his membership of a separate social caste. Contact with the outside world, and especially with Indians and Burmese during the Second World War, stimulated a dislike of dependent status, which, though its first expressions might be trivial, meant that colonial governments had to battle against a deep and growing suspicion of their every action. In these circumstances, however far the doctrines of Christianity and the interests of the Churches might tend towards an upholding of the right and just action of the State, towards the moderation of racial antipathies and towards the avoidance of violence, that influence could only be weakened by the official association of the missions with the State.[1]

It was as much in the interest of the colonial governments as in that of the missions that the strengthening of the Churches, as Churches, under responsible and experienced African leadership, should now assume an absolute priority over the social services, which the missions had initiated, and

[1] The propaganda directed by the Bataka leaders against the Anglican Bishop of Uganda in 1949 may be cited in illustration of this danger. See the Report of the Commission of Inquiry into the Disturbances in Uganda during April 1949. Entebbe, 1950, p. 113.

which they had carried on and extended as the salaried agents of the State. For the Church, whether Roman Catholic or Anglican, Lutheran or Presbyterian, was the only institution of which the African was consciously and by outward initiation a member, which was wider than his own tribe and wider than his own race. As such, it was a corporation of unique value in the plural society which was moving towards self-government in East Africa. Within the Church there was still a host of specialist functions of vital importance which only the missionary from Europe would for some time be able to perform. Theological education would have to be continued and vastly expanded in the Catholic Church; in the Protestant Churches it would have to be related not merely to the daily needs of the subordinate clergy working in primitive parishes, but raised to the level necessary for the maintenance of some standard of doctrinal orthodoxy. The production and distribution of Christian literature was a technical problem which would continue to need the co-operation of western Christians for its solution. The organisation of appropriate lay movements within the Churches, such as 'Catholic Action' or the 'Mother's Union' or the 'Student Christian Movement' would call for special missions of limited duration by European pioneers. In the fields of medicine and education lay missionaries could continue to play an important part in setting professional standards. Within the pastoral ministry, and not necessarily in the highest positions only, missionaries, and especially Roman missionaries, filled vacancies which could not easily be abandoned. But the fact remained that by the end of the period the time for missionary self-effacement was drawing near. The missionary's duty was within the Church; and no advantages could outweigh the dangers of prolonging the separate identity of the mission as an employer over against the Church.

When it came to planning the transition from dependence to independence the problems facing the missions were certainly simpler than those which faced the colonial governments. The baptism administered by Rebmann to the first East African convert in 1851 had conferred a citizenship which knew nothing of the invidious distinction between a 'British subject' and a 'British protected person'. When Bishop Steere ordained John Swedi to the diaconate in 1879, the first commissioned officer of the East African Church was admitted into the same ministry as the European missionary. When Pope Pius XI consecrated Mgr. Joseph Kiwanuka to the Episcopate in 1939, the power to admit men into the universal Catholic priesthood was entrusted to East African hands.[1] In the Protestant Churches European clergy and laymen[2] had long been accustomed to sit as minorities among Africans in governing synods and assemblies. The attractive political theory of indirect rule, implying as it did the ability of a central administration composed entirely of Europeans to guide the evolution of a wide variety of indigenous systems of government into confederacies large enough and efficient enough to hold their own in the modern world, formed no part of missionary policy, which would at least escape the embarrassments of

[1] The Right Rev. Abere Balya, Assistant Bishop in Uganda since 1947, was the first East African to be consecrated to the Anglican episcopate.

[2] Including, in the Anglican Church, the chaplains to the European Communities and non-missionary laymen from those communities.

having suddenly to introduce Africans to the highest levels
of government just as the political momentum was shifting
from European to African hands.

*   *   *   *

5

Viewed as a factor in the total of European activities in
East Africa, the missionary movement was relatively most
powerful during the early years of contact. At a time when
the political and commercial interests of Europe had been
confined to the coasts of the Indian Ocean, missionaries had
already penetrated to the lake regions of the interior. They
had built and planted, taught and governed, while British
financiers were hesitating over concessions, while Bismarck
was still an opponent of colonial expansion. Their enthusias-
tic support of the cause of African freedom had led them
from the first to an attitude of aggression towards the Arabs
which was considered highly impolitic by the British
officials at Zanzibar, who, for all their own efforts against
the slave-trade, were seeking to use Arabs rather than
Africans to promote their country's interests in East Africa.
When a portion of the Arabs reacted to the German
occupation of the coastlands by trying to create an empire
of their own in the interior, it was the missionary voice,
protesting that African interests would be better served by
a European occupation, which was heard in the constituencies of England. When, finally, the Church Missionary
Society had committed itself and its adherents to political

support of a bankrupt British company, it was probably the ecclesiastical interest which swayed a Liberal Government's decision to intervene.

During the first generation of European rule the missionary factor in East Africa reached its greatest strength. While the embryo administrations were engaged in the prosaic tasks of establishing law and order, providing communications and wrestling with the most elementary problems of taxation and justice, the missions, already fledged, were directing great popular movements in religion and education, were introducing western medicine and promoting new and revolutionary economic activities. The phenomenal progress of Uganda at this time was due above all to the political and social revolution set in motion by the so-called religious wars and by the expansion of Christianity which followed them. During this period the desire to communicate western civilisation along with Christianity was both fully developed and unselfconscious; and yet it is significant that the symptoms which it produced were those of a cultural renaissance rather than a social cancer. The diffusion of new ideas was spontaneous and widespread; tribal structures, though profoundly altered, remained alive; there was no deracinated élite, as there was to be when mission education under government direction became more formal and more selective.

After the First World War, with the setback suffered by conventional Christianity in the West, and with the impetus given to colonial development by the economic impoverishment of Europe, the missionary factor was gradually but steadily outpaced by secular forces, although by reason of its established interests it was able to participate in development and in some measure to influence its course. The fact that in a country which was suitable for European settlement economic development nevertheless took a form which encouraged Africans themselves to become producers rather than to be merely the humanely ordered labour supply for European enterprise, was very largely due to missionary representations in the political sphere. The speed with which educated Africans were able to join in the work of stimulating development, as chiefs, as civil servants, as doctors, as technical officers, as schoolmasters, was due to the initiative with which missions undertook with government aid to build a professional system upon their own educational foundations. Nevertheless, by the end of the Second World War the missions were but a partly pensioned company of the European regiment, considerable mainly by reason of their immense and unique following among the African people as represented in the indigenous Church.

Seen from the viewpoint of East African Christianity, the missionary movement from Europe acquires a different perspective. The freed-slave settlements at the coast, the long caravans toiling inland with bales of cloth and printing-presses and steamers in sections, the political struggle with the Arabs, the competing nationalisms of the missionaries themselves, were but the preliminaries to the planting of the Church. The martyrs and confessors of Buganda were a radiant exception to the general rule that the converts of the pioneer period were Christians from circumstance rather than choice. It was not until the surge of popular evangelism into the strongholds of tribal paganism during the early

years of European rule that the faith achieved any widespread victory, and even then it was characterised by the
impermanent enthusiasm of a lay movement. The age of the
catechists may have marked the zenith of the missions, but
it was only the dawn of the Church. It has only been in the
most recent period that indigenous Christianity has grown
from infancy into adolescence and given proof of a momentum and a continuity not wholly derived from its European
founders. During the thirty-five years from 1914 to 1949, while
the missions have been declining, or at least ceasing to
expand, the membership of the Church has increased five-
fold. The African clergy has grown from an experimental
nucleus working in strict subordination to the ordained
missionary, into an established order, in some places responsible for the entire conduct of the regular pastoral work. In
so far as the Church has become indigenous it has also
become financially self-supporting. All its non-Roman
denominations have started upon the path to constitutional
self-government.

The problems which beset the Church in East Africa
today arise less from rival beliefs of local origin than from the
unbelief and half-belief of the secular west. The initiative
of Christianity over tribal paganism is at present so firmly
established that it would be surprising if, even with greatly
reduced missionary support from Europe, the indigenous
Church failed to double its present numbers during the
coming generation. The danger is rather that, under
the stress of political and social change, it may start to
disintegrate at the centre while it is still expanding at
the circumference. Missionary enterprise in secondary

education during the past twenty years has ensured that the majority of the secular leaders of East Africa during the immediate future will be in some sense Christians; but it is significant that the ministry is the one profession which has not so far gained from higher education. There is a real possibility that a Church led by peasant priests may come to be increasingly spurned and ignored by the educated minority which will come in the future to exercise the greatest share of political power. In these circumstances it is possible that the decisive act of the missionary drama lies still in the future, and that it is in the theological colleges, in the secondary schools, and above all in the impact of European Christianity upon visiting students from Africa, that the future legacy of thè missionary factor relatively to that of the secular forces of the 'European Conquest' will be finally determined.

SELECT BIBLIOGRAPHY

I. Books and Pamphlets

Ashe, R. P., *Chronicles of Uganda*, 1894.
Bates, M. Searle, *Data on the Distribution of the Missionary Enterprise*, 1943.
Battersby, C. F. Harford, *Pilkington of Uganda*, 1898.
Becker, J., *Die Katholische Kirche im neuen Afrika*, Geneva, 1947.
Bell, G. K. A., *Randall Davidson*, 1935.
Bouniol, J., *The White Fathers and their Missions*, 1929.
Buell, R. L., *The Native Problem in Africa*, New York, 1928.
Catholic Handbook of East Africa, Mombasa, 1932.
Chamberlin, D., *Some Letters from Livingstone, 1840–72*, 1940.
Church of Scotland Foreign Missions Committee: *Kenya, 1898–1948*.
Coats, V. T. *David Charters*, 1925.
Congrégation du St. Esprit: Aperçu Historique, Paris, 1936.
Coupland, R., *East Africa and its Invaders*, 1938.
Coupland, R., *The Exploitation of East Africa*, 1939.
Cust, R. N., *An Essay on the prevailing methods of evangelising the non-Christian World*, 1894.
Delegatio Apostolica Africae Orientalis et Occidentalis Britannicae: Status Missionum anni, 1945–6, Mombasa.
Dubois, H., *Le Répertoire Africain*, Rome, 1932.
Education in East Africa, New York, 1924.
Eliot, C. N. E., *The East Africa Protectorate*, 1905.
Elmslie, W. A., *Among the Wild Ngoni*, 1899.
Frere, H. B., *East Africa as a Field for Missionary Labour*, 1874.
Goodwin, H., *A Memoir of Bishop Mackenzie*, 1864.
Goyau, G., *La Congrégation du St. Esprit*, Paris, 1937.
Goyau, G., *Un grand Missionnaire: Le Cardinal Lavigerie*, Paris, 1925.
Hailey, Lord, *An African Survey*, 1938.
Heanley, R. M., *A Memoir of Edward Steere*, 1888.
Hore, E. C., *Tanganyika*, 1892.
Johnson, W. P., *My African Reminiscences*, 1898.

Jones, H. Gresford, *Uganda in Transformation*, 1926.

Kitching, A. L., *From Darkness to Light*, 1935.

Krapf, J. L., *Travels and Missionary Labours in East Africa*, 1860.

Latourette, K. S., *A History of the Expansion of Christianity*, 7 vols., 1937–45.

Leblond, G., *Le Père Auguste Achte*, Paris, 1904.

Livingstone, D., *Missionary Travels and Researches in South Africa*, 1857.

Livingstone, D., *Narrative of an Expedition to the Zambezi and its Tributaries*, 1865.

Livingstone, D., *Last Journals*, 1874.

Livingstone, W. P., *Laws of Livingstonia*, 1921.

Livingstone, W. P., *A Prince of Missionaries*, 1931.

Lovett, R., *A History of the London Missionary Society*, 1899.

Lugard, F. D., *The Rise of our East African Empire*, 1893.

Maples, Chauncey: *Letters and Journals*, 1897.

Mazé, J., *La Collaboration Scolaire des Missions et des Gouvernements*, Algiers, 1933.

McDermott, P. L., *I.B.E.A.*, 1893.

Moir, F. L. M., *After Livingstone*, London, 1923.

Mott, John R., *The Decisive Hour of Christian Missions*, 1910.

Murray, S. S., *A Handbook of Nyasaland*, 1932.

Nicq, A., *La Vie du Vénérable Père Siméon Lourdel*, Paris, 1896.

Parker, J. I., *Interpretative Statistical Survey of the World Mission of the Christian Church*, 1938.

Philp, H. R. A., *A New Day in Kenya*, 1936.

Proposed Scheme of Federation of Missionary Societies working in British East Africa, Nairobi, 1913.

Richter, J., *Tanganyika and its Future*.

Schmidlin, A. J., *Die Katholischen Missionen in den deutschen Schutzgebieten*, Hamburg, 1914.

Smith, E. W., *The Christian Mission in Africa*, 1926.

Smith, H. Maynard, *Frank, Bishop of Zanzibar*, 1926.

Stock, E., *History of the Church Missionary Society*, 3 vols., 1899; IV, 1916.

Swann, A. J., *Fighting the Slave-hunters in Central Africa*, 1910.
Thoonen, J. P., *Black Martyrs*, 1941.
Towards a United Church, London, Edinburgh House, 1947.
Tucker, A. R., *Eighteen Years in Uganda and East Africa*, 2nd edition, 1911.
Ward, G., and Russell, E. F., *The Life of Charles Alan Smythies*, 1890.
Ward, G., *Letters of Bishop Tozer and his Sister*, 1902.
Wilson, G. H., *History of the Universities Mission to Central Africa*, 1936.
Witty, S. W. W., *Medical Missions in Africa and the East*, 1922.

2. PERIODICALS

Africanae Fraternae Ephemerides Romanae, 1930–48.
Allgemeine Missionszeitschrift, 1873–1914.
Central Africa, 1883–1914.
Church Missionary Intelligencer, 1849–1906.
Church Missionary Review, 1907–18.
Evangelisch-Lutherisches Missionsblatt, 1894–1912.
International Review of Missions, 1912–45.
Jahresberichte der Missionsgesellschaft zu Berlin, 1890–1913.
Jahresberichte der Brüdergemeine, 1899–1912.
Jahresberichte der Evangelisch-lutherische Missionsgesellschaft, 1894–1912.
Missions Catholiques, 1868–1914.
Missionsberichte der Missionsgesellschaft zu Berlin, 1890–1913.
Missionsblatt der Brüdergemeine, 1899–1912.
Nachrichten aus der ostafrikanischen Mission, 1894–1912.
Zeitschrift fur Missionswissenschaft, 1914–35.

3. GOVERNMENT PUBLICATIONS

Hansard, 1869–97.
Accounts and Papers, 1887–8, LXXIV; 1893–4, LXII; 1898, LX; 1900, LVI; 1905, LVI.

Despatch on Native Labour, 1920. Cmd. 873.
Despatch relating to Native Labour, 1921. Cmd. 1504.
Indians in Kenya, 1923. Cmd. 1922.
Report of the East Africa Commission, 1925. Cmd. 2387.
Report of the Commission on Closer Union of the Dependencies in Eastern and Central Africa. 1929. Cmd. 3234.

4. OTHER PRINTED SOURCES

Reports of the World Missionary Conference. Edinburgh, 1910.
Reports of the International Missionary Conference. Jerusalem, 1928.
Reports of the International Missionary Conference. Madras, 1938.

5. UNPUBLISHED TYPESCRIPTS

Capon, M. G., *A History of Christian Co-operation in Kenya*, 1947. Copy in archives of Kenya Missionary Council.
Hanna, A. J., *The History of Nyasaland and North-Eastern Rhodesia, 1875-95*, London. Ph.D. 1948.
Hollingsworth, L. W., *The History of Zanzibar, 1891-1913*, London. Ph.D. 1951.

6. UNPUBLISHED DOCUMENTARY SOURCES

 (i) Correspondence relating to the Lake Tanganyika Mission of the London Missionary Society, 1877-88, in the archives of the L.M.S., Broadway, Westminster, in boxes marked Central Africa Mission.
 (ii) Correspondence relating to the C.M.S. mission in the area now included in the Diocese of Central Tanganyika, 1876-1930, in the archives of the C.M.S., Salisbury Square, E.C., in packets marked successively Nyanza, Usagara and Tanganyika.
 (iii) Selected correspondence between the Foreign Office and the British Consulate in Zanzibar, 1875-84, printed copies, formerly the property of Sir John Kirk, in Rhodes House, Oxford.

(iv) Correspondence between the Foreign Office and the British Consulates at Zanzibar, Mozambique and Zomba, 1885–94, in the Public Record Office, Series F.O. 84. Correspondence relating to the missions to Uganda of Captain Macdonald and Sir Gerald Portal, in the Series F.O. 2.

(v) Correspondence relating to the origins of Christian co-operation in Kenya, 1908–18, preserved at the Church of Scotland Mission, Kikuyu. Minutes of the Kikuyu Conference of 1913; and correspondence between the Protestant Missionary Alliance and the Secretary for Native Affairs and the Secretary of State for the Colonies, 1918–25, in the archives of the Kenya Missionary Council, Nairobi. Correspondence of Dr. J. W. Arthur relating to his mission to England in 1923, as the representative for African interests in the Indian Question, C.S.M., Kikuyu.

(vi) Correspondence of Dr. J. H. Oldham relating to Land and Labour in Kenya and Indians in Kenya, 1919–23, in the archives of Edinburgh House, Eaton Gate, S.W.1., in files marked 'East Africa—Native Labour' and 'East Africa—Indians'.

INDEX

Africa Inland Mission, 171, 225 n, 228, 236 n

African International Association, 46, 48, 49

Andrews, C. F., 260–1

Anglican Church, 171, 218–19, 227, 232, 236, 240, 243, 287; see also Church Missionary Society and Universities Mission to Central Africa

Anti-Slavery Society, 89, 153

Arabs (and Swahilis), 4; trading sphere of, 29–33; 37, 51–2; and missions at Mombasa, 54–6, 67, 70; Kirk and, 84–6; Germans and, 96–103; political activities, in Buganda, 103–8, 133–4, 135–8, 139, 140; Lake Tanganyika, 109–13; Nyasaland, 113–16; 158–9

Arthur, J. W., 223 n, 228 n, 249, 250 n, 259 n, 261–2

Augustana Lutheran Synod of North America, 238

Baker, Sir S., 27, 28, 67, 99 n

Barghash, Seyyid, 89, 101, 107, 108 n

Benedict XV, Pope, 234

Benedictines, 163–4, 237, 284 n

Berlin I Society, 165–7, 175, 180, 197–8, 205–6, 214

Berlin III (Bethel) Society, 96, 167, 175, 181, 205, 214

Blantyre, see under Church of Scotland Mission

Buganda, 29, 31; missions to, 40–1, 48; Egyptian interest in, 67–8; missions under Mutesa, 73–8; under Mwanga, 103–8; Muslim-Christian war, 134–8; first treaties, 138–40; Lugard and the religious wars, 140–9; British Protectorate, 156–60; expansion of Christianity in, 182–7

Burton, R. F., 7, 27, 28, 29

Buxton, Sir T. F., 3rd Bart., 89–90, 170

Capuchins, 237

Church Missionary Society, 4; Mombasa mission, 5–9; and freed slaves, 16–19, 25, 26; Freretown, 53–6, 82–3; Buganda mission, 39–41, 73–8, 87–8, 103–8, 129–49; and the occupation of Uganda, 149–60; in Tanganyika, 41, 166–7, 198, 237–8, 267; in Kenya, 169, 171, 176, 199, 223–6; in Uganda, 182, 184–6, 188–93, 209–21, 237

Church of Scotland Mission, Nyasaland, 36–7, 58–60, 61–2, 121–3, 126; Kenya (Kikuyu) mission, 170–1, 173, 199, 222, 223 n, 225, 236, 240, 249

Churchill, Winston, 255, 257

Consolata Fathers, 170, 199, 237

Cust, R. N., 25, 47

Davidson, Archbishop, 221, 227, 252, 255–7, 261, 268–9

Education, 16, 18, 22, 23–6, 39, 60–3, 72 n, 77, 174–5, 179–81, 184–6, 199–201, 205–6, 212–15, 263–71, 274–82

Egyptian penetration of E. A., 28, 67–9; opposition to, 87–9

Emin Pasha, 112, 130–33

Erhardt, J. J., 6–8, 27

Free Church of Scotland Mission, 35–6, 56–7, 59–60, 62–3, 65, 86–8, 92, 119–21, 217

Frere, Sir H. B., 19–23, 25, 26

Freretown, 25, 53–6, 82–3